Will O' the Wisp: Madness, War and Recompense

Roger Newman

W & B Publishers
USA

Will O' the Wisp: Madness, War and Recompense ©
All rights reserved by author.

W & B Publishers

For information:
W & B Publishers
9001 Ridge Hill Street
Kernersville, NC 27284

www.a-argusbooks.com

ISBN:9781635543506

This is a work of *fiction.* All of the characters, organizations and events portrayed in this novel are either products of the author's imagination or used fictitiously.

Book Cover designed by Dubya

Printed in the United States of America

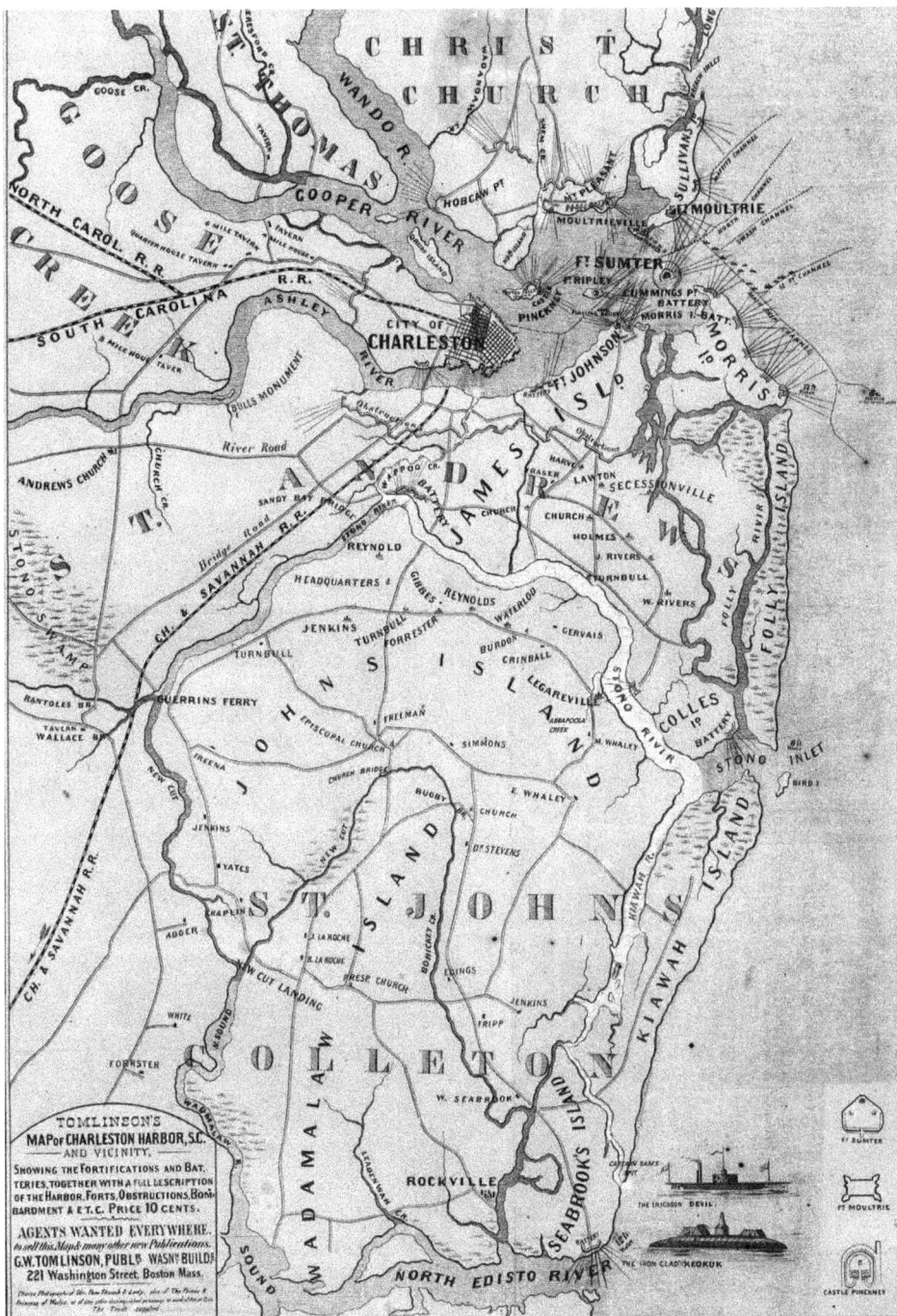

CHRIST CHURCH

ST. THOMAS

GOOSE CR.

WANDO R

COOPER RIVER

HOBCAW PT.

MT. PLEASANT

MOULTRIEVILLE

SULLIVANS I.

FT. MOULTRIE

NORTH CAROL. R.R.

QUARTER HOUSE TAVERN

6 MILE TAVERN

MILE HOUSE

SOUTH CAROLINA R.R.

ASHLEY

8 MILE HOUSE TAVER

FT. SUMTER

RIPLEY

PINCKNEY

CUMMINGS PT. BATTERY

MORRIS I. BATT.

CITY OF CHARLESTON

ASHLEY RIVER

FT. JOHNSON ISL'D

MORRIS I.

BULLS MONUMENT

River Road

ANDREWS CHURCH

CHURCH CR.

ST.

ANDREWS

JAMES ISLAND

SECESSIONVILLE

LAWTON

HARVEY

FRASER

CHURCH

HOLMES

J. RIVERS

TURNBULL

W. RIVERS

FOLLY RIVER

FOLLY ISLAND

STONO

SWAMP

SANDY BAY

STONO RIVER BRIDGE

REYNOLD

HEADQUARTERS

JENKINS

TURNBULL

FORRESTER

REYNOLDS

WATERLOO

GERVAIS

BURDON

CRINDALL

LEGAREVILLE

STONO RIVER

COLLES I.

BATTERY

RANTOLES BR.

GUERRINS FERRY

TAVERN

WALLACE R.

JOHNS ISLAND

EPISCOPAL CHURCH

FREEMAN

SIMMONS

ABBAPOOLA CREEK

M. WHALEY

STONO INLET

BIRD I.

IREENA

NEW CUT

CHURCH BRIDGE

RUGBY

CHURCH

E. WHALEY

JENKINS

YATES

NEW CUT

DR. STEVENS

CHAPLIN

ST. JOHNS ISLAND

ADGER

J. LA ROCHE

J. LA ROCHE

PRESB. CHURCH

BONICKET ST.

EDINGS

JENKINS

KIAWAH ISLAND

HOA WAH R.

NEW CUT LANDING

WADMALAW RIVER

WHITE

FRIPP

FORRSTER

COLLETON

W. SEABROOK

SEABROOK'S ISLAND

WADMALAW SOUND

ROCKVILLE

NORTH EDISTO RIVER

CH. & SAVANNAH R.R.

TOMLINSON'S
MAP OF CHARLESTON HARBOR, S.C.
— AND VICINITY.

SHOWING THE FORTIFICATIONS AND BAT-
TERIES, TOGETHER WITH A FULL DESCRIPTION
OF THE HARBOR, FORTS, OBSTRUCTIONS, BOM-
BARDMENT & E.T.C. PRICE 10 CENTS.

AGENTS WANTED EVERYWHERE,
to sell this Map & many other new Publications.
G. W. TOMLINSON, PUBLR. WASHN. BUILDR.
221 Washington Street, Boston Mass.

FT. SUMTER

THE ERICSSON DEVIL.

FT. MOULTRIE

THE IRON CLAD KEOKUK

CASTLE PINCKNEY

Chapter 1

December 20, 1860

Institute Hall

The three boys were of an age somewhere between old enough to be captured by belief in their own righteousness and infallibility, but not old enough to realize the consequences of arrogance and impertinence. Of an age still trusting in a nurturing mother's capacity for comfort and protection, but not old enough to understand a grown man's proclivity for intolerance and violence. Old enough to enter a tavern for bark juice and beer, but not old enough to know when to stop drinking and go home.

The true depth of their Unionist views was anyone's guess. Their hairless chins suggested the absence of a well-constructed world view or adequate life experience to inform good judgement. They were of an age when moral compasses swung wildly before a coming storm. An age that misjudged true North as the cardinal point they wanted to travel on this night. Tragically, an age that took delight in the emotions that could be stirred by a vociferous, but unpopular contrarian argument. Not old enough to know that raw passion, when picked, would bleed.

Withdrawal from the Union was being actively debated just a few blocks over at Institute Hall. Insurrection was the only topic of conversation anywhere in Charleston, and especially at the Poinsett Tavern on Elliott Street. Cooperationist versus secessionist insults had been hurled back and forth across the tavern floor for most of the evening. The boys called slavery barbaric and the slavery proponents dismissed as ignorant. In God's eyes, all men were equal, and the enslavement of black men and women was an abomination. The invectives rapidly became more personal. Insults eventually turned into threats as the three boys continued to rail against the sin of slavery. The threats turned into shoving when the boys began to sing the camp tune "John Brown's Body." "As he died to make us holy, let us die to make men free."

The agitated day laborers pinned the boys against a back-wall intent on adjusting their attitudes. The boy who had proven himself the greatest agitator pulled a penknife from his pocket and insolently impaled it into a wooden tabletop. His overly dramatic reveal of what was no more than a lady's letter opener elicited nothing but laughter from the overheated men.

A broad, red-bearded Irish tavernkeeper with a large knotted shillelagh pushed his way between the boys and the incensed workingmen. "I'll be damned if I'm going to be here late scrubbing blood from the floorboards. It's time for you boys to leave and that's not a suggestion."

Warning off the infuriated regulars, the tavernkeeper ushered the boys out a side door away from the taunts of the angry men. Pointing his shillelagh at the most hot-tempered of the three, the tavernkeeper warned them away. "Next time you're thirsty for a drink find another saloon. Better yet, stay at home and suckle from your momma's teat."

The loudest of the three hollered back and shook his fist at the tavernkeeper and jeering men. "Nobody throws a McGinley out of his own bar. When I come back it'll be at the front of a slave army and we'll drink wherever we want."

Satisfied with their defiance, the boys gathered themselves in the alley that ran beside the Poinsett Tavern. There was discussion of a more accommodating tavern over on Church Street. They never made it.

Fear of a slave rebellion was ever present in the Southern consciousness. Constant rumors of Northern plots to incite a slave insurrection only heightened that corrosive anxiety. The boy's imprudent boast touched this raw nerve. The men in the tavern were no longer satisfied with just throwing the three condescending schoolboys out. The most brutish of the men rallied his drinking mates, "No way those abolitionists are going to move onto another public house to sow their seeds of slave revolt. If they really want to celebrate the martyrdom of John Brown, we can accommodate them!"

At the head of the alley, the boys were met by a dozen men from the tavern. The boys were young, angry, and imbued with an alcohol-fueled willingness. They had muscles born of an inevitable, but unearned hormonal surge. The tavern men had muscles which had been hammered hard against the anvil of heat, humidity, and heavy lifting. The boys mistook the impending confrontation for a schoolyard tussle. They were mistaken and should have been running in the opposite direction.

It was over by the time the boys recognized it had begun. The mouthy boy stepped forward, brandishing his pen knife, but no more abolitionist proclamations came from his open, but silenced, mouth. The leader of the lathered mob sank a serious hunting knife deep into his belly, taking the wind from his throat. The smallest of the boys went down after the first fist. He curled into a fetal position and was stomped by leather work boots. His cowardice saved his life. The most imposing of the three boys grabbed a loose piece of wood and waded in. He took out two men, but his bravery cost him a crushed skull as he was swarmed from behind. The boys were left bleeding out in the alley as the men returned dispassionately to the tavern. No songs would be written about this first skirmish in Charleston's march to secession.

At approximately the same time, over on Meeting Street, delegates streamed out of Institute Hall. It was a clear, crisp perfect night. A brass military band trumpeted the delegate's arrival along with the hurrahs of a crowd who had filled the street hours earlier. The South Carolina Ordinance of Secession had just been unanimously ratified. No Charlestonian would ever know the building again as anything other than Secession Hall.

South Carolina's secession fuse had been burning slowly for decades. Charleston, more than any other city, embodied the state's unruly spirit. South Carolina's powerful politician-philosopher John C. Calhoun had been the most strident and bellicose proponent of state's rights. Calhoun eloquently argued that states could legally void any Federal law it deemed unconstitutional. In Congress, Calhoun was known as the Great Nullifier.

That constitutional belief was tested when Calhoun served as Vice-President under Andrew Jackson. South Carolina decided it was unwilling to pay a federally imposed tariff and threatened to raise a militia to enforce their nullification. At a private White House dinner, "Old Hickory" Jackson leaned across the table and threatened a naval blockade of Charleston and a willingness to have Calhoun immediately hanged for sedition. The Federal tariff would stand. South Carolina was humiliated and John C. Calhoun dramatically resigned the Vice-Presidency, only to be immediately elected back to the U.S. Senate by the affronted citizens of South Carolina.

Calhoun's other bedrock belief was in the "right of property" which was, in Calhoun's opinion, the basis of all civilized societies. Personal property was inviolable, even if human. The Constitutional right to property ownership was Calhoun's legal argument in defense of human bondage. The Negro was a child-like dependent who needed benevolent protection and fostering of their spiritual well-being. No man, and no state, should be subjected to a Federally mandated, but Constitutionally unlawful, confiscation of that property.

While Calhoun railed against Congressional actions he found odious, unjust, and oppressive to the South, he did not favor obliteration of the Union. In reflective moments, Calhoun could divine the coming political discord between North and South. If he continued to champion "State's Rights" and the Constitutional protection of slave ownership, the ultimate result would either be the dissolution of the Union or a destructive civil war.

Regretfully, Calhoun never gave more robust voice to his fears or a less incendiary voice to his indignation. Had he devoted his political skills to improving the Union, rather than championing narrow Southern self-interests, he may have realized his presidential ambitions and spared the South the conflict now on the horizon. Sadly, few men take advantage of the opportunity to reconsider their lives and bearings amid the rapidly changing currents of history.

The foundational cracks in the Union espoused by Calhoun were subsequently exploited by a parade of Southern nationalists promoting a narrative passionate enough to stir men to action, move them into the streets, beat the drums, and shout down the opposition. A narrative fed by wealthy, but never wealthy enough, planters and merchants. A narrative endorsed by compliant pastors of limited conscience who had long forgotten the yearning for freedom that drove their forefathers to fight England for independence.

Most influential were the insurrectionary newspapermen like Robert Barnwell Rhett, Sr. and Jr. who owned and edited the Charleston Mercury. The senior Rhett purchased the newspaper in 1857 with money obtained by mortgaging slaves from his plantation. Robert Barnwell Rhett, Sr. dreamed of being the president of a new Southern Republic while the younger Rhett was the editor-in-charge peddling the message of severance to a pliable public with incautious fanaticism. Southern secession was their goal and they stooped to all manner of rascality to achieve it.

While Rhett senior was a fire-breathing ideologue, Rhett junior was a southern-fried Machiavelli, expert in the black art of propaganda. The Charleston Mercury served the public a daily dose of twisted news, cunning insinuation, and the constant hammering of secessionist themes. "Barny" Rhett, Jr. was a skilled caricature artist who understood that the virtue of secession required a vice to set itself against. That foil would be the repugnant nominee of the Black Republican Party, Abraham Lincoln. Ignoring Lincoln's basically even-handed legislative record, the Mercury's editorial page screamed that Lincoln was a full-blooded abolitionist with a heart as hard and black as onyx. Rhett's caricatures portrayed Lincoln with a stooped, long-armed, monkey-like posture, with heavily shaded skin and raggedy dress, suggesting a lack of purity in his bloodline. The Mercury described him as "sooty and scoundrelly in aspect; a cross between the nutmeg dealer, the horse swapper and the night man."

The Scotch-Irish workingmen of Charleston were continuously threatened with the possible loss of what little they had to freed slaves with even less. "Barny's" editorials neglected to point out the historical reality that these same working-class whites would be the ones fighting and dying to preserve a right to property they did not own and never would.

Despite incessant haranguing, Charleston was slow to rile. Secessionist hectoring and outrage would flame, then smolder in the face of Charleston's unhurried pace and conservative nature. Charleston's charms provided too many diversions from rebellious indignation. Charleston's elite balanced their radical politics with an equally ardent taste for balls, regattas, horse races and seasonal plantation parties. The disingenuous tactics of the Charleston secessionists, however, continued to apply pressure to the wedges they had so carefully placed into societal cracks.

The threat of slave revolt was the greatest crack to be exploited. Of Charleston's forty thousand residents, only 23,000 were white. Over 13,000 were slaves and another 4,000 were free persons of color. Older Charlestonians remembered Denmark Vesey's slave rebellion of 1822. Although Vesey and his followers were betrayed and executed in a mass hanging before any white blood could be spilled, Charleston lived in dread of having its throat slit in the night. Slave-owners also feared irretrievable financial loss. Insurance companies happily covered enslaved chattel but carried specific provisions that absolved them of any responsibility for reimbursement of slave property lost in an insurrection.

At the edges of the Meeting Street crowd were dozens of mounted police in dark blue uniforms, cockaded hats, shiny swords, and pistols on their hips. No one mistook them for crowd control. Every night at ten minutes till nine, drumbeats rang out across the city signaling slaves and freemen to get off the streets before the St. Michael's church bells rang the nine o'clock hour. The penalty for a black man breaking curfew was a flogging at the city jail on Magazine Street. The cheering crowd gathered outside Institute Hall drowned out the wails from those bound to the whipping posts. The mounted police outside Institute Hall were there to subdue any perceived threat among the black population or from "traitorous whites." None of the mounted police had been called to aid the three boys in the alley outside Poinsett Tavern.

Secession became a certainty just months earlier in the same Institute Hall. The Democratic Nominating Convention of 1860 had been given to Charleston in hopes of blunting its insurrectionist leanings. The main floor seated approximately one thousand Democratic delegates from around the country. More than 2,000 of Charleston's most vociferous revolutionaries filled the galleries overhanging the floor.

The Democratic Party was at political loggerheads, evenly split between the supporters of a strong Federal Union championed by "Old Hickory" Andrew Jackson and the state's righters of John C. Calhoun. The party had fractured over the issue of allowing slavery in the new Western territories and the position the Democratic Party should take on the 1857 Dred Scott decision. In Dred Scott, the Supreme Court ruled that the legislatures of the new Western territories had no authority to ban slavery.

The presumptive Democratic nominee was Senator Stephen A. Douglas, the "Little Giant" from Illinois. Douglas orated the position of popular sovereignty, believing the settlers of new territories should have the right to decide for themselves about slavery. The Southern Democrats demanded that the party specifically endorse the Dred Scott decision preserving the possibility of slavery in the new West. Dred Scott was immensely unpopular in the abolitionist North and Douglas recognized that his endorsement of it would seal his defeat.

Moderate ground was fast disappearing topography and the prevailing winds were gusting hard against compromise. To the deafening cheers of the radicalized Charlestonians in the galleries, the South Carolina delegation puffed out its chest and walked out of the Democratic convention followed by the delegations from most of the other Southern states. The Northern Democrats reconvened in Baltimore a short time later and nominated Stephen Douglas. The pro-slavery Southern Democrats met in Richmond and nominated the current Vice-President, John Breckenridge, with no expectation of his winning in November. The pro-slavery, pro-secession Southern Democrats had other November expectations. They correctly calculated that Breckenridge would draw enough support away from Douglas to assure that the hated Republican candidate, Abraham Lincoln, who opposed expansion of slavery into the Western territories, would win. Southerners like Rhett senior and junior trusted that Lincoln's election would be the final hammer strike to the blunt end of the wedge. The foundation of the Union would finally be split apart.

Within two months of Lincoln's election, the South Carolina Secession Convention was gaveled open in Charleston's Institute Hall. In contrast to the contentious Democratic Convention, the Secession Convention was a festive four days of boastful speeches, masculine pomposity, and simplistic, empty-headed arrogance. The one hundred and sixty-nine delegates weighing the question of secession were treated to all of Charleston's comforts and indulgences including theater, outdoor picnics and concerts in Charleston's parks and parade grounds. Rebellious conversation dominated the fancy parlors and piazzas along the high battery and spilled over into smaller venues such as Charleston's numerous saloons, gambling halls, and whorehouses.

The few remaining Unionists were drowned out by the fiery articulacy of the secessionists who dominated the convention floor. No white man should ever be subjected to the menial, back-breaking work of cotton cultivation, scraping a boat hull, or clearing a field of stumps. The anti-slavery drift of the Democratic party had to be throttled and emphatic voice given to indisputable property rights. Constitutional protection was required to preserve the right to hold slaves. If not the U.S. Constitution, it would be another.

The moral justification for slavery was clear in the mind of every secessionist. In a refined city like Charleston, Negro slaves lived far superior lives to those in the free North. What is the value of freedom when reduced to begging for a decent paying job and suffering the want of adequate food, clean shelter and, most importantly, a benevolent master? A master who provided for all needs in exchange for simple obedience and hard work. Tasks to which the white master believed that the Negro to be so well-matched.

On the convention floor, pastors read from the first epistle to Timothy where Paul warned of the dangers of associating with men who disturbed the relationship between servant and master. Most of Charleston's ministry viewed the slave trade as the greatest missionary work ever done by man. In speeches taken directly from their Sunday sermons, ministers reassured delegates of the propriety of their humanity. "Abolitionist efforts to destroy the master-slave relationship are unholy, corrupt and destitute of truth. Africans joyfully acquiesce to slavery as part of the natural arc of their existence. What the institution of slavery brings to the Godless heathen is empirically good. The African is disorganized and ungovernable; best suited to the simple and easily directed cultivation of tropical crops. Slavery is a blessing to the African race and a system of labor anointed by God. To believe in God, one must accept slavery as divinely ordained."

For those opposed to secession, it was heartbreaking that the power and beauty of the liturgy could be so badly misused by educated men. Chapters of the Bible revealing the antipathy of Jesus to the notion of servitude were murdered by self-serving clergymen. To the enlightened ecclesiastical minds of the Holy City, it was not self-evident that all men are created equal.

A roll call vote was demanded. The Ordinance of Secession was read, and an apprehensive silence quieted the room. "Samuel T. Atkinson," was alphabetically first called. Samuel Atkinson was a knowledgeable man who understood the vital role that South Carolina and its statesmen had played in the Revolutionary War and in drafting the new nation's Constitution. At the same time, Samuel rationalized that his revolutionary grandfathers had gambled their lives in seeking independence from a tyrannical government. They would understand.

Samuel Atkinson responded with a subdued, but firm, "Yea," which was the first of a unanimous declaration.

Each delegate signed the document and then exited the Secession Convention to the embrace of an adoring crowd. Hats were thrown in the air and tears of joy were shed. The roar of approval was that of a single mind and voice. The sense of a Southern Nationalist revolution was palpable. Bonfires were lit on every street and the celebrants moved from house to house as public officials came out to their moonlit piazzas to endorse secession, raise a glass of rich Madeira, and smoke a celebratory cigar. The gathered delegates and fine ladies of Charleston with wide-brimmed hats and parasols celebrated their new reality on the gas-lit streets of the first city of the new South.

Other states would certainly follow South Carolina's lead. The delegates had carried out God's divine will, and the South was now set on a path to fulfilling its destiny. The streets were slick and clean from an earlier rain and the fine plastered fronts of Charleston's stately mansions gleamed like the marble of ancient Rome. For those who were apprehensive, they kept it to themselves. The chance to change anyone's mind or hold back the tempest was long past.

Those who should have known better either did not recognize the coming calamity, or worse, believed that terrible times could be turned to their benefit. For Charleston's wealthy, powerful, and socially privileged, secession was the end of Southern spoliation. Gold collected from the sale of cotton and other Southern natural resources would be used to build a new Southern infrastructure of factories, shipyards, and railroads. The port of Charleston would become the epicenter of a booming free-trade, tariff-free republic. Charleston's dock-side warehouses would always be full, and its water-side real estate values would rise.

Another cerci accompanying secession would be the wiping out of all Southern debt to Northern banks; a not inconsequential benefit to Charleston's planters and merchants. Those same men would enjoy the permanent protection of slavery, the plantation economy, and the Southern way of life. The new Southern Republic would reopen African slave trade. As the number of available slaves increased, their cost would fall. Even the working man might be able to afford a slave. For the Southern elite, secession was anticipated to offer an excellent return on investment.

Samuel Atkinson lingered behind as the delegates exited onto Meeting Street. Atkinson turned a final time and contemplated what had just occurred in the now empty Institute Hall. Decorating the far wall was a mural of a curvaceous Southern maiden with a sly smile on her lips and a dagger in her hand. Her blade was pointed menacingly toward a world globe. Atkinson shivered with a disquieting premonition of the disorder to come.

Chapter 2

January 6, 1861

White Gold

News of secession spread like a grease fire, and although anticipated, it was still stunning. Jack Whitesides Holmes of Christ Church Parish east of Charleston had been intently following the deliberations at Institute Hall. Jack Holmes was the grandson of the Christ Church Parish shipbuilder, Francis Marion Jones, founder of the F.M. Jones Shipyard on Shem Creek. Jack had been a carpenter's apprentice since childhood and eventually the head shipwright at Jones Shipyard. Jack Holmes had built everything from barges to luxury yachts. He sensed that the Ordinance of Secession would bring new demand.

The son of a shipbuilder and sea captain, life on the rivers and coastal waters of the Lowcountry was all he had ever known. Jack shared a dispositional synchrony with the ebb and flow of the tides and a lifetime of experiences that tethered him to the Lowcountry waterways. When asked where he was from, Jack would joke, "I was born in the Lowcountry salt marsh with pluff mud in my diapers."

Jack's reputation as a shipbuilder and sea captain was unmatched. The superior craftsmanship of his work at the F.M. Jones Shipyard had provided for a comfortable life. Life on the water had rendered Jack windswept, steeled, and ruggedly handsome. Jack possessed great personal magnetism and self-confidence. He married his childhood sweetheart, Mary Ann Gleeson, and they had been blessed with four children. Thomas Henry, now nineteen, was the oldest and he had also grown up on the water working alongside his father. The next oldest was Eliza who had just turned seventeen and the younger two were George Chapman and Frances.

Jack Holmes was apolitical. Life on a ship had taught Jack the non-negotiable importance of being a realist. His only thoughts regarding secession were to consider its foolhardiness. Jack was not ignorant of the North and saw through most of the bunk being written and asserted by the passionate, but willfully uninformed. Jack's visits to Northern ports revealed the vastness of the industrial differences between the regions. Jack owned no man, woman, or child and considered slavery hateful. He had never placed a human being of any color in the hold of a ship he captained. No slaves toiled either at his home, shipyard, or on his ships. His abhorrence of slavery was absolute, but also insignificant. Jack understood that slavery was an economic imperative for the South and that secession was solely about the preservation of human bondage.

Jack was equally certain that secession could not be peaceably accomplished. Jack would not hesitate to defend his home and his state from the armed aggression he knew would inevitably follow. At the same time, however, Jack knew in his heart that the preservation of enslavement and financial self-interest were insufficient justifications for rebellion.

From a practical perspective, European arms, munitions, and other industrial products would be the South's lifeblood. Without massive European support, any conflict with the North would invariably become a war of attrition that the South could not survive. Jack could not imagine a scenario where the Union did not attempt to blockade Southern harbors. Nor could he imagine those same harbors and sea lanes not remaining open to him. With a quality ship and his knowledge of the Lowcountry coast, there was no Federal blockade he could not successfully elude.

To purchase European steamships, locomotive engines, railroad iron, munitions and other vital industrial products, the South would have to trade its greatest resource, South Carolina's Sea Island cotton. Jack called it "white gold." The Sea Islands were a perfect niche for the growing of cotton. Its inventive planters had developed a silky strain of cotton with long fibers and a creamy white hue. Sea Island cotton was the finest in the world. Premiere textile manufacturers in Europe demanded the luxurious cotton varietal and would pay any price. England had the greatest taste for Southern cotton, feeding more than three thousand textile mills and three-quarters of a million British textile workers. Expanded and uninterrupted cotton trade with England and other European countries could potentially generate sufficient trade to sustain a new Southern Republic and lure foreign investors.

A single successful transatlantic shipment of "white gold" to the textile mills of Lancashire generated enough hard cash to pay for the vessel, its crew and a belly-full of returning cargo which could be sold for a handsome profit. An attempted blockade would only raise the asking price for cotton even higher.

Knowing that the Ordinance of Secession would be ratified, Jack Holmes had met two week earlier with his brother-in-law, George Alfred Trenholm. Jack made George a straightforward proposal. Jack would build the fastest and most stealthy blockade runner ever put to sea. Trenholm would fund its construction and provide all the necessary iron, boilers, engines, and other mechanicals from England. Jack would own and captain the ship. Profits from each successful run would be split fifty-fifty.

George Alfred Trenholm's grandfather had been a loyalist to the British crown and had immigrated to Holland during the Revolutionary War. After the overthrow of British rule, the Trenholm family returned to Charleston. The oldest son, William Trenholm, became a sea captain and sailed for Saint-Domingue where the Trenholm family had briefly lived during their wartime exile. William went to Saint-Domingue to marry the daughter of a wealthy French landowner, the Comte de Greffin. Disappointed to learn that the Comte de Greffin had already married off his eldest daughter, William wed her sister, Elizabeth Irene de Greffin, instead. William and Irene married in New York, and lived there briefly, before relocating back to Charleston.

George Alfred Trenholm was born in 1807, one of William and Irene's seven children. George's mother and father both died in 1824, ending George's formal education at age sixteen and forcing him to find work with John Fraser and Company, one of Charleston's leading exporters of Sea Island cotton.

Strikingly handsome and imposing in presence, George Trenholm was also industrious and ambitious. After John Fraser's death in 1854, the "under-educated" George Trenholm ascended to the position of senior partner and principal owner. His minority partners included Theodore Wagner, his brother Edward L. Trenholm, James T. Welsman, and Charles K. Prioleau. The business flourished as never before under George's leadership. John Fraser and Company became the world's leader in the export of raw cotton, loading up to 20,000 cotton bales every morning. The firm bought large steamships to carry their cotton to every major European port.

George Trenholm overcame an orphaned childhood and lack of academics to become the richest man in South Carolina, if not, the entire South. He owned several stately mansions, dozens of commercial warehouses, and much of the Charleston waterfront. Trenholm gained major shareholder interests in the banking world as well, becoming part owner of the thriving Bank of Charleston. George Trenholm built an empire on the backs of African slaves and a slave economy that his father, William, brought to Charleston from the slave-driven French plantations of Saint-Domingue. In addition to the waterfront, Trenholm's empire included almost two thousand acres of Lowcountry rice and cotton plantation land, thousands more of pineland near Abbeville, cotton presses, a rice pounding mill and the Planter's Hotel. Each of these profitable businesses were sustained by hundreds of slaves and long village rows of slave cabins also owned by George Alfred Trenholm.

In the way that the brass-barrel lens of a collodion wet-plate box camera gathers light, George Trenholm's charm, graceful manner, and business success gathered friends and admirers to him. One of those Trenholm admirers was Jack's sister, Anna Helen Holmes. Because of her grandfather's shipbuilding business and their docks off East Bay Street, the Holmes family and the Trenholm family were well acquainted. So well acquainted, in fact, that George Trenholm married the beautiful and independent Anna Helen Holmes while his brother Leonard Trenholm married Anna's younger sister, Eliza Bonsal Holmes. During his courtship of Anna Helen, George came to know Anna's oldest brother, Jack. Despite vastly different upbringings and social circles that rarely overlapped, they shared a friendship and commonality of independent spirit.

On his now cleared mahogany desk, George Trenholm ran his hands over the design plans for the graceful and powerful blockade runner that Jack Holmes proposed to build. George shared Jack's vision of what was to come. Continuous European trade would be essential to compete with the more populated and industrialized North. With ships like the one he was looking at, both Jack and George concurred that any Northern blockade could be rendered ineffectual. With more than three thousand miles of Southern coastline, the lumbering men-of-war of the moth-eaten U.S. Navy would be no threat to open sea trade with

England, France or whoever else was interested in the cotton, timber, turpentine, linseed oil, grains, ham, bacon, and lard filling Trenholm's warehouses. With the right captains, the South could survive on the trade provided by a fleet of swift blockade runners. Jack Holmes was just such a captain and the only man he would trust to build it.

Jack also appreciated that George Trenholm was the perfect partner. No one in the world had more contacts or understood the commodity market for cotton better than George Alfred Trenholm. In the world of cotton, George Trenholm was the man who set the price. A partnership with his brother-in-law to build this blockade runner would mean financial security for his family in the face of probable upheaval.

With a handshake the two men became inextricably linked to the future of the new Southern Republic and the deliverance of Charleston. Jack had already named his new ship, *Will O' the Wisp.*

Chapter 3

March 27, 1862

Will O' the Wisp

Captain Jack Holmes took his customary position. He awkwardly draped his gangly six- foot-three-inch frame over the small crosstree fitted on the foremast. He was most comfortable when the ship's best man was at lookout. Many blockade runner captains offered their lookouts an extra dollar for every sighted sail from the crosstree, but also docked the lookout's pay three dollars for every sail first seen from the deck. Captain Jack never trusted anything based on a carrot or the stick. With the safety of his ship at stake, Jack relied only on his own two eyes.

The *Will O' the Wisp* was moving swiftly through a black void with its paddlewheels beating froth from the sea. Captain Jack was content and in total control of the ship, its crew, its direction and seemingly even the night. Not a muscle twitched as a spidery fork of lightening leapt from one invisible thunderhead to another, briefly illuminating his ship to any Union lookout or gunnery officer within a mile. The crew's anxiety grew as the *Wisp* drew closer to the shallow bar outside the Charleston harbor. Captain Jack drew strength from the power he felt beneath his feet, his trust in the *Wisp*, and his familiarity of the waters of the Lowcountry. The crew drew strength from its captain. No captain in the rapidly growing Charleston blockade running fraternity enjoyed more respect than Captain Jack. In his mind's eye, Jack clearly saw the *Wisp's* passage through the channels of a rising ocean floor.

Captain Jack had moved in and out of the Charleston harbor with impunity during the first year of the war. The Union Blocking Squadron was woefully inadequate. The few legitimate warships in the squadron were old and slow, while the remainder were rotten-hulled relics appropriated from the New England whaling fleet. Jack had steamed through the blockade more than a dozen times already with rarely a sighting and never a scratch. On this run, he had carried more than 7,000 pounds of Sea Island cotton to Nassau valued at almost two million dollars. Now on return, the hull was full of sorely needed war supplies and merchandise destined for the Confederate troops and merchants of Charleston.

Even with his unblemished record of success, Jack remained vigilant on the crosstree. Times were changing. The Union fleet grew with each passing month. Majestic old sailing ships of the line were being relieved by new, faster, steam-powered cruisers. The Federal captains were learning blockade runner tactics and developing countermeasures. They were also increasingly resentful of always being the loser in a nightly game of hide-and-seek.

The Charleston Mercury published monthly statistics demonstrating the clear rise in the number of blockade runners being captured, run aground, or sunk by the prowling Federal wolf packs. The *Will O' the Wisp* crew was unconcerned with those statistics. Numbers did not apply to the *Wisp*. The *Wisp* had delivered on every cargo with which she had been entrusted. The elusive *Will O' the Wisp* was described as a "veritable phantom ship" by the Charleston Mercury. Despite the troubling monthly statistics, the Mercury reassured its readers that, "No ghost could move more silently among the Yankee junkers. The *Will O' the Wisp* appears to be able to cast a spell which closes the eyes and obscures the glass of our maritime sentries."

The *Will O' the Wisp* was a three hundred-ton dual side paddlewheel steamer with the graceful lines of a yacht. She was 190-feet in length with a narrow 22-foot beam. The hull was Lowcountry live oak and red cedar harvested from the timber-rich Christ Church forests along the Wando River. The side paddle wheels were powered by top of the line English oscillating steam engines. The pilot house was located just behind her sharply angled and telescoping smokestacks which could be lowered to the deck minimizing the ship's stamp on the horizon. Every line and feature of the *Wisp* had been created under the hand of master carpenter and shipbuilder, Jack Holmes.

The *Will O' the Wisp* was specifically built to run a wartime blockade and she took to the water like a Chesapeake Bay Retriever. Her long, low hull only showed eight feet above the waterline and was painted a dark blue-gray. Her low silhouette and minimal masting allowed her to be overlooked at dusk and virtually disappear at night. Even during the day, her blue-gray color blended with the sea and sky at the merge of the horizon. She burned clean Welsh anthracite coal yielding only thin white smoke. When steam had to be blown off, it was done underwater, muffling the discharge. The galley carried two dozen chickens for both their eggs and the fryer, but Captain Jack forbade any cocks for fear of a dawn crow that might alert a nearby Yankee fox.

Even when fully loaded, the *Will O' the Wisp* drew only nine feet of water allowing her to easily pass over the Charleston bar. She exuded a fast look and those looks were not deceiving. The *Will O' the Wisp's* powerful engines could push her to a maximum speed of fifteen knots when sprinting across the South Atlantic from Charleston to the Caribbean Islands.

On a moonless and cloudy night, the *Wisp* blended so perfectly with the surrounding sea that she could pass within one hundred yards of a Union lookout without being detected. Captain Jack depended on stealth and had no intention of exchanging fire with a Federal blockader. The *Will O' the Wisp* didn't carry even an eighth of an inch of iron plating. Speed and invisibility were their advantage and the lack of armor assured that the *Wisp* could outrun anything in the Atlantic Squadron.

In addition to Captain Jack, four other officers walked the deck, including Jack's nineteen-year-old son, Thomas Henry Holmes. Thomas Henry, like his father, had inherited an affinity for the sea and a slightly higher than normal salt content in his blood. The *Will O' the Wisp* carried a crew of twenty-eight which included deck hands, firemen, coalmen, two cooks, a doctor and a leadsman. Each member of the crew had been individually selected by Captain Jack and were all experienced Lowcountry watermen.

Jack's chief engineer was Copper Joe, half white, half Cherokee. Jack and Joe's relationship pre-dated the birth of Thomas Henry and no one on the crew knew when or how they had met. When the call went down the engine room tube for more power, Copper Joe fearlessly squeezed his boilers for every pound of steam they had to give. The rubbery, red knots of a steam burn that shined across the right side of Joe's face, shoulder and back was all the testament needed to both his toughness and commitment.

Jack's pilot was Bennett Gibbons, a childhood friend who had sailed with Jack for years. Having grown up sailing the inlets, fishing the creeks, and hiding in the spartina grass, Bennett was the only person who knew the Lowcountry coast as well as Jack. Bennett could smell a Yankee cruiser before it could be seen. Ignorance or cowardice on the part of the pilot were responsible for far more intercepted cargoes than the tactics of the Federal blockaders. Neither of those words had ever been used in a description of Bennett Gibbons. Along with the captains, pilots took the greatest personal risk in blockade running. Captains and pilots were never exchanged. If captured, both Jack and Bennett would sit out the remainder of the war in a putrid mud dugout masquerading as a Federal prison.

Intensity mounted during the final hours of a blockade run. The captain and the pilot had to thread a needle through snarled Federal sentinels and hit a harbor channel less than a half-mile wide. Moreover, it had to be done at night, without lights or cues from a coastline so flat and featureless that the first sign of proximity was usually a sparkling thin white ribbon of riffling surf.

Captain Jack's departure from Nassau had been selected to coincide with a new moon and starless, low late winter sky over the Charleston harbor. From the pilot house, Bennett could barely make out Captain Jack on the crosstree only 30 feet away. Jack's slouch hat covered his thick curly black hair. The intensity of Jack's stare was accentuated by a poorly trimmed black goatee with just the first traces of gray. A black canvas duster covered a six-shot pistol on his hip and a twelve-inch Bowie knife in a scabbard attached to his belt in the small of his back. Both were quickly accessible through the splits in his duster. Jack's lips were pulled tight across his teeth and his cobalt blue eyes peered unblinkingly into a blackness so dense you wanted to scoop it aside with your hands.

Smoking on deck was strictly prohibited with Captain Jack granting himself the only exemption. A deep-bowl pipe was clenched between Jack's teeth with its glowing tobacco embers shielded by his free right hand. Light from the engine room hatchways was blocked by heavy tarpaulins which amplified the heat in the ovens where the firemen and coal heavers toiled. Even the binnacle was shrouded so that the helmsman had to peer into a small conical aperture to see the dimly illuminated compass. The *Will O' the Wisp* was a black hole in the water, undetectable except for the muffled engines and the rhythmic beat of the paddle floats.

The deck crew crouched motionless behind the bulwarks in wary anticipation. From the crosstree, Jack saw nothing, but sensed something. He raised his fist in the air.

Jack whispered to his son, Thomas Henry, who stood beside the foremast, "Better cast the lead. We're getting close. Tell Copper Joe to slow the engines and come to a full stop."

The order was passed down the engine room tube while the leadsman, Caleb, slowly made his way to the forechains to cast the lead obscured in the shadows of the foremast and sweptback smokestack. Even with underwater venting the crew tensed, knowing the danger of their engines blowing off steam when unexpectantly stopped. Copper Joe's experience, and taking the engines down slowly, would lessen the risk, but a sudden belch of steam could betray their position.

Two minutes later, Thomas Henry whispered back to his father, "Sixteen fathoms, sandy bottom, sir."

"We're farther out than I anticipated and southward of the channel." Captain Jack ciphered for a second and then added, "Two points to port and ahead slow. Resound in fifteen minutes."

"Captain," Thomas Henry responded respectfully, "that's going to steam us back into the belly of the beast."

Captain Jack blew out a puff of pipe smoke and replied, "Maybe I better put this thing out."

"Maybe so, sir."

The next sounding satisfied Jack that he was at the mouth of the channel and he signaled back to the pilot house. Bennett whispered down the engine room tube to Copper Joe, "Ahead easy."

The *Will O' the Wisp* crept forward to minimize the sound of the turning paddle wheels. Despite the *Wisp's* snail's pace and extra canvas tarps hung over the paddle boxes the beating floats were still dangerously loud.

Suddenly, Thomas Henry grabbed Captain Jack's arm and pointed into the darkness. "Off the starboard bow, close," Thomas Henry mouthed in silence.

Captain Jack stared but could not see anything. Still, he trusted his son and respected his younger eyes. Thomas Henry had proven his worth many times.

Too close to risk cutting the engines, Captain Jack whispered back to Thomas Henry, "Starboard a point and steady." He patted his son on the back and pointed to the pilot house. Thomas Henry took off quickly crouching low behind the bulwarks.

The starboard tack was an immense gamble. Moving closer to the Yankee gunship increased the likelihood of being seen or heard. However, if spotted, the change in course would close the distance and render useless the cruiser's most powerful guns. Guns the *Will O' the Wisp* had no iron to withstand.

Moments later, Jack was finally able to make out what Thomas Henry had already spotted. A long, two-mast cruiser sat silently in the water about fifty yards to starboard. Jack calmly relit his pipe and pointed forward. They passed the cruiser undetected while the crew silently prayed and thanked God for the *Wisp's* protective veil. They were also thankful for the Union Navy's nightly ration of grog.

Leaving the cruiser safely behind, the crew let out a collective breath. Relief was short lived. Within five minutes, Captain Jack pointed from his perch on the crosstree. This time he shouted back to the pilot house, "Steamer on the port bow. She knows we're here and is closing fast."

All heads turned.

"Hard a-starboard and full ahead," Captain Jack hollered.

Jack took another long draw off his pipe and laid his head back to scan the night sky. Survival would depend on the *Wisp's* distance from the Charleston bar. The horizon was turning the color of a dark purple bruise suggesting they were alarmingly close to the break of dawn. Jack's mental calculations were interrupted by an angry shot of hot iron which tore through the rigging five feet above Jack's head. The steamer was closing fast and firing at intervals from her bow gun.

The *Will O' the Wisp* sliced through the combers like a thick, broad knife as she pounded her way toward shore. The quivering of the deck under his feet confirmed that Copper Joe was giving him every bit of power that could be coaxed from her steam boilers. The Union cruiser bow chaser barked again. The projectile whistled above his head and plunged into the sea twenty yards in front of the *Wisp,* throwing up a white geyser of salt water.

Captain Jack calmly surveyed the damaged rigging above, the Union steamer behind, and then forward to scan for signs of the Charleston bar. An unnerved crewman shouted a request to dump cargo. Captain Jack waved him off. "Negative. There'll be no need. Our new friend will pull up soon."

In her hold, the *Will O' the Wisp* carried a load of war contraband including rifles, bayonets, gunpowder, and coils of lead from which bullets would be made. When chased, many blockade runners would dump their cargo, especially heavy lead coils, to reduce weight and increase speed.

The crewman may or may not have been assured, but no one questioned Captain Jack. The two vessels were now steaming virtually bow to stern toward the bar. A hoarse shout escaped across the water, "Stop or we'll sink you!"

Captain Jack shouted down the engine room tube, "Pile on the coal. We need all you've got."

Copper Joe, his exotic face black with coal dust and dungarees smeared with dirt and grease screamed at his coal heavers, "Shovel like your miserable lives depend on it." It did.

Copper Joe's eyes remained focused on the steam gauge and he pumped his fist when the needle pushed past one hundred percent. Smoke poured from the *Will O' the Wisp's* twin smokestacks, and she responded like a thoroughbred under Copper Joe's whip.

Realizing that the *Will O' the Wisp* had leapt ahead, the Yankee cruiser maneuvered into position to use its prodigious broadside of cannon. For a brief period, the Federal warship was close enough that the swirl of a Union bos'n's pipe and Yankee curses could be heard across the narrow, black ribbon of water between the ships.

Finding the range with its broadside, one Union shell lodged in the fore hold abaft the ship's funnel while another exploded the top of the foremast, showering the deck with wood and metal splinters. Knocked from his vantage point on the crosstree, Captain Jack rose calmly from the deck, brushed the wood chips off his duster, and retrieved his pipe which had skittered across the deck.

The *Will O' the Wisp* was now creating distance between itself and the Union steamer. In a final desperate attempt to stop the *Wisp's* escape, the cruiser fired one more broadside. When the deck crew raised themselves up from flat on their bellies, they were astonished to see Captain Jack still standing near the foremast. Silhouetted against the sun, now low and blood orange at the horizon, Captain Jack had never moved. With his hat flying behind him on a cord and his black duster tails flapping, Captain Jack squinted into the wind and salt spray searching for the approaching bar.

Just then, the breaking dawn was punctured by a flash and roar from a barely visible, but now awake, Fort Sumter in the center of the harbor. The single shell from the big guns of Fort Sumter was a warning to the Union gunboat to keep its distance. With their prideful final broadside falling 50 yards short, the Federal cruiser turned and sulked out of range. Within another few minutes the *Will O' the*

Wisp was safely over the Charleston bar as the sun fully emerged on the eastern horizon.

Not one in ten captains would have denied the request to dump the lead coils. No one wants to drop their profit into the sea, but survival is always most important. Captain Jack would never jeopardize his crew's safety for a ton of coiled lead. The crew was his responsibility, his lifelong friends, as well as his son. But in this case, his reasoning had been certain: an objective calculation of speed, distance, weather, armament, and resolve. His algebraic mental mathematics informed him that dumping cargo would not only be militarily and financially unwise, but most importantly, unnecessary.

As the *Will O' the Wisp* approached the dock at the east end of Calhoun Street, Captain Jack finally allowed himself a smile that slyly separated his moustache and goatee. Jack nodded at his old friend Bennett Gibbons in the pilot house who vigorously pumped his fist in response.

Chapter 4

March 28,1862

Plantation Economy

Captain Jack spent the day supervising the off-loading of his cargo into the warehouses of his partner, George Trenholm. The offices and warehouses of John Fraser and Company were located on the North Central Wharf at the foot of Cumberland Street. The wharfinger, James Hibben, would be taking responsibility for the delivered goods. Hibben was an old friend and Jack would not parley with anyone else but James. Delivery of the cargo was not complete until James signed off on the paperwork.

It was a crisp, invigorating early spring morning and Jack surveyed the buzz of activity going on around him. Nothing about the wharf front suggested the new Republic was struggling. Wagons, trollies, slaves, soldiers, and Scotch-Irish stevedores crowded the docks. Broad-shouldered hoisting horses lifted vital military cargo and necessities destined for the shelves of Charleston's merchant shops out of the *Wisp's* hold. The North Central wharf was servicing a half dozen ships owned by George Trenholm, or his company, and a half dozen more with other diverse ownership. Jack was proud of both himself and his fellow captains for eluding the Federal gunboats and quietly delighted that Union cannon shot had not removed his head from his shoulders. Jack also acknowledged a bit of weariness recognizing that as soon as the *Wisp* was emptied, she would be re-loaded with bales of Sea Island cotton for another outbound journey.

Part of Jack's weariness was his disdain for human bondage. Every ship was being loaded or unloaded by slave labor. His bales of "white gold" had been planted, harvested, and hauled to the North Central wharf by other even less fortunate slaves. This was a rich man's war being fought to safeguard a profitable Southern plantation economy. It was a misgiving that plagued him.

Charleston had been the commercial epicenter for the Atlantic slave trade. More than three hundred slave ships and forty thousand chained Africans entered Charleston harbor, more than any other North American port, during the first decade of the nineteenth century. The descendants of those original African slaves now numbered in the millions. More than half of the white families in Charleston were slave owners. Virtually all considered the Northern abolitionists to be hypocrites. It had been Northern slavers who sailed into Charleston's harbor and Northern business consortiums who collected the money from Negro bondage and sale.

Transatlantic slave commerce was declared illegal in 1808, but that did little to slow their trade in Charleston markets. Importation of slaves from the Caribbean Islands remained legal and the profitable smuggling of African slaves continued. Most of Charleston's slave trading, however, consisted of the buying and re-selling of domestic slaves already under ownership as well as their children born in country. The separation of husbands from wives or mothers from children was not a concern as the preachers taught, and everyone believed, that the Negro did not share the same sense of family as did Christians.

The prosperity of Charleston City was as intimately entwined with the business of slavery as it was with the exportation of cotton, rice, and other commodities. A sales commission was paid to the city whenever a slave was sold at a downtown market. The city levied annual property taxes based on the number of owned slaves. The city required the purchase of a business license and a compulsory work badge before an owner could hire out his slaves to others. Even freed slaves were forced to pay a capitation tax or face re-enslavement for failure to pay. Slavery had established deep roots as an agricultural necessity. Cotton and rice planting and picking were back and spirit-breaking work which demanded slave labor. The success of the Southern plantation economy, and the South itself, had become dependent on slavery for its social, political, and financial identity. Charlestonians could not imagine it any other way.

Jack Holmes' grandfather had owned slaves purchased off slave ships out of Newport, Rhode Island. Those slaves had worked on the family's indigo plantation and in the shipyard. When the estate was left by will to Jack and his siblings, he came to own eight old and heavily tattooed Africans. They spoke a dialect that neither Jack nor any of his other workers could understand. Jack repudiated the family legacy and declared the eight men free and paid them for their work at the shipyard. Jack rebuilt their cabins with real beds and glass pane windows. He replaced clay chimneys with brick and deeded the small houses to the freed men. Jack despised the inadequate excuse that slavery was all they had ever known. Despite being unable to ask them, Jack was certain they had once enjoyed freedom and full manhood. Few friends, neighbors or co-workers at the shipyard questioned Jack's benevolence toward his former slaves. It was a sore subject for Jack, and he was not known to take criticism well. Jack was never without the bill of sale for those eight Africans which he kept as a reminder of his family's Simon Peter moment of denial.

At Ryan's Mart on Chalmers Street, naked men, women, and children were sold in an open auction no different than livestock. Young women screamed and pleaded to not be separated from their men or children. They fell to their knees, beating their hands on the ground and heads against their cages. Contorting their faces into masks of pain, they screamed again and again until their voices failed them. It strained Charleston's long practiced tolerance and sense of propriety to excuse the shocking inhumanity of Ryan's Mart. But it did.

Young, strong bucks or unfortunate women cursed by beauty or fertility brought the highest bids. Sea Island planters paid as much as $1,500 for the strongest appearing field hand. Just as a Northern industrialist would reinvest in a successful production line, Southern planters would reinvest their profits into the purchase of more slaves. As a result, black slaves outnumbered whites by more than ten to one in most of the coastal cotton growing communities.

For Southern planters, it was axiomatic that cotton could only be profitably grown with slave labor. The British empire had failed to sustain their cotton plantations in the West Indies after abolishing slavery in 1838. There was not a reasonable price that a free man, black or white, could be paid to muck out creek beds and stoop for days on end under a blistering tropical sun to pick cotton until their fingers bled.

Northern abolitionists considered Southern slave masters godless, morally reprehensible, and ignorant. Godless and morally reprehensible were arguable, but not ignorance. Southern slaveholders developed advanced management and accounting techniques long before their adoption by Northern factory owners. Even though considered barbaric by most in the North, the plantation economy was based on a sophisticated business practice model.

A young slave in good health was considered a "prime" field hand, while an injured field hand, a child, or breastfeeding mother might be valued as half or three-quarters of "prime." Valuing workers as fractions allowed planters to more easily evaluate their enslaved workers as simple commodities. Like a piece of factory equipment that lessens in value over time, planters used complex formulas to track the value of their slaves. Slaves might appreciate as they grew stronger or developed new skills such as blacksmithing, carpentry, distillery, or mid-wifery. They depreciated with illness, injury, or older age. Pre-printed productivity books allowed for production of charts and graphs clearly illustrating the need for human labor and precise workforce planning.

Plantation overseers were salaried middle managers who ran the operation. The overseer implemented productivity standards for each slave each day. Rewards such as extra food, clothing or time for conjugal relations were used as incentives to increase output. Punishment for failure to meet productivity standards was far more liberally applied. Men and women were expected to harvest eighty pounds of cotton per day while children had smaller quotas. Slaves received a lash of the whip for every pound short of expectations.

Slaves were also leased out to work at other jobs in town or on other plantations. Male slaves worked on the docks, in hauling, as chimney sweeps or as apprentices to other skilled workers. Female slaves received badges that allowed them to work as domestics, dressmakers, cooks and wet nurses. These arrangements allowed for slaves to remain profitable even when no longer satisfactory for field work.

While pastors praised the fatherly and God-fearing plantation owner on Sunday, everyone understood the brutal realities associated with the other six days of the week. As a matter of human nature, when given absolute power over another, the refined veneer of civility will soon be worn through by self-interest and maliciousness. A deep thin vein of sadism runs through the bedrock of most men. In some, it is a thick rich strike which goes far beyond proper actuarial business practices.

For the South to remain the world's supplier of high-quality cotton, and for its economy to thrive, it must collectively ignore the moral issue of slavery. Most

Southerners believed that abolitionists were religious fanatics and posed an existential threat of governmental intrusion into a vital private commercial enterprise. Rather than argue the immorality of slavery, Southerners chose to debate its constitutionality. Southern leaders thundered about the constitutional right to hold private possessions, but Jack, and every other thoughtful Southerner, knew that secession was about protecting the South's massive capital investment in human property and the necessity of enslaved labor to generate future wealth.

The unloading of cargo from the *Will O' the Wisp* was completed by late afternoon. Jack was pleased because a serious storm appeared to be gathering out over the ocean. Purple and slate gray thunderheads had piled up and were rolling towards the coast on the crest of a rising onshore breeze. Its potential fury was unknown, but furtive glances from the stevedores toward the horizon had motivated the swift unloading of the Wisp's cargo crates.

The last cargo to be unloaded came from Captain Jack's private cabin. A privilege enjoyed by each ship's captain was the ability to speculate on merchandise that could be carried on board in their own cabin. These items usually occupied little space in relation to their value, ranging from sewing needles to French wines. Jack's preference was for small boxes of medicine.

The South was almost entirely dependent on the blockade runners to bring in medicines, hospital supplies and surgical instruments from Europe. The lack of adequate medical and surgical supplies resulted in routine amputations for wounds that could otherwise be repaired. This carnage was evident in the piles of arms and legs accumulating outside the Confederate surgical tents. Those tents were generating an army of needlessly limbless Southern men.

Jack had purchased approximately ten pounds each of morphine and quinine off a French steamer in the Bahamas for three thousand dollars in gold. The morphine and quinine were worth approximately one hundred dollars per ounce. Jack's two cartons could bring more than thirty thousand dollars back in Charleston. Captain Jack personally supervised the loading of the morphine and quinine into a dockside carriage with one hand on his pistol. He would personally deliver it to the Medical College hospital. Jack's service to the slave economy was making him a wealthy man, but his hypocrisy extended only so far. He would donate the medicine to the Medical College hospital.

As Jack drove his carriage across the peninsula, his thoughts turned from profits to costs. Despite the bustling commercial hum of the docks, the optimistic talk of politicians and generals, and the endless charm of Charleston's lovely avenues, Jack knew that things were changing. His recent return to Charleston had been his closest scrape yet with Union cannon shot. An ever-growing list of the families he knew had now been touched by bloodshed in one way or another. Childhood friends had been killed at Bull Run. A weekly list of the missing, wounded, and dead was appearing on the back page of the Charleston Mercury. The majority of those wounded or dying for the cause had never owned slaves, never been a guest at a party where a slave had served and had no family fortune to protect. The plantation economy had never worked for the enslaved. Maybe it did not work for as many whites as originally believed.

Chapter 5

March 29, 1862

Moves to Make

Jack returned to the wharf after sundown in the greasy illumination of downtown gas lamps. Electricity flickered out over the Atlantic and wind gusts smelled of metal and ozone. The wharf side was now quiet with the ships casting ominous shadows in the light of a lone barrel fire two docks over.

Jack fell asleep in his cabin to the sound of raindrops as fat as musket balls splatting on the deck above. Whatever heavy weather God chose to unleash tonight at least would not be accompanied by an incensed Union warship with a broadside of twelve large cannons suddenly emerging from a black cloudbank one hundred yards to starboard. The gentle rocking of the *Wisp* against its mooring and the pinging of metal mast rings quickly transported Jack to the peacefulness of his dreams.

An insistent knock on his cabin door awakened Jack earlier than he had hoped. He opened it to a member of his deck crew escorting a small black boy. The boy was just over waist high and probably ten years old, light brown in color with a scrofula scar on his neck. He looked like a miniature, albeit shabby, Confederate soldier. His military cap too big for his head as was his Confederate tunic. Although badly frayed, the youth had shined the brass buttons of his tunic proudly. His butternut-colored wool pants were unevenly cut-off at the knees and his feet were inadequately shod in homemade shoes constructed from a piece of leather and rolled palmetto fronds.

"Cap'n, this boy came on board this morning and claims to have an important message for your eyes only."

"Well, what you got for me?"

The boy smiled broadly as he reached into his coat pocket for a folded piece of paper. "Miss Piexotto say give this only to you."

Grace Piexotto was the Madame at the Brick House on Beresford Street off King. There was no classier brothel in Charleston than the Brick House which offered women of all shades. The message was brief. Copper Joe had gotten wallpapered and in a row with another patron leading to his arrest. Jack needed to get down to the city jail as soon as possible. Copper Joe had beaten up a well-known planter of means. When Copper Joe beat someone up, it tended to be serious.

"Thank you, son. Please let Miss Piexotto know that I deeply appreciate the information.

Fletcher, please make sure this young trooper gets a good breakfast before you send him back to Miss Piexotto."

"Yes sir, Cap'n. Son, you up for some bacon and biscuits with honey?"

The smile got even broader.

As they walked forward to the ladder topside, Jack reopened his cabin door. "Fletcher, also find this little man a new pair of shoes. Some that fit. You can't be running up and down these cobblestone streets with your soles flapping and toes hanging out."

The crewman and the young boy began to ascend the stairs when Captain Jack called to them once more, "Fletcher, please let Thomas Henry know that I'll be leaving the ship this morning for the Fraser and Company offices. He'll have the ship until my return."

"Yes sir, Cap'n. Mister Thomas is already on deck."

Despite the escalating Federal efforts, there was still a long line of blockade runners crowding the East Bay docks, each being loaded with 200-pound bales of cotton pulled from George Trenholm's dockside warehouses. Jack wondered if the docks would still be as crowded in a years' time.

Just a week after the firing on Fort Sumter, Lincoln ordered the blockade of Southern ports from South Carolina to Texas. With the subsequent secession of North Carolina and Virginia, the blockade was extended to the Potomac River. Lincoln declared the South to be in a state of insurrection and ordered any ship, including neutral vessels, attempting to enter or leave a Southern port be seized, cargo confiscated, and the ship brought to the nearest Union port for proceedings against her as a prize of war.

Lincoln's advisors had argued against a blockade fearing it would be viewed internationally as an act of war unintentionally bestowing a legitimacy on the Confederate states as a foreign nation with whom the Union was now in conflict. Lincoln wagered, however, that a Union blockade was the best means of segregating the South from the rest of Europe both economically and diplomatically.

The Charleston Mercury derisively proclaimed the blockade to be an empty threat. With hundreds of harbors, river mouths, inlets, and bays available to the Confederacy, a blockade would be impossible for the Union to enforce. The citizens of Charleston were more offended than concerned. Blockade was an outrageous affront and motivated by the desire to punish Charleston for its bombardment of Fort Sumter.

Jack was more circumspect. He assumed that Charleston harbor would be a prime blockade target and key measure of the blockade's success. He also realized that the blockade was evolving. A Union line that previously consisted of harbor tugs, coal barges and refugees from the Staten Island ferry service had been replaced by serious warships, capable captains, and crews. The Union was building and purchasing top of the line steam-powered cruisers outfitted with deadly batteries.

Admiral Samuel Francis DuPont commanded the Southern Atlantic Blockading Squadron. He raised a task force of fifty ships and twelve thousand men and sailed them south of Charleston to Port Royal. Port Royal Sound is a natural deep-water harbor perfectly placed to provide a refitting and resupply base of operations for the blockade of both Charleston and Savannah. Port Royal was also inadequately defended.

DuPont's armada arrived outside of Port Royal Sound on November 4, 1861. The overmatched defending rebel forces were driven from their positions by a devastating naval barrage and skedaddled across surrounding cotton fields to escape into the woods and marshes. The invasion and occupation of Port Royal had been achieved without the loss of a single drop of Yankee blood. Admiral DuPont pushed up the Broad River to Beaufort effectively cutting off the inland waterway connecting Savannah and Charleston. The news that a major Union naval base and army garrison were encamped less than one hundred miles to the south was met with disbelief by the citizenry of Charleston. The looming Union presence would not be Charleston's first disquieting experience.

Jack was not the only one who sensed a turning of the worm. The hundreds of shirtless black slaves and free blacks trundling enormous cotton bales across the docks were far more animated and boisterous than Jack could ever remember. The slaves and the drivers shouted to each other across the narrow strips of water between the docks in the virtually incomprehensible cacophony of the Gullah dialect. Jack understood as much Gullah as any white man, but you did not have to be fluent to appreciate the obvious high spirits. Normally, the overseers and dock managers aggressively suppressed slave chatter. This morning, the slaves did not find their presence as intimidating as usual.

The slave community had been stirred to excitement by the election of the man they called "Massa Linkum." News of the ongoing war for their freedom was overheard on the street and over dinner service. Important news was secretly disseminated by word of mouth. By now, every slave in Charleston would be aware of DuPont's garrison in Beaufort. The increased attitude and sass among the enslaved dockworkers was being answered by the familiar and increasingly frequent crack of the bull whip.

Jack walked the bustling cobblestone street leading to the door of John Fraser and Company at Number One Cumberland Street. Black matrons hawked fresh fish from canvas tent-covered markets and younger women sold oysters and vegetables from push carts. Shoe-shine boys and cigar peddlers shouted for attention. Bar maids beckoned from the front door of one room taverns promising cheap beer and rum along with countertop lunch specials of hot-buttered corn pone, dried fish, pickled eggs, and pig's feet.

Jack waited in an outer office for about half an hour while George Trenholm and his partners finished a meeting with two Confederate officers and several other Charleston businessmen. When they emerged from Trenholm's conference room, George embraced his brother-in-law. "Jack, wonderful to see you. You're looking pretty good considering the reports I received."

"What reports were those?"

"Word on the wharf is that you'd gotten your butt shot off."

Jack laughed, "The Yankees did seem more interested than on my prior trips into port. They expressed displeasure with my failure to heed their hail. They bellowed some, but it just passed through my rigging."

Trenholm clasped Jack on the shoulder and turned to his guests, "This is Jack Holmes, captain of the *Will O' the*

Wisp, the most successful blockade runner on the Atlantic coast. I've lost track of all his successful runs, but my accountants know he's never lost a dime. Take a good look, gentlemen, because he's a phantasm, and if you blink twice, he and the *Wisp* will be gone."

Trenholm formally introduced Jack to each of his guests. The higher ranking of the two Confederate officers made a point of energetically shaking Jack's hand. "Captain Holmes, on behalf of the Confederate States of America, I want to thank you for your invaluable service. Our successes on the battlefield would not be possible without the weapons and munitions you and the other blockade runners have been so effectively providing."

"Thank you, sir. I'm obligated to do what I can," Jack replied.

George also made a point of introducing his brother-in-law to Christopher Gustavus Memminger. Jack was aware of who Memminger was, although they had never formally met. Christopher Memminger was Trenholm's financial advisor and one of his oldest friends. President Jefferson Davis had selected Memminger as the Secretary of the Treasury for the Confederacy. Although not quite as tall as Trenholm, Memminger was also ruggedly handsome with deep-set blue eyes and wavy light brown hair. During the hysteria of pre-war Charleston, Memminger's aloof demeanor rubbed some people the wrong way. Memminger had no tolerance for uninformed conversation and offended many who found him curt. He had few words and little time for those who failed to interest him. Other than George Trenholm, Memminger's list of interesting men was not long.

Prior to secession, Memminger had been mercilessly lampooned by "Barny" Rhett, Jr. and the Charleston Mercury for being a political moderate and a submissionist to a Northern controlled Union. Memminger's commitment to the cause was questioned as he employed many free persons of color and owned no slaves. Memminger was analytic, even-tempered, and opposed the war on practical grounds that had nothing to do with secessionist ideology. Because of his openly expressed pre-war reservations, many were surprised when Jefferson Davis selected him as Secretary of the Treasury. Davis, however, had to have a cabinet member from South Carolina and chose to overlook the blemishes on Memminger's ideologic purity.

Memminger considered himself a cooperationist as opposed to a submissionist, however, both positions were ridiculed for lacking the moral or physical courage to be a Southern nationalist. Wisely, no one ever accused the imposing Christopher Memminger of lacking either of those virtues to his face. Only after the election of the abolitionist Lincoln did Memminger leave compromise and conciliation behind in favor of his city and state.

"A pleasure, Mr. Memminger. You appear to be far less the blue-belly than I've heard described."

Trenholm pointedly looked down to the floor and the others looked at Memminger for his response to Jack's provocative greeting. There was a tense stillness for several seconds before Memminger broke into a laugh.

"So, I understand you must be a subscriber to the Charleston Mercury, Captain Holmes. Never has so much opinion been constructed so bereft of any facts. It's my favorite rag when I wish a quantity of cranks and a minimum of common sense."

"You do seem to be a favorite editorial subject of little "Barny" and his blustery father. I'm sure you take it as a badge of honor," Jack added with a sly smile.

Memminger smiled as well. "I believe the elder and younger Rhett have both been standing too close to their own incendiary rhetoric. It's seared their hair and fried their brains. I trust in my belief that their self-aggrandizing ambition and continuous search for the highest horse will inevitably lead to a hard fall. While I do not give a whit for the favor of the Rhett's opinion, I do look forward to their certain self-immolation."

"May I quote you on that for the record?" Jack asked with mock seriousness.

"I'd prefer you not," Christopher Memminger replied with another laugh.

Several of the other guests expressed their agreement with Secretary Memminger's appraisal of the Rhetts. After a round of handshakes, the guests bid their adieu to George and Jack who retired to Trenholm's inner office. Jack noticed that the gracious smile was now gone from his brother-in-law's face. Not many could perceive when George Trenholm was stressed. Jack was one of the few. "Is everything okay at home, George? How are Anna Helen and Eliza?"

"They're fine. At least Anna Helen is. Can't speak for Eliza. Remember, she's married to my dim-witted brother," which George punctuated with a laugh. "How is my favorite sister-in-law, Mary Ann, and the children?"

"Thomas Henry's fine. He's standing watch on the *Wisp* as we speak. I have not yet been over to Christ Church, so I'm unsure regarding the rest of the family. We'll probably take the *Wisp* over tomorrow for repairs. I am looking forward to seeing Mary Ann. More after this trip than most."

"As well you should. I'm surprised that Mary Ann didn't come over to meet you at the dock."

"Then you don't know Mary Ann as well as you think you do. There's no way she's coming across the river to meet a scruffy and smelly old tar who's just spent two weeks out on the salt."

"I take your point," Trenholm responded while pinching his nose to tease his brother-in-law. "I did hear that your Lizzie is working as a nurse at the hospital. That is unsettling and extremely challenging work, Jack. You should be very proud of her."

"We are. I just hate for her to witness such mayhem. She comes home completely tuckered out."

"George Chapman must be close to sixteen. Are you going to take him onto the *Wisp* as crew? Or, do you want to get him on a good ship?" George Trenholm grinned and clapped Jack on the shoulder.

"Actually, just sixteen. Mary Ann and I are going to have that conversation as soon as I get home. Mary Ann does not want George anywhere near this war. Of course, he's ready to volunteer. I don't think it's smart to have all three of us on the *Wisp*, but I also don't want him burrowing like a mole in a muck-filled army trench."

"I agree, Jack. Make me a promise that you and Mary Ann won't make any final decisions until I've had a chance to look into a couple of prospects."

"I appreciate you taking an interest in George Chapman's welfare."

"Anything for my favorite brother-in-law, and best captain."

"What was going on with that group? I sensed some angst around the edges of your gathering."

George Trenholm sighed and rubbed his eyes with both hands. "The loons have been left in charge of the asylum."

The two men sat in plush leather covered chairs and a stout black woman Jack had seen many times previously brought them a silver platter with hot biscuits, wildflower honey and slices of green apple. Two cups of hot hibiscus tea were poured. After a few thoughtful sips, Trenholm shared his concerns.

"Ever since the initial shelling of Fort Sumter, I've been trying to make others understand the inherent business realities of this war. The lack of business aptitude displayed by the leaders of the Confederacy is astounding."

George had long ago learned to separate hubris and magical thinking from clear vision and a realistic business prospectus. After another sip of tea George continued. "Contempt for the Yankees has blinded too many of our leaders from seriously considering the South's constraints and needs."

"So, what has happened?" Jack asked.

"Despite my counsel, and that of Secretary Memminger, President Davis and the rest of his Cabinet has made one reckless miscalculation after another. Davis believed that a Civil War would cost the Union both Southern trade as well as that from several border states who were leaning towards secession. Davis estimated that Lincoln would not have the belly for such a gamble and would bend to Northern business interests who would counsel appeasement instead of economic disruption. They were wrong on every damn count."

George caught himself and took a sip of tea to regain his composure. "What has set us back the most, however, was Davis' decision to withhold Southern cotton from the international market. Jefferson believed that the huge textile factories of Northern England and France, starving for raw material, would force their governments to, at least, recognize the Confederacy, if not actually join the war as a Southern ally in exchange for free cotton trade."

"England wants the trade but has no interest in another war with America," Jack interjected.

"Of course, they don't. I exhausted myself arguing the folly of this policy and foretold the misfortune that would follow. Both Britain and France had large enough stockpiles of top rail cotton that a Southern cotton embargo would hurt but not be crippling. I have spent enough time in Liverpool and London to know that the moral sentiment in England is not with the South on the issue of slavery. While the unemployed English working-class textile workers are angry, that anger is tempered by their anti-slavery sympathies. Davis' cotton embargo was a cataclysmic miscalculation."

George Trenholm considered Jefferson Davis to be the dimmest of wits, especially regarding financial matters. While "King Cotton" wielded significant economic power, it was not truly royal. Queen Victoria, however, was, and she was not going to recognize the sovereignty of the Confederate States of America or go to war on behalf of the slave-holding Southern states.

George continued, "As Lincoln predicted, Queen Victoria declared British neutrality last May. As a result, the cotton embargo did nothing but starve us of European cash and investment for the first two years of this war. Rather than banking the gold necessary to wage war we hoped that either Lincoln would lose his nerve or that England would fight for us. Well, wish in one hand and spit in the other, and see which one fills up quicker. I fear we've squandered the opportunity to become independent of Northern domination."

"I am sorry to hear that, George. I know that you must be immensely frustrated."

"I am, Jack. I have worried since day one that Southern secession would be doomed by the oversupply of clamorous speechmakers demonizing Northern abolitionists and an undersupply of pragmatic legislators and businessmen who understood the need to confront the limitations of an agrarian South."

Those limitations were obvious to anyone who seriously considered them. The South was rich in raw materials, but its wealth was primarily tied up in land, slaves, and cotton. More than eighty percent of the Union's manufacturing capacity and sixty-five percent of the railroad system were in the North. Once, shortly after secession, while staring from the soon to be shuttered windows of the New York City offices of John Fraser and Company, Trenholm lamented to an assistant, "There is more manufacturing capability within my view than in the entire South. God help us."

Iron could be mined in the South but could not be forged into steel or machined into precision tools. Only the Tredegar Iron Works in Richmond could provide experienced casting of large cannons or roll the two-and-a-half-inch iron plates essential to a modern navy. Birmingham, Alabama had some modest iron forges, but most other Southern foundries were little more than small town blacksmiths. The South was rich in coal and timber but lacked an adequate transportation system to get those raw materials to manufacturing centers. The South needed to expand its railroad system and replace its worn rails and steam engines.

The only two major shipyards in the South were Norfolk, Virginia and Pensacola, Florida. The former was a bustling, first-rate naval yard with two huge ship building houses. However, it had been destroyed when the Federals evacuated at the beginning of the war. The latter in Pensacola was only fitted for refurbishing and repair rather than new construction. Smaller shipyards, such as F.M. Jones Shipyard on Shem Creek, were scattered along the Southern coast, but almost all lacked the capability to build or equip a warship of even moderate tonnage. What infuriated George's sensibilities the most was that the ramshackle tugboats and worn-down passenger steamers that comprised the Confederate navy had been purchased at exorbitant prices exceeding the new construction costs of war ready gunboats.

The South did not even possess the ability to weave its own raw cotton into a finished product. Virtually all the domestic textile mills were in the North. It was infrastructure the South lacked, not will. There was plenty of coal, iron, and timber in the South, but it was either under or on top of remote hillsides. Who would mine it, harvest it and, given the poor transportation systems in the South, get it to the few legitimate factories capable of manufacturing the tools of war?

"In the meeting just concluded, I advised Christopher and the others that the Confederate States of America should immediately buy up all the cotton and cotton futures in the South and sell it to England for a treasury full of gold rather than withholding it in hopes of a political acknowledgement that's never going to come. The gold bullion received in exchange for the Confederate cotton bonds could both repay the planters and establish the essential credit of a Confederate central bank. With that gold we could build or purchase a fleet of armed ships for a retaliatory blockade of Northern ports. Cutting off the supply of raw materials to the North would neutralize their massive industrial advantage and increase the pressure on Lincoln for a negotiated end to the war. It is also conceivable that once English and French textile mill owners purchase the cotton bonds, they will finance their own merchant fleet to retrieve their cotton bales. Union seizure of those merchant ships on the high seas might precipitate a direct military confrontation which is exactly what Jefferson Davis has been hoping for."

George had been preparing this business plan ever since Lincoln ordered his naval blockade. Trenholm closed his office in the heart of New York's financial district and opened new offices in Nassau and Bermuda under new names. To ensure that the South was not cut off from European markets, Trenholm smuggled cotton, turpentine, tobacco, and timber out of Charleston and other southern ports on board more than sixty steamers he either owned or had invested in. These small steamers made for those neutral British islands where they off-loaded their cargo onto large European merchant ships. The most reliable of those steamers was Jack's *Will O' the Wisp*.

George also opened a branch office, Fraser, Trenholm and Company, in Liverpool. Trenholm's Liverpool office functioned as a bank, taking Confederate notes in exchange for the gold acquired from the trading of cotton and other goods. Confederate agents in Europe would then use that gold to purchase everything from warships and cannons, to rifles and bullets, to sewing needles and soap.

"The key is the gold," George concluded. "We have to nationalize the cotton and cotton futures and sell them in Europe for the hard currency we'll need to wage war."

Listening to George talk, Jack found it troubling that his risk, and the greater risk for many others, might prove to be in a futile fight.

George sensed Jack's alarm and smiled reassuringly. "Don't worry, Jack. There're always other moves to make."

"You need to know that it's already getting tight out there. It used to be a day sail. Now, mistakes can be lethal. Even if you know what you are doing, there are no longer any guarantees. We were totally dark when that Federal cruiser came up on us the other night."

"I don't have to worry about you, Jack. You are the best there is, and no ship is as stealthy as the *Wisp*. She is an apparition, and if anyone does see her, she'll show them her heels. Just like she did the other night."

"I appreciate your confidence, but I promise you, the risk is escalating with every run."

"I know. That is why we're partners on the *Wisp*. We're in this together. That's also why I wanted to see you today. I have some precious cargo I need you to take to Nassau on your next run. They're special envoys I need to get to England."

"Envoys?"

"Yep. Like I said, there're always more moves to make. I'm depending on you to get them there safely."

"Consider them in Nassau. Any more you can tell me?"

"Not right now. Too many ears. Once you've made your repairs and plans for departure, I'll fill you in. In the meantime, I thought you might appreciate this."

George handed Jack a folded piece of paper. "One of the Confederate officers gave me this intercepted message from one of the Federal captains in the South Atlantic Blockading Squadron. It was on a captured packet steamer being sent back to Washington."

Commander John Downes of the Federal gunboat Huron reported, "I would be glad if I could impress upon you some faint notion of how disgusting it is to us, after going through the anxieties of riding out a black, rainy, windy night at three fathoms of water, with our senses on alert for sound of paddles or sight of miscreant violation of our blockade, and when morning comes to behold him lying placidly inside of Fort Sumter, as if his getting there was the most natural thing in the world, and the easiest."

Jack smiled as he read.

Chapter 6

March 29,1862

Sugar House

Before leaving George Trenholm's office, Jack explained the situation with Copper Joe. He was blowing off some steam at the Brick House and got into an altercation with a pompous plantation owner. Jack did not know who had initiated the fracas, but that was irrelevant. Interactions with the Charleston City police did not go well for half-breeds. Joe's attitude had probably been adjusted a half-dozen times already.

Trenholm was a member of the State Marine Battery Commission which made him responsible for the seaward defense of Charleston. It was unclear what authority this actually conferred to him, but everyone in Charleston knew his name and position. George also never assumed anything was not or should not be under his personal jurisdiction. George promptly wrote a detailed note to the Commissioner of Police demanding Joe's release and designating him essential to the maritime defense of Charleston. Further, it instructed the police to extend all courtesy and latitude to Captain Jack Whitesides Holmes and the *Will O' the Wisp* crew. There was no question as to whether Trenholm's letter would be sufficient. The Commissioner of Police would toe the mark.

While capable of walking a pitching foredeck amid ocean swells, Jack appreciated any opportunity to walk on solid ground. Charleston's streets and alleyways were exploding with multi-colored azaleas proclaiming spring's arrival. A short-lived thundershower had blown through during his meeting at Trenholm's office. The wet sheen on the slate roofs coalesced into thin streams of rainwater sluicing down the elephant ears and banana leaves. The last remains of the thunderstorm coursed between the cobblestones carrying waxy magnolia leaves back to the river.

Private horse drawn carriages steered by well-liveried slaves crackled along the rutted crushed-oyster shell streets. Their destination were the Georgian mansions along East Bay and Battery Streets overlooking the seawall at the tip of Charleston. As the peninsula narrowed, the grand homes got packed closer together and set at acute angles to the street allowing the piazzas to catch the harbor breezes. The mansions had backyard slave quarters, cook houses, and exquisite gardens protected by iron fences and gates, topped with sharp spikes for security in the event of a slave uprising.

Behind those iron fences, conversations regarding the war were still overheated, captive to a narrow self-indulgent patriotism. However, the notion of a quick Confederate victory was now gone. Jack wondered if the patriarchs of those mansions still viewed their spiked gates and fences as protective or whether they were beginning to feel caged.

Jack stopped to appreciate a beautiful side garden adjacent to an unassuming single house. The war hadn't yet touched this tiny enchanted patch of Charleston. The garden was weed less, mulched with woodchips, bordered by carefully trimmed monkey grass and planted with camelia and oleander bushes. Creeping jasmine vines, daffodils, and paper whites were beaded with small crystalline water droplets which gleamed like diamonds. The garden had been tended to with affection.

The fronds of a prickly palmetto tree next to the garden rustled against a whisper of a breeze. Jack's eyes rose to a second-floor balcony decorated by iron grillwork tangled with blood-red bougainvillea. His eyes met those of a young girl, as bright and pretty as a rosebud. Jack nodded his appreciation for her garden and noted a flush pickling her throat before she turned away, unsure why she was embarrassed by being noticed. The young girl on the balcony embodied everything he loved about his home and reminded him of his daughter Lizzie. He offered a brief prayer that the coming years would not steal her life, or worse, her innocence.

The City Jail was located on Magazine Street. It was an ominous, four-story crenellated fortress built at the turn of the century. The dank cells were crowded with more men, lice, and rats than should ever co-exist. The building reeked of stale sweat, human filth, and fear. The nerves of any still sane man were frayed by the bloodhounds penned in the prison yard who howled all night. Gallows stood in the same prison yard where slaves were left hanging as a warning to others until the stench became overwhelming.

The jail held runaway slaves, free blacks who violated curfew, felons, deserters, and suspected spies. There was also a wing where black sailors from visiting ships were required to stay until their vessels left port as a precaution against them provoking the slave community. The building exuded misery and despair. Jack was furious that this was where his chief engineer and friend had been taken.

The Captain of the Guard was arrogant and unmoved. He had encountered innumerable outraged ship captains. If they could keep their crew's mizzen mast in their pants, off the grog and out of the brothels, they wouldn't be in this situation. The Captain of the Guard changed his tune when Trenholm's letter was produced. Copper Joe was produced a few minutes later.

Both of Joe's eyes were blackened and swollen nearly shut, his lower lip split, and the chipmunk-like swelling along his jawline made Joe almost unrecognizable. Joe was limping badly and needed assistance to walk. Jack was trembling with anger, knuckles blanching as he unconsciously balled and unballed his fists.

"Joe, you okay?" Jack asked without taking his eyes off the police captain.

"Fine, Cap'n. Sorry to have brought you down here. Man said some things I couldn't walk away from. Probably should have, but I think I was a bit tight." His words were almost unintelligible.

"Don't worry about it, Joe. Sorry I didn't get down here sooner. Mr. Trenholm wrote a letter demanding your release."

"I'll thank him, sir," Joe mumbled through his fattened lips and possibly broken jaw.

"No need, Joe. The *Will O' the Wisp* doesn't sail without you, and Mr. Trenholm has an important run planned for us."

"I'm ready, Cap'n. When do we sail?"

"Not right away. You'll have plenty of time to get fit."

"Fit as a fiddle right now, sir. These boys slapped me a few times with their handbags. Nothin' that would keep me from being seaworthy."

"I don't doubt you, Joe, but the *Wisp* needs a few repairs. They must've knocked a few memories out of you. The *Wisp* took some hits when you didn't deliver the speed I asked for."

Copper Joe laughed, and his striking, but incongruous, light blue eyes sparkled for the first time. He quickly grimaced and held his jaw with both hands. "Don't make me laugh, Cap'n. I haven't forgotten anything, and we was flyin'."

"We weren't movin' any faster than you are. Why ya hobbling?"

"One of the guards decided that I looked more like a slave than a chief engineer. I spent a good bit of yesterday on the treadmill over at the Work House. Got my left foot caught. Hurts, but it ain't broken."

Jack Holmes was an affable, easy going man who dutifully took his family to Sunday sermon whenever he was in port. Captain Jack was a different breed of man, and not one known for turning the other cheek. It was Captain Jack that was now glaring at the Captain of the Guard. His face flushed, and he repeatedly wiped his lips with the back of his hand as he decided whether to leap at the jailor's throat. After thirty tense seconds, Jack exhaled loudly and gathered himself. He looked at Joe and then slowly brought his eyes back around to meet those of the Captain of the Guard. Jack calmly and coldly informed him, "If I ever see you again, I'll cut your heart out."

The Captain of the Guard was smart enough to not respond.

Jack helped Copper Joe outside and they looked for a carriage. As they waited, both Copper Joe and Jack could hear screams emanating from the adjacent thick-walled Work House. Few white men had ever seen the inside of the Work House, but everyone knew of its brutality.

The Work House was a former sugar warehouse and most referred to it as the Sugar House. Owners who wanted a slave disciplined, but were too refined to do it themselves, sent them to the Sugar House to be punished for a fee. Slaves who forgot their place were sent downtown for "a little sugar." Like Pontius Pilot, owners could wash their hands, and the Sugar House would get their slave's mind right. Every slave in Charleston understood that "a little sugar" meant a day of unthinkable cruelty.

The Sugar House contained a huge treadmill which had originally powered the grinding of cane. Slaves sent to the treadmill had their hands tied above their heads and their feet tied to wooden planks. Their planked feet were used to turn the treadmill blades. If the slave slipped or faltered, the plank could become trapped between the rollers of the treadmill dislocating or fracturing an ankle or leg. A bullwhip encouraged effort on the treadmill.

The screams devolved to shrieks. The shrieks became more intermittent before deteriorating into the sub-human wails of a tortured animal. Captain Jack was familiar with screams of all types including those that ended with grown men pleading for their mother. He could differentiate the screams of pain from injury and the sound of the mortal soul escaping the body. This was a scream with which he was unfamiliar. Jack removed his slouch hat and rubbed the back his neck. Copper Joe saw an agitation the captain rarely revealed aboard ship.

"Joe, wait here. I'll return directly."

"Captain, your letter won't help you in there," Copper Joe warned. "I deserved my whippin'. That poor fella probably does too."

"Nobody deserves that," Jack said solemnly.

Copper Joe shook his head and felt sorry, but not remorse, for the man about to receive the captain's reproach. Jack Holmes was tall and well-knit, and most would describe him as having a friendly countenance. His family, friends and partners knew him as honest, loyal, and kind. He could be charming when charm was required. Joe, however, knew another side of Jack Holmes that could emerge from the shadows when Jack was wrathy. Jack Holmes was a man equally ready for either a hearty exchange or violent confrontation. Jack's preference was for the former, but that would, in no way, restrict his expeditious execution of the latter. Joe judged the latter to be more likely in this situation.

A teen-aged black boy was bound to a whipping post at the far end of the room. The whipping post was about eight feet tall, crowned with an octagonal block with iron clasps for securing the slave's wrists. The boy's tone indicated he was either unconscious or dead. His back had been laid open in a half dozen places. His gray woolen pants were soaked with blood over his buttocks and down the backs of his thighs. Standing ten feet away from him was a man with a long raw-hide whip draped around his neck and a bucket of water in his hands.

Captain Jack's arrival registered on the periphery of the man's focused and malicious intention. He wordlessly waved Captain Jack away and then threw the salted water onto the boy's flayed back provoking new screams. He was annoyed to look back and discover that Captain Jack had not left.

"I think he's done. It's time to cut him down," Jack shouted as he walked across the room toward the municipally sanctioned sadist.

Most of the re-educators in the Sugar House were either mulattos or free blacks. Captain Jack wondered if this hideous man might fall into a different, inexplicable category. The smallness of his head and repulsive facial features looked incestuous and certainly only engendered disappointment in those who bred him. His eyes were unnaturally close together and beetle-browed. Curly black hair rose from his ears, nostrils, and neck collar, but not from his head. His teeth were tiny, notched and the yellowish-brown color of concentrated urine. Smaller versions of such men emptied the chamber pots from underneath whorehouse beds. Larger versions ended up in places like the Sugar House.

The straw in the room was saturated with the fetid smell of urine, stool, and blood. Even that stink was overwhelmed by the foul stench of unwashed hair, body odor, decayed breath, and cruelty emanating from this half-man. Sweat and grime permeated his Confederate wool. His fingernails were ringed by dirt and pared to a point.

"Git on out now, sir. This ain't none of your bidness. I'm workin' this boy for his master. He's payin' the city for me to work'm good."

Captain Jack stepped closer. "I'm making it my business. I don't care what his master wants or has paid for. He's not here, but I am, and I'm tellin' you that this boy is done."

Jack had spent his entire adult life captaining his own ship. The safety of that ship, its crew and Jack himself required that his orders be instantly followed. A ship's captain without absolute authority is no captain at all. Crossing a shallow bar at top speed in pitch blackness under the threat of Union cannon made no allowance for debate or discussion. On board ship, there is only one voice, and Captain Jack's orders were followed immediately and without question. If not, there were unfortunate consequences.

The overseer stared back, similarly surprised by someone unprepared to be subservient. His self-worth had never been measured by any other metric than the pain he could inflict on others. He had never experienced pity, he fed on fear, and felt only mistrust of anyone untrussed. Puzzled by this man's intrusion into his place of work, he just turned his back on Captain Jack and prepared to administer another flesh slicing lash.

"Mister, I told you to stop, and I meant it," Jack ordered, pointing his finger at the overseer.

In the blink of an eye, a bullwhip cracked, and a curled streak of blood appeared on the back of Captain Jack's outstretched left wrist. Jack withdrew his hand like it had been struck by a water moccasin. A smirk appeared on the overseer's face. Jack could not see it as a blood red rage rose from his chest and his vision narrowed to a black shrouded tunnel. The Sugar House had just become the deck of the *Wisp* and a line had been irrevocably crossed. There would be no more discussion, only consequences.

Jack reached his right hand behind his back and between the slit in his black duster. The overseer's smirk disappeared when Jack withdrew a gleaming twelve- inch Arkansas toothpick. It was a weapon that had but one purpose and the cretin recognized that purpose immediately.

The overseer cracked the whip again just missing Jack's face. As Jack ducked away, the overseer picked up a pitchfork and advanced on his new prey. Jack moved behind a thick hand-hewn timber post to protect himself from the raw-hide's bite.

The whip cracked on each side of the support beam to keep Jack cowered. Jack could not allow himself to be trapped in a confined space by this vicious troll and his pitchfork. The overseer thrust the pitchfork to the right of the timber post and Jack took off to the left leaping on the treadmill. Jack scrambled to the top working the blades with his hands and feet.

The overseer's whip wrapped itself around Jack's calf with searing effect and began to drag Jack down. A downward slash of the Bowie knife severed the whip just before another thrust of the pitchfork would have found flesh.

With the whip cut, Jack leaped backwards off the rolling treadmill and landed on both feet behind the malignant overseer. Jack wrapped his right arm around the oaf's neck and with his left hand drove the Bowie knife to the hilt beneath the lowest left rib. Jack drug the knife upward through the diaphragm to where the heart would have been if he had one. The overseer fell forward impaling himself on the tines of the pitchfork which had fallen from his hands and become stuck between two treadmill paddles. The pitchfork and the treadmill lifted the overseer lifelessly into the air like a heathen offering as its rollers slowly came to a stop.

Copper Joe entered the Sugar House and viewed the tableau set before him. "Jesus, Captain. What in damnation happened here?"

"We had a disagreement over the extent of the boy's flogging. He was unprepared to listen to reason."

"He made a bad call."

"Time will tell. Help me get this kid off the post."

The black boy appeared to be about the same age as Captain Jack's son, George Chapman. His green eyes stood in stark contrast to his skin which was so black it shined like freshly mined coal. The bloody red muscles of his back also stood out in relief against the radiant onyx of his torso.

Copper Joe splashed the boy's face with water, covered his wounds with some clean straw, and then wrapped him tightly in a discarded tunic which probably belonged to his now dead tormentor. The boy did not utter a sound as Joe applied the horse straw and clothing. He stared slack jawed at the man who had whipped him, now dangling lifelessly twelve feet above his head, and bleeding out like gutted hog.

"Captain, we gotta git outta here, or we'll end up flayed open too. Except, after our flayin' we ain't goin' back to a jail cell. We goin' to the gallows."

Jack was unfocused, shaking and breathing heavily, as the adrenalin drained from his body. Copper Joe called to him twice to capture his attention. "Yes, let's get back to the *Will O' the Wisp* and then back across the Cooper River to Christ Church," Jack finally responded.

Jack and Joe helped the black boy out of the Sugar House. Joe's fear had temporarily cured his limp. A couple blocks away from the Sugar House, a more composed Captain Jack pulled them into an alley.

"What's your name, boy?" Jack asked.

"Vanderhorst," the boy replied.

"I don't mean your master's name. What's your real name?"

The boy's eyes got big. Was this a trick? Most slaves chose surnames for themselves but never used them in front of their master or any whites. It was an assertion of their own identity and a dangerous repudiation of their master's claim on their soul.

"Come on, what's your real name. We don't have time for games."

After several seconds of looking from Captain Jack to Copper Joe and then back again, he spoke. "Ezekiel."

Captain Jack now had his full attention and laid it out for him. "Okay, Ezekiel. Here are your options. You can head on back to the Vanderhorst mansion and tell them what happened. A man you did not know killed the overseer and turned you loose. I'd appreciate it if you don't give them much in the way of our description."

"Massa Vanderhorst ain't going to be happy about dat."

"No, he's not, Ezekiel. He's going to have to repay the city for the damage at the Sugar House and they're going to hang you no matter what you tell them or what they believe. Your second option is to hide here in the city until nightfall then try to sneak out of town into the countryside. The Yankees are camped down in Beaufort which is about ninety miles south of here. They'll protect you if you can make it there. It's a damn long way. I'd say it's most likely you'll be captured and killed for being a runaway."

"Mista, I ain't never been north of Boundary Street or that far south of the city."

"Your third choice is to come with us. I'm a ship captain, and this is my Chief Engineer. We're heading across the Cooper River to Christ Church tomorrow. We can put you off upriver near the swamps. Slaves have been cutting timber north of Charleston for years and sneaking off into the woods. They call themselves Maroons and live on high ground deep inside the swamp. They have fresh water, wood for shelter, and there's ample fishing and hunting. Ain't nobody found them out 'cause there ain't nobody really lookin'. They're close enough to some of the surrounding plantations that you can sneak back and visit with any relatives you might have there. The Maroons live a hard life, but they're free."

"Suh, I ain't got nobody on dem plantations or anywhere."

Captain Jack looked at Joe who shrugged and then nodded. "Or, you can stay with us on our ship. We'll find something you can do. It'll be hard work, but I'll pay you fairly. There aren't any slaves on my ship. We sail back and forth to Bermuda, Nassau and Cuba where most people look just like you. I'll set you off on any of those islands whenever requested, no questions asked."

"Do I have to get off?"

Both Joe and Captain Jack grinned. "If you work hard, don't drown, and still want to stay, you can sail with us for as long as you'd like. It's only fair for you to know that the Yankees try to blow us apart every time we leave the harbor."

"What's da name of ya ship?"

Copper Joe responded, "It's called the *Will O' the Wisp* and it's the best damn ship in the Atlantic."

Captain Jack gave Copper Joe a gold coin and instructed him to take Ezekiel back to the *Wisp* and tend to his lacerations. "They're probably not lethal, but recovery will take time. Keep Ezekiel out of sight. Take him to Dr. Southgate's cabin. The doc has treated the cat-o-nine tail's bite on more than one occasion. Suppuration and blood poisoning are both risks, but Ezekiel is young and should heal up okay."

"Will do, Cap'n."

"Joe, also have Dr. Southgate take a look at your ankle and jaw. I can't have my chief engineer hobbln' and mumbln' around."

"No need to worry about me. I'm good to go."

"Right," Jack replied with a look that told Joe his request was not a suggestion. Jack reached into his coat pocket and produced a diamond-shaped and numbered bronze badge. Jack pinned it to Ezekiel's new jacket.

"I always carry a few extra," Captain Jack explained to Joe. "In case anybody gets nosey."

The badges distinguished hired out slaves from free blacks. The badges also identified the type of work a slave was expected to be doing.

Copper Joe studied Ezekiel's badge. "I'm not positive this boy's gonna pass as a cooper."

"Only a one in three chance that any policeman you meet can read, but still probably best to keep off the main thoroughfares."

"Why ain't you comin' with us, Cap'n?"

"I got to clean this mess up, Joe."

"That ain't a good idea, boss. That's a bloody one in there and a slave is missing. The locals don't care that man was evil. They like him evil. I say we leave them scratchin' their heads and let the devil take the hindmost."

"Can't do that Joe, but don't worry. I'll fix it. You get Ezekiel back to the ship and get the engines ready to go. Tomorrow we are heading for Christ Church."

"Alright Cap'n, but if you ain't back to the ship by nightfall, we'll all be coming back down here with pikes and truncheons to git ya."

"I know you will, Joe, and so do they. That's how I know I'll be back."

Chapter 7

April 26, 1862

War Profiteers

The *Will O' the Wisp* spent almost three weeks on Shem Creek undergoing repairs. Jack had now returned to the East Bay wharf where the *Wisp* had been re-loaded with a king's ransom in Sea Island cotton. Southern plantation owners sold their cotton for five cents a pound. The frantic textile mill owners in England would pay sixty. With a capacity of seven hundred bales, the *Will O' the Wisp* would earn over $400,000 delivering this cotton to Nassau. The *Will O' the Wisp* was joined on the docks by more than a dozen other runners. Trenholm and other smart financiers were purchasing anything that would float. Two successful runs generated so much profit that even loss of the ship, cargo, and crew on a third run was still a lucrative investment.

Coming onto the deck, Jack noticed Bennett Gibbons and the wharfinger, James Hibben in animated conversation on the wharf side. Joining them, Jack inquired, "What's going on, Bennett? Doesn't seem like we're making preparations."

"We had an incident overnight and weren't sure how you'd want to handle it," Bennett replied.

"Does it have anything to do with a confrontation down at the Sugar House and a missing slave boy?"

"No, nothing like that, Captain. That's what I'm talking about," Bennett said, pointing back toward the *Wisp*.

The words "Judas Iscariot" were painted across the *Wisp's* hull in whitewash.

Bennett continued, "I've told James this is his responsibility. He's accountable for security on the docks and it's clearly inadequate. He doesn't agree and doesn't want to pay for repainting."

The disappointment in Jack's eyes was obvious. "I don't care who did this. Just cover it up with an oilcloth and have it repainted immediately. By immediately, I mean by this afternoon. I'll pay for it, James, but I expect security to be improved."

"Thank you, Jack," James Hibben answered. "I was telling Bennett that this is one of several incidences that have occurred over the past couple of weeks. The Charleston Mercury has been printing editorials accusing blockade runners of being war profiteers. Mr. Trenholm hasn't been mentioned by name, but everyone knows who's the he-bull in the ring."

"Any mention of the *Will O' the Wisp*?"

"Only to celebrate her successful runs, but again, everyone knows that she's one of Mr. Trenholm's ships."

"Thank you, James. Bennett, get the repainting done quickly. I want to leave for Nassau as soon as the moon is new."

James Hibben was wrong about who had title to the *Wisp*. Jack's ownership agreement with George Trenholm for the *Will O' the Wisp* was unique. Their partnership, coupled with the *Wisp's* incredible success, had made Jack wealthy. George had invested much of Jack's accumulated wealth in British banks as pound sterling to assure its safety. The money would be there for his family regardless of what might happen to him or with the changing fortunes of war. Still, the "Judas Iscariot" defacement stung him.

Denunciation was harshest when it contained an element of truth.

The Confederate War Department had established rules directing the activities of Southern blockade runners. The C.S.A. had placed the export of cotton in government hands after Jefferson Davis finally recognized the folly of withholding Southern cotton from European markets. Half the proceeds from all cotton and tobacco sales in Europe were credited to the Confederate treasury and used to pay for military supplies. One half of the cargo hold of every returning blockade runner was reserved for those military supplies needed by the Confederacy. The War Department issued further regulations prohibiting importation of luxury goods or "unnecessary" articles not for common use. Importation of "unnecessary" goods could result in heavy fines and penalties.

These latter regulations were the ones that "Barny" Rhett had harped on in his recent editorials. The Charleston Mercury called out speculators and profiteers as an anathema to polite society. "Barny" railed that the high-end luxuries in the blockade runners' hold arrived at the expense of critical military needs and everyday necessities like salt, sugar, coffee, cloth, candles, and soap. Never subtle, Rhett questioned the patriotism of the blockade runner owners and their dedication to the cause. War profiteers were also being routinely attacked in political speeches and outraged jawing in church courtyards and high battery parlors. With the war becoming a more desperate fight than anticipated, the expectations of the blockade runner were now greater. It was easy to connect the dots between those editorials and political speeches and "Judas Iscariot" scrawled on the hull of the *Wisp*.

Ignoring C.S.A. regulations, George Trenholm speculated heavily in luxuries and other commercial goods that he sold at inflated prices to Charleston merchants or directly to the Charleston elite through private auctions. Among the plantation owners there was still a taste for fancy French silk, Spanish Marino wool, South America alpaca fleece, French millinery and sadly, expensive mourning veils. George was an entrepreneur and believed he had little to offer the Confederacy other than his exquisite understanding of business. George could not and would not separate his commitment to financial success from his role as a servant leader to the Confederacy. George believed that one enabled the other. Jack understood that George was trying to thread an exceptionally fine needle. Moreover, they were literally and figuratively in the same boat. Jack was unsettled to be on the wrong side of public opinion.

George made no public excuses for his business model or expressed any private fear of C.S.A. penalties. Fraser, Trenholm and Company of Liverpool represented the Confederate treasury in Europe and banked the gold generated by the sale of C.S.A. cotton, tobacco, or other imported commodities. That gold provided the credit required to back the purchase of Confederate supplies needed for the war effort. As required by regulation, George filled half of each runner's cargo hold with C.S.A. military supplies which he delivered at an undervalued fixed price. George balanced that loss in the other half of his cargo hold with every manner of luxury to which the planter elite had become accustomed. To George, European china, Persian rugs, silk slippers, fine leather boots, cigars, Scotch whiskey, and Spanish Madeira were all "necessary" goods. The C.S.A. turned a blind eye to these importations as George knew they would.

There were only a few, including Jack, who were aware of the many sacrifices George Trenholm had made to preserve the South's ability to wage war and support its economy. George had exchanged more than a third of his personal wealth in gold for Confederate notes to forestall inflation. He used his European influence to promote the Southern cause and generate financial donations. George also allowed the head of the Confederate Secret Service to operate out of his Liverpool office. George personally covered the entire cost of the network of Southern agents in Europe by placing them all on his own company payroll.

Bennett Gibbons draped his arm around Jack's shoulder. "Jack don't let this get under your skin. They don't understand how much we're doing for the cause or the risks we're taking."

"Don't they?"

"How could they? They don't consider that the food they put on their table, the clothes on their backs and every bit of equipment used by their army must be smuggled in by us. Smuggled through a line of warships intent on blowing our butts out of the water. Smuggling is a risk no one would ever take without the chance to make a profit."

"I know, but the vandals aren't entirely wrong. In part, our profit does come at their expense."

"Even if we invariably step on each other's toes, the people who painted "Judas Iscariot" on the side of the *Wisp* don't really have anyone else to dance with. If it weren't for us, the boys in butternut gray would not be marching into battle in quality leather shoes, with a haversack full of food, a fine Enfield rifle, and enough bullets to set the Yankees on the run."

"I don't know, Bennett. Sometimes it just doesn't feel right."

"Maybe, it is and maybe it isn't. What I know for sure, is that you are the last man on these docks who should be feeling guilty. I know that you donate those medicine vials you bring back in your cabin. The crew knows that you pay them more generously than any other captain, and always in hard British gold or pound sterling. Do you think the crew doesn't know that other blockade runners lease slave crews to increase their own profit? Shake it off, my friend, especially if you're going to take us on another run tonight."

Left standing alone on the East Bay quay, Jack realized that Bennett was right, at least about the need for him to get focused on the task ahead. He was responsible for a valuable ship and a valuable cargo. He could hear the rhythmic thumping of the steam presses which had made outward-bound cotton runs even more profitable. Planters now brought their bulky cotton bales by barge or wagon to the cotton presses which compressed them to roughly half their original size. With smaller bales, the potential profit for each run almost doubled. Once in place, Jack's deck hands jammed the cotton bales tight into the holds with screw jacks. Turning the screw jacks just a few more times allowed more bales to be added. Every available inch of the *Will O' the Wisp's* hold and deck space was tightly packed with white gold.

Once loading and repainting was completed, Jack signed the necessary paperwork with James Hibben. He also set his own guards around the ship. Jack and his wife, Mary Ann, had plans for a farewell dinner at Ashley Hall, the downtown home of George and Anna Helen Holmes Trenholm. George and Anna Helen hosted a similar dinner every time the *Will O' the Wisp* left Charleston. It was a party that acknowledged, but did not discuss, the fact that family and friends might not see each other again.

After the events of the day, Jack would have difficulty not viewing George and Anna Helen's dinner as a last supper. Jack wondered how Judas Iscariot must have felt that night, a disingenuous guest with thirty pieces of silver in his pocket. The notion of betrayal in any form was abhorrent to Jack.

Chapter 8

April 26, 1862

Ashley Hall

It was dusk when Jack and Mary Ann's carriage rolled through Ashley Hall's towering wrought-iron gates. The sunset west of the Ashley River had set the sky on fire with curling fingers of red, pink and violet flame. Purplish-orange clouds domed the dying sun. Enough light remained in the day, however, to appreciate the meticulously groomed grounds of Ashley Hall. The Rutledge Avenue mansion was pillared and stately, reflecting the stature of the man who lived there. A splendid landau drawn by a pair of high-spirited bays followed the Holmes' carriage through the open gates.

On the front steps, Jack and Mary Ann introduced themselves to a young man named James Morris Morgan who was returning from an afternoon ride with one of George Trenholm's daughters. James Morris Morgan had been staying with the Trenholm family for a couple of months and was now sparking the lovely Helen Trenholm. The Ashley Hall foyer was dominated by a one-of-a-kind flying spiral staircase and the luxurious aroma of old Madeira.

A young slave girl greeted them with a silver tray of wine glasses. Jack caught her eye as he thanked her for the wine. Every slave learned to be deferential as a matter of survival. A lifetime of submissive servitude had trained her in the unctuous arts, but she had not mastered her eyes. The hate in her eyes was beyond conscious control.

Glowing embers deep in her eyes reflected injustices that had begun at birth on a straw mat over the cold dirt of a slave cabin floor. A father who had been sold and shipped away before imparting any conscious memories. Held in the bloody hands of a mother physically and emotionally exhausted from picking prickly cotton bolls all day under a blazing sun. Odium tempered to a fine hard edge by watching the white overseer first taking older sisters, and later herself, to the deep grass to satisfy his feral urges. Selection as a house slave did little to change a lifetime of humiliation. Condemnation and dismissal were a daily reminder of her place, and the Sugar House awaited if she forgot.

Only her eyes revealed the detestation she felt for every white man she had ever met. It was a carefully considered act of defiance. Lashes could be poulticed, fractured bones set, and broken teeth pulled, but they would never take her eyes. Every slave quickly learned they were a commodity, and a blind slave was far from prime.

Jack Holmes held her gaze for several seconds after accepting the glass of Madeira. He considered it remarkable that so few white men could read a story written in such bold print. It surprised and troubled him that such loathing could reside in the beautiful home of his friend and sister. What could be better than working for George and Anna Helen at Ashley Hall? Looking into the slave girl's eyes, he already knew the answer.

Jack's sister, Anna Helen, was the oldest, most independent, and outgoing of all of William and Sarah Ann Holmes' children. Anna Helen was as masterful at carpentry and joinery as Jack. She could hunt, fish, and sail as well as any man. Anna Helen was also the prettiest girl on the Lowcountry coast with ice blue eyes, high cheekbones, and long, wind-tangled auburn hair. It was that beauty and wild spirit that caught the attention of the dashing George Alfred Trenholm.

Anna Helen breezed among the assembled guests with ease and grace, bringing a smile to all she touched. Jack was certain that Anna Helen treated the house slaves well and could not possibly be responsible for what he had seen in the slave girl's eyes. Jack believed that Anna Helen shared his distaste for the holding of human chattel. Jack would talk with Anna Helen about this young girl when the chance presented itself. There must be someone overseeing the house slaves who is mistreating them.

Anna Helen and George soon brought over their two special guests to meet Jack and Mary Ann. The man was introduced as James Dunwoody Bulloch, one of George's most trusted managers in his Liverpool office. It was a canard that fooled no one. Bulloch was a short, burly man with a barrel-chest and broad, strong shoulders who looked as if he might burst from his suit at any moment. Bulloch was the head of the Confederate Secret Service in Europe and would be as out of place in a manager's office as a bull in a china shop. He nodded a greeting, but his face remained impassive except for an intensity which burned deep in his eyes as well.

Bulloch had been born in Georgia and joined the U.S. Navy as a midshipman in 1839. At the outbreak of the war, Bulloch resigned his fourteen- year commission in the U.S. Navy and volunteered to serve the Confederacy. Captain Bulloch was sent to England in June of 1861 to secretly arrange for the building of a fleet of commercial raiders that could disrupt Northern transatlantic shipping. As cover, Captain Bulloch was assigned to work out of the offices of Fraser, Trenholm and Company in Liverpool.

Captain Bulloch's efforts were clandestine in order to skirt the English Foreign Enlistment Act. Under that law, British shipbuilders could not build, equip, or arm any vessel for a belligerent foreign government. However, the textile mills of Lancashire had fallen quiet. Thousands of English working men were unemployed, and business was business. The British Maritime courts conveniently ruled that if the ship, armaments and naval crew did not come together in British territory then it did not constitute an armed expedition under the Foreign Enlistment Act.

George Trenholm introduced James Bulloch to the Merseyside shipbuilders William Cowley Miller and John Laird of the Birkenhead Shipbuilding yard. Bankrolled by almost a million dollars in gold from the sale of Confederate cotton, Bulloch found these men to be willing partners.

The first steam ship Bulloch commissioned was the *Oreto,* built to full battleship specifications but without its battery or ammunition. The *Oreto* sailed from England under a British captain and flying British colors. At sea, the *Oreto* rendezvoused with a merchant steamer carrying guns, naval supplies and Confederate Naval officers who happened to be looking for a ship to call their own. Transfer of title was made at sea to Adderly and Company of Nassau, the local agents for Fraser, Trenholm and Company. The *Oreto* was re-commissioned as the lethal man-of-war, *C.S.S. Florida.*

Bulloch's second ship was an even larger, three-masted topsail schooner equipped with a powerful auxiliary steam engine, called the *Enrica.* After the *Oreto,* its construction did not go unnoticed by U.S. officials who reported the *Enrica* as a violation of British neutrality laws. Under intensifying scrutiny from British authorities and threat of seizure, Bulloch invited several of Liverpool's social elite to take an innocent and festive maiden sail down the River Mersey. The *Enrica* sailed on the evening tide accompanied by the tug *Hercules.* At the mouth of the river, Bulloch informed the guests that the *Enrica* would need to be out all night for sea trials and he would accompany the invited guests back to Liverpool on the *Hercules.* The *Enrica* sailed on with a British crew to the Azores where she was outfitted with guns, ammunition and supplies. Once again,

Trenholm's agents transferred her title and the *Enrica* was renamed as the *C.S.S. Alabama.*

Captain Bulloch's return to Richmond had been to report on the progress with the *C.S.S. Alabama* and to raise a crew of Confederate naval officers. George explained that he needed Jack to get Captain Bulloch back to Nassau where he would rendezvous with the *Alabama's* new naval officers coming separately from Richmond before taking an English steamer to meet the *C.S.S. Alabama* in the Azores.

Jack immediately realized that the risk associated with the upcoming run had increased dramatically with Captain Bulloch on board. Captain Bulloch was persona non gratis on two continents. There was no chance that Bulloch's transatlantic operations had escaped the attention of the Union's network of spies. Jack smiled and shook Bulloch's massive hand while lifting his glass with the other.

"A pleasure to meet you, Captain Bulloch. Here's to a safe and swift trip to Nassau."

"I'm sure it will be. Your reputation precedes you, Captain Holmes. I was specifically instructed by Secretary of the Navy Mallory to come separately to Charleston so I may be transported in your capable hands."

Mary Ann Holmes was impressed by Captain Bulloch's military bearing, propriety and purpose. She was proud that Jack was transporting him to meet the new officers and crew of the *C.S.S. Alabama.* She was not as enthused about the other special guest that Jack would have on board.

In the earliest days of the war, the hazards associated with blockade running were considered so slight that both women and children frequently made the runs between Charleston and the Caribbean Islands. Many sailed on to European destinations. However, as things had become more dangerous, women were no longer accommodated. Jack's other passenger would be Miss Belle Boyd of Martinsburg, Virginia.

An ardent Southern nationalist, Belle Boyd was unsatisfied with the assumption that her war effort would be restricted to bandaging festering wounds or praying with the mortally wounded. She was an outstanding horsewoman and knew every river, stream, valley, path or pass along the border between Virginia and Maryland. Soon after the battle of Bull Run, she became a member of the Confederate intelligence service smuggling communiques back and forth across Union lines either sewn into her riding habit or rolled into her coiled hair. President Jefferson Davis had personally asked George Trenholm to arrange Miss Boyd's safe passage out of Charleston. Whatever she was carrying needed to be personally delivered to someone of importance in Europe. Belle Boyd was frequently asked to carry such communications when it was imperative that they be well received.

Belle was said to be intelligent and well-read. Mary Ann noticed within minutes of her arrival in Trenholm's parlor that Belle Boyd was also clever and charming, essential gifts for a woman who trades in manipulation. Belle Boyd had an athletic build, long blond hair in tight ringlets and striking green eyes. She captured the attention of every man or woman whenever she entered a room. Mary Ann saw Belle Boyd for who she really was, an iron fist in a velvet glove.

Scandalous stories of Belle's ability to enchant Union government officials, army and navy officers and even utilitarian clerks in the War Department were well known. Her charms supplied the South with a ceaseless flow of top-secret maps and plans, blueprints, and orders for both the Federal army and navy. While happy for these small Southern victories, the women at Trenholm's dinner party discretely questioned the boundaries of Belle Boyd's patriotism. Whispers which had never bothered Belle Boyd. Mary Ann said nothing impolite but was annoyed that Jack would be giving this woman his captain's berth on the way to Nassau.

As captain, Jack had other concerns with Belle Boyd on board. Not for his crew who all knew better. Not for any concern over her being a member of the fair sex. In Jack's experience, women face dangerous circumstances at sea with far more composure than their male counterparts. Maybe a greater innate curiosity that prevails in the face of peril. Maybe the suffering of childbirth allows women to compartmentalize their natural fear of death.

Jack's concern was for Belle Boyd's less attractive personal characteristics. Belle had a fierce, hair-trigger temper and no tolerance for fools. Another captain described Belle Boyd as the most shrewish harridan he had ever encountered. The devil-may-care Belle Boyd also had the type of courage that most would describe as recklessness. On a ship, it was the type of courage that brought jeopardy to others.

Dinner was sumptuous, as it always was, at a dinner party hosted by George and Anna Helen. Barbequed pork shoulder and rice pilaf was accompanied by a fine French wine. Between courses, Mary Ann expressed her disapproval of the upcoming trip by her irritated and deafening silence.

Anna Helen orchestrated the dinner like a maestro. She had installed a button in the floor at her end of a long mahogany dinner table which when stepped on rang a bell in the pantry. The number of rings signaled the need for wine, appetizers, the main course, or dessert. Besides its efficiency, the system was also designed to exclude servants from the dining room. Word of mouth following a dining table discussion regarding the prosecution of the war was a major source of information in the slave community.

The dinner's crowning moment was the highly anticipated and flamboyant arrival of a splendidly dressed older servant carrying a silver tureen of terrapin stew. The guests murmured with excitement as other servants placed a special terrapin fork at each place setting. The terrapin fork had both a tong for the terrapin meat and a bowl for the soup broth. Terrapin stew was the most elevated of culinary efforts and a highlight at all of George Trenholm's elite dinner parties.

Terrapin stew had been originally eaten by the slave populations of the Tidewater area between Virginia and Maryland. The soupy stew was served over a starch of African origin and was a cousin of creole gumbo. Over time, the African food traditions were appropriated by the white masters. The name terrapin itself was an Algonquian Indian word that translated as "good tasting turtle." The successful preparation of terrapin stew was a mark of pride for a host like George Trenholm.

George's slave who had mastered the technique enjoyed such a reputation that he did virtually nothing else. The turtle's head was severed, and the carcass hung upside down for hours to bleed out. It had to be dissembled and butchered carefully, removing the nails, scales and shell along with the entrails. Key was making sure that the gallbladder was not perforated which would impart a bitter taste to the turtle meat. If fortunate enough to find eggs within a she-turtle, they would be hard boiled and added to the soup. George's ability to afford a slave with the talent to prepare such a sophisticated fine dining dish was a matter of societal prestige.

Jack knew that George lived extravagantly. It was not Jack's life, but it was the life of an international financier and businessman who had been successful beyond measure. Both men and women were drawn to George Trenholm who captured them with his piercing gaze, sweet, distinctive smile, and charm. George's brilliant conversational powers held all around him under a rapturous spell.

Uniquely, George could be both dignified and intimidating at the same time. It was a duality that he had frequently used to business advantage. Tonight, at the head of his own dinner table, he engaged his guests with irresistible charisma and buoyant conversation. Even when not speaking, George would stare at you intently with his unblinking eyes holding your attention. His commitment to you and whatever you were saying reminded Jack of a springer spaniel pointing out a covey of partridges.

After allowing everyone to savor the delicious aroma of their terrapin stew, a small cadre of servants circled the table sprinkling a mixture of finely chopped spring onion tops, parsley, dill, and celery leaves on top of the stew as a garnish. Croutons crisped in duck fat were also passed. The original server circled the table offering a dram of sherry to top off the presentation. Moans of satisfaction soon began to arise from around the table.

Knowing George's preference, Jack asked the question that many were wondering, "George, is this a Chesapeake Bay Diamondback Terrapin?"

"I wish it were. The king of all turtles; revered for its delicacy and flavor. Sadly, our recent disagreements with the North have made them hard to come by. My man, Justin, has discovered that the Shem Creek snapper makes for an extremely fine substitute."

"Well, he's absolutely right. I, for one, cannot tell the difference."

"Thank you, Jack. Sounds like you're angling for another bowl," George responded eliciting general laughter.

"Honestly, George. This is a different version than Justin has prepared before. I like it even better."

"Most people prepare their turtle soup Philadelphia-style with heavier cream and mace. They add cayenne and ground white pepper, but I think that overpowers the mild flavor of the turtle meat. Philadelphians also prefer brandy to a skim of sherry, but those people are pagans. In Baltimore they make their turtle soup with a clear, buttery broth, but I find it a little bland."

"Justin's inspiration comes from where?" Belle Boyd inquired.

"Justin came to me from New Orleans. His New Orleans version is a bit more piquant with a spicy tomato broth and darker roux. Justin calls it his mammy's Creole Snapper soup."

Mary Ann asked if the chopped hard-boiled eggs were turtle or hen.

George smiled. "Justin would never divulge such a sensitive preparation detail."

"Pity," said Belle Boyd seated beside Captain Bulloch. "I imagine I could entice him to reveal his secrets." Belle Boyd smiled wickedly at her own impertinence and seemed to be looking directly at Mary Ann Holmes.

Jack dropped his head realizing just how long the carriage ride home would be. Maybe he would have a second bowl of soup.

After dinner, Anna Helen invited everyone to the wide second floor piazza for continued conversation while enjoying tea and a special homemade dessert. Anna Helen had collaborated with the women in the kitchen to capture the perfect proportions of molasses, brown sugar, tiny hand-ground African runner peanuts and coconut to produce sweet tasting, figgy-textured "monkey meat." Anna Helen was proud of how the dessert had turned out. The cooks had also sliced some fresh peaches which complemented the "monkey meat" perfectly.

The men hung back, abusing Trenholm's parlor with the smell of strong cigar smoke, strong brown whiskey, and strong language. Jack was pleased to see the thin quarter moon almost completely obscured by a bank of clouds in the east. Tomorrow would be a perfect night to run.

George Trenholm called everyone together and announced that he had received an important telegram. It was signed by Stephen R. Mallory, Secretary of the Confederate Navy, and instructed James Morris Morgan to report for duty as a member of the Confederate Navy assigned to the *Will O' the Wisp* under the command of Captain Jack Whitesides Holmes. Everyone knew that George Trenholm had arranged for the appointment for his protégé.

There were handshakes and toasts all around. Young James was mightily pleased and repeatedly promised Captain Holmes that he would do his level best. George pulled Jack aside and asked him to take care of James Morgan.

"George, you know there can't be any preferential treatment. He starts at the bottom the same as everyone else, including Thomas Henry. It's the only way for him to gain the respect of his crewmates."

"Understood. No special treatment requested. Just make a good sailor out of him. I'm thinking about sending him to the Naval Academy."

"That I can do, George. He'll come back a different man."

"That's all I'm asking. Thank you."

"George, I'm sorry for putting you in the middle of that unfortunate situation down at the Sugar House."

Trenholm smiled back with a twinkle of insolence in his eyes. "Nothing to apologize for, Jack. From what I'm told, it was a comeuppance long overdue. The miscreant lashed the wrong man and paid for it. However, when you return, I'd warn your crew to avoid the city police. Hard feelings may persist."

"Excellent advice. I will pass it along."

Jack Holmes then turned to his newest crew member. "Seaman Morgan, my advice would be to end your evening now and get some sleep. Tomorrow night will be a long one. Are you prepared?"

"Absolutely, sir. I'm ready for duty."

Chapter 9

April 28, 1862

Salt Fires

A cloudless night delayed the departure of the *Will
O' the Wisp* by twenty-four hours. It was a calculated risk. A
fully laden ship sitting dockside was certain to create
suspicious visuals for the ever-present Union spies along the
waterfront. That risk was accepted in anticipation of the
heavy clouds now walling up on the horizon. Tonight, the
Wisp would sail for Nassau underneath a starless sky and in
the shadow of a new moon. Captain Jack soundlessly
signaled the crew to throw over the lines.

Jack's plan was to leave the harbor heading north
against the backdrop of Sullivan's and Long Island before
turning and beginning his dash to open sea. The sky was
black on black and a chilling breeze was raising a mist off
the water's surface. The best of all possible scenarios would
be for that mist to coalesce into a midnight fog. Blessed with
both fog and a moonless night, safe passage was virtually
guaranteed.

A complete blockade of Charleston would require
coverage of thirteen miles of surrounding ocean. While the
Union blockading squadron had expanded to twenty
steamers, it was still woefully inadequate to button down
every possible route of escape from Awandaw to the Stono
Inlet.

Captain Jack's plan of running against the backdrop of Charleston's northern barrier islands would make the *Will O' the Wisp* virtually impossible to spot. Steaming close to shore, however, was risky in the absence of well illuminated landmarks along the maddingly monotonous coastline. Jack liked to make use of the salt fires which he knew to be burning at specific spots along the Sullivan's and Long Island beaches.

Salt had become an expensive commodity since the start of the blockade. Several families on the barrier islands had taken to boiling saltwater in large iron kettles on the beach to produce their own salt as well as a salable commodity. It was a slow process requiring fires to burn constantly day and night. Jack knew all of these families and could pick out each salt fire as corresponding to a specific barrier island location. The salt fires were Captain Jack's personal landmarks which informed his mental map as to the *Wisp's* exact position and the location of the channels that would take him to open sea.

Some captains coordinated with the local Confederate forces to set up a series of coastal lights to guide their exit and return to harbor. Jack worried that the Union blockaders might take notice of new, unexplained beacons on shore and preferred to rely on the ever-present salt fires. As per usual, Jack chose to wager on his own sailing experience.

Some Federal captains tried hanging powerful masthead searchlights for use on night patrol. Illuminated as they were, it created an impressive tableau of Federal authority, but also made it child's play to avoid them in the dark. The Federals soon learned the folly of masthead lights; however, even in the dark, the blockade remained a simple riddle to solve.

Bored Federal lookouts spent tedious hour after hour on high alert peering into blackness for sign of a nearly invisible prey. Eternal vigilance was an unsustainable standing order. Many successful blockade runs owed more to an untimely nap than they did to the skill of the runner captain. Among Union captains, assignment to the Charleston blockade was considered the worst possible duty. Union captains referred to Charleston as a "rat hole" due to the multitude of navigable rivers and inlets up and down the Lowcountry coast. Realizing their naval careers hung on interdiction success, assignment to the Charleston blockade had proved to be highly demoralizing to both captains and crews.

The Union captains were also aware of the strain that was being placed on their ships. Winter storms, buffeting winds and heavy seas damaged rudders, rigging and hulls of vessels constantly on patrol. Needed maintenance often exceeded the ability of the crew and the ship-based machine shops. Consequently, Union frigates were frequently missing from the blockade line, having abandoned their post to pursue repairs either in Port Royal or Northern shipyards.

Even when seen, blockade runners were hard to stop. Hitting a low-slung, fast moving runner in heaving seas and pitch blackness was far more luck than skill. The only range-finding system available to the blockaders was line-of-sight and experience, both of which were in short supply. Union naval ordinance was also of poor-quality after weeks or months at sea. The Union blockaders fired calcium flares with every possible contact providing brief, but brilliant illumination over a wide area. Given the frequency with which they were fired, the calcium flares were often more effective in identifying the location of Union cruisers than they were in spotlighting a nearby blockade runner.

Even when a blockade runner was discovered, their shallow draft usually offered them escape back across the bar. The big Federal cruisers could not get any closer than a half mile or so of the shallow channels used by the blockade runners without putting themselves at risk of grounding. As the blockade dragged on, the usual sing out of, "Sail-ho!"

was replaced by the more frustrated, and angrier cry of, "Black Snake." Captain Jack took pride in this new reputation.

Although supremely confident of success, Captain Jack still took all precautions, especially considering his important passengers. All lights were doused, except of course, Captain Jack's pipe. The binnacle was hooded, and the fireroom hatch covered by a tarpaulin. Captain Jack and Thomas Henry were stationed to port and starboard, respectively. Bennett Gibbons manned the pilot house which had been wrapped in hawsers and chain cable for protection. Steam pressed cotton bales were piled around the engine room hatches protecting the boilers and coal stores from hot shot and shells.

Cotton bales were also stacked behind the bulwarks to protect the crew from small arms fire and exploding oak and cedar. Loose timbers were laid across the deck to protect the crew below from any downward shots at close quarters. Copper Joe had rigged a hose from the boilers that could spew scalding hot water on potential boarders. No one dared cut corners on the *Will O' the Wisp* crew. The men assigned above deck went below to the engine room to smear their faces with coal soot. The heavers, stokers and boiler tenders were already known as the "black gang" because of the filthy work of servicing a coal-fired boiler. Some of the "black gang" were former slaves, but some were pasty-white Scotch-Irish immigrants. It was impossible to tell the difference.

Captain Jack strode the deck between the big paddle wheel boxes. He signaled Bennett Gibbons that the *Will O' the Wisp* was ready to turn to sea. The timing was perfect. The *Wisp* would hit the Charleston bar when the tide was at its highest. With a hold bursting with pressed cotton and timber, the *Wisp* was low in the water and Jack was glad to be passing over the bar at tide's peak.

Captain Jack chatted quietly with both Captain Bulloch and Belle Boyd who insisted on remaining on deck despite Jack's preference for her to remain in his cabin below. The excitement of the run and potential consequences of failure fueled a rush of adrenalin that kept both Belle and Bulloch topside. A brewing nor'easter made it uncomfortably cold. Captain Jack promised to bring up some buckets of hot embers from the fire boxes once the *Will O' the Wisp* was safely past the blockade.

The *Will O' the Wisp* was about five miles past the bar when the forward lookout shouted, "Smoke, dead ahead."

Captain Jack ran forward and took the long glass from the lookout. He was unable to spot the ship on the horizon but confirmed the spindly wisps of smoke against the low- lying clouds. Jack asked Thomas Henry to go to his cabin and fetch the English colors from a variety of flags he kept in his steamer trunk. The ruse of hoisting English colors was unlikely to work but might create an element of confusion that could be used to their advantage.

The *Will O' the Wisp* continued to race forward, all eyes straining to identify the source of the smoke. No sound was heard other than the unwelcome but unavoidable clapping of the side-wheel paddles. Captain Jack continued to scan the horizon until he spied a double line of Union blockaders. Two of the larger vessels were already steaming directly toward the *Wisp* while another two were still at anchor. Several smaller gunboats were also cruising restlessly. Jack was shocked by the clustering of so many ships of the line directly in his path and so far out to sea. Despite miles and miles of open ocean, the Yankees had somehow known exactly where to position themselves to intercept the *Will O' the Wisp*. The only explanation was that Union spies on shore had predicted the night of the *Wisp's* departure and had somehow divined that Jack would use one of the northern channels off Long Island to reach open sea.

The shadowy forms of the large Union ships became clearer as they closed the distance. Spirals of smoke rising from the other two indicated they were firing their boilers as well. They would steam toward his flanks. The Union ships were too close and moving too fast to consider turning tail and trying to make it back across the now distant bar.

A dangerous encounter was looming, and the *Wisp* had nowhere to run.

Jack shouted, "Full speed," down the engine room tube and the vibration of increased revolutions could be immediately felt followed by the heavier pounding of the side paddles. That sound was soon overlaid by the windward roar of heavy guns and the scream of sizzling iron. A bursting shell carried away a tier of cotton bales piled on the starboard deck while another slammed into the ship's structure. The *Will O' the Wisp* trembled with the impact.

"What's the damage?" Captain Jack demanded.

"Two shells, sir. One exploded among the cotton bales. No structural damage but one crewman wounded. Not severe. A large shell passed through the deck about two feet above the water line. It penetrated the starboard side coal bunker but didn't explode," answered a boatswain.

Jack hesitated, realizing that had the shell exploded in the coal bunker the *Will O' the Wisp* would've been blown to bits and no man left alive.

A trail of sparks flared from the nearest frigate. It was a Drummond calcium rocket which exploded in a blinding white light. The flash revealed two Union cruisers in stark relief positioned to administer a dreadful broadside of heavy cannon fire. Another rocket was fired over the *Will O' the Wisp* and Jack could see the cannon ports being opened. In response, Captain Jack ordered his deck crew to fire two identical calcium rockets at a right angle to his actual course in hopes of confusing the warships closing on his position. The ruse did not work.

The trap had been set well. The *Wisp* was boxed in. The nearest vessel continued to close and fired her bow chaser. A shell sizzled over the foredeck but made no impact. A veil of white smoke enshrouded the second frigate and Jack knew they had luffed up an enormous broadside. Several shells hissed themselves into the sea just thirty yards short of the *Wisp* followed by muted but still resonant submerged explosions. The top half of a smokestack sheared away while another shell passed through the fo'c'sle and a seaman.

A large solid projectile boiled through the side of the ship and struck the sandbags piled around the boilers. The 32-pound shot bounced over a steam drum and ricocheted off the overhead beams carrying away some of the engine room ceiling and the head of a coal heaver. A dense cloud of oak splinters and iron shavings filled the engine room, shooting through the clothes and face masks of the engine room workers like tiny arrows. The engine room men were surprised by the small rivulets of blood they discovered running down their arms, legs, face, and chest. They kept heaving, knowing they should already be dead, and soon would be, if they lost steam power.

Captain Jack took the damage reports grim-faced and without response. He glanced quickly at the Union frigates continuing to close from three directions leaving him no place to run. Jack approached Captain Bulloch and Belle Boyd just as another shell burst overhead showering them with enough debris that even the most seasoned sailor would have hit the deck. Neither Bulloch nor Belle even flinched.

"Miss Belle were it not for your presence on board I would burn the *Wisp* to the water's edge rather than give her over to those Yankee bastards. Excuse my language."

"Captain, do as you must and do not pay any deference to me. I am unafraid, and uncaring as to my fate, except for the possibility of returning to a Federal prison. I will never again be placed in one of those filthy Yankee cages. There are many things worse than death. Burn her if you must. I will happily take my satchel to the bottom of the Atlantic in preference to handing it over to those sons of bitches. Excuse my language."

Captain Jack smiled and turned to Captain Bulloch who nodded his agreement, "Don't let those scoundrels take her."

After thanking Captain Bulloch and Belle Boyd for their support, Captain Jack consulted with Bennett Gibbons and his son. He stared silently at the oncoming Federal frigates making his decision. "It's too late to burn her. We must yield."

The crew was silent as Captain Jack ordered the *Wisp* turned into the wind. "Bennett, tell Copper Joe to shut down the engines. Thomas Henry, strike the colors." Thomas Henry hesitated, and Jack could sense his reticence. Blockade runners had standing orders to destroy their vessel and cargo if capture threatened. Close to shore, most captains would purposely run aground. At sea, it was expected that the cargo be dumped, or the ship razed. "Thomas, do as you've been ordered, then return to my side. Do not assume that the Yankees have taken the *Wisp* yet."

With his engines stopped and white flag clearly visible, the closest Federal cruiser reached hailing range yet continue to fire. A projectile hummed just over his and Belle Boyd's head while another shattered a bulwark tearing the arm off a member of his deck crew.

Captain Jack exclaimed to no one in particular, "Those God damn bastards, don't intend to give us quarter. They'll damn sure regret that decision."

A loud, coarse voice bellowed out over the water between the two ships. "Steamer ahoy! We mean to either board you or pour a broadside into you. One shot, or if we see the first flicker of a fire, you'll have made a fatal choice."

Captain Jack signaled to Belle Boyd who scurried below decks to feed her dispatches into the engine room fire box. Captain Bulloch stood with Jack.

"Stand down," Jack yelled loudly to his crew for the benefit of the faceless voice across the water. Captain Jack then spoke quietly to Bennett Gibbons, Captain Bulloch, his son, and a stunned James Morris Morgan. Jack pointed at a long boat being lowered from the Federal blockader. "Allow the long boat to grapple alongside," Jack ordered. "Thomas, take James and a handful of men down to the quartermaster's hold and retrieve a dozen Enfield rifles, bayonets, side pistols, and cartridge boxes with forty dead men each. Tell the remainder of the crew to quietly collect axes, clubs, and hand spikes and prepare to protect themselves from a boarding attempt. Bennett, tell Copper Joe to have one of his men bring up his steam hose."

Before they left, Captain Jack gave his officers further instructions, "Make no sign of haste, and tell the men to stay down behind the cotton bales. No one is to move until I signal. Their arrogance will be their downfall. Those Yankees will never stand on the deck of the *Wisp*."

Captain Jack held a second conversation with Copper Joe through the engineer's tube. "I'll need full speed the second I ask for it."

"You'll have it, sir."

Ten minutes later, Jack, Thomas Henry, and Captain Bulloch stood alone on the deck as the Union longboat tied alongside. A Union naval lieutenant and ten marines rose from the longboat with weapons drawn and announced their intention to board.

"I would advise against that," Captain Jack replied as twenty of his crew stood with rifles, pistols, and spikes from behind the bales of cotton.

"Throw your weapons over the side and retake your seats in the longboat, or my men will pick you off one at a time. It'll be shooting fish in a barrel."

"What is this treachery? You lowered your flag and now you'll lay down your arms. This ship is our prize and we intend to board you."

"Like hell you will, Lieutenant. You and your men have only one chance of surviving this, but you'll have to be smarter than you've been so far. We intend to sail on with you and your men tethered to our side. You'll be released in your longboat as soon as we're safely out of range. That assumes, of course, your frigates don't open fire. At this range, your man-of -war would certainly sink us with one broadside. We're prepared for that eventuality. However, your frigate's broadside won't sink us without first painting our gunwales with the blood and brains of you and your men. Are you and your marines prepared for that? Time for you to make a fatal choice."

The checkmated Union lieutenant quickly called back to his ship, instructing them to hold their fire and not pursue.

Copper Joe opened up the engines and the *Will O' the Wisp* began to churn away from the stymied Union warships. True to his word, Captain Jack released the longboat as soon as the Union frigates disappeared on the horizon.

Red-faced and splenetic, the Union lieutenant cursed at Captain Jack. "You're the lowest yellow dog on the sea and have brought shame to your crew to do this after lowering your flag."

"Don't lecture me, lieutenant. You fired on us with our flag stricken. We raised the white flag and you showed us no mercy. You murdered one of my crew. Our actions are sufficiently honorable once you revealed your low intentions. This will reflect on your register of naval service, not mine."

The livid Union lieutenant responded, "There will be no place on these waters for you to hide. We'll hunt you mercilessly."

"I'm sure you will. If you ever want to find me, I will be at the helm of this ship. It is the only hiding place I've ever needed. I wish you luck in hiding from the report on how this prize was so clumsily lost. Your naval career is more certainly over than if your captain had opened fire with you tied alongside."

The crew of the *Will O' the Wisp* jeered and hooted at the Union officer and his men as their longboat drifted away from the *Wisp*. Jack was not proud of the seamanship that had led to the *Wisp* becoming ensnared. Nor was he comfortable with the bushwhacking of the Union longboat. At the same time, he anticipated his discomfiture would pass quickly.

Weightier than his own embarrassment, Jack understood that his escape would soon become a rallying cry for the entire Union blockading fleet. The *Will O' the Wisp* would never again be given the option of surrender, nor would he or his crew ever have the option of Federal prison. Their lives were now bound exclusively to their sailing skills.

Captain Jack pulled the plug from the engine room tube. "Joe, let's get the hell out of here."

"Aye, aye, Captain. Did you get to use the steam hose?" Joe responded hopefully.

"Sorry, Joe. We didn't, but maybe next time."

Chapter 10

April 29, 1862

Salad Oil

Captain Jack kept the whip to the *Will O' the Wisp's* twin boilers throughout the night. The cloud banks to the northeast had consolidated and were ominously dark. More than the impending storm, Jack feared the high blood of the Union captains he had hoodwinked. Few things possessed the single-minded motivational power of vengeance. Jack explained to Bennett that he wanted to stay ahead of the foul weather, whether it came from the northeast or from behind.

Morning of the following day, Copper Joe sent a runner to Captain Jack suggesting that the *Wisp* be shut down. Their pace through the night was placing a dangerous strain on the *Wisp's* engines. If the engine's ball bearings became overheated, they could freeze up, disabling the engines and paddle wheels. Four hours at dead stop would allow the bearings to cool and boiler seams to relax. Being dead in the water made everyone nervous, but no one knew the engines better than Copper Joe.

No longer pushing southeast, the thunderstorm soon caught up with the *Wisp*. Spindrift blew across the deck and bands of rain came in horizontal sheets. The *Will O' the Wisp* pitched and rolled in the churning sea and water surged over the decks. Jack ordered the hatches battened down and all but essential crew below decks. Lightening sizzled through an enveloping blanket of angry, energized clouds and thunder crashed incessantly.

The lookout on the stern called out, "Sail ho!"

"Where away?" Captain Jack answered.

"Right astern, sir, and in chase."

It was a miracle that the lookout had spotted the topsails of the Union steam frigate through the bank of clouds. It was likely one of the blockaders from the night before but Jack could not yet tell which one. To make up distance, the Union vessel was using both sail and steam. Riding on the crest of a storm, the addition of sail could add three or four knots to a frigate's top speed.

Captain Jack ran down to the engine room and found Copper Joe. "How are the bearings?" he barked.

"Probably could use another hour or two to completely loosen up."

"We don't have it. Union frigate bearing down on us."

"I'll have us going in ten minutes," Joe answered.

Copper Joe ran to the ship's galley and grabbed a gallon tin of salad oil and a bucket of lard. The dumbfounded galley mates followed Joe back to the engine room and watched him pour the salad oil and slather the lard over the bearings. The engines were fired, and the ball bearings rolled smoothly. Joe had the *Wisp* under steam in less than five minutes and she was soon slicing through the white horses.

With only steam against steam and sail, Captain Jack calculated they would be overtaken by midday. He neutralized the frigate's advantage by turning the *Wisp* into the wind. His gambit was rewarded when the Yankees were forced to clew up and furl their sail. Jack ordered Copper Joe to soak some of the cotton bales in turpentine and feed them into the boiler fire. The resultant head of steam pushed the *Wisp* safely out of cannon range.

Jack did not understand why the frigate never fired when it had the chance. Possibly the captain felt that a salvo would be wasted in such heavy sea. The *Wisp's* forward deck had a turtleback design allowing her to force her way through big waves. The resultant diving and rising motion of the *Wisp* as she plowed through the rollers made her an impossible target. Jack also suspected that the Union captain was convinced of his ability to overtake the *Wisp* and did not want to damage his anticipated prize. That captain's lust for retribution would be a costly miscalculation.

The chase continued all day into the gathering darkness. The *Wisp's* big tubular boilers could generate an incredible amount of steam pressure. Without any heavy equipment aboard, and lacking armor or armaments, the *Wisp* was capable of exceptional speed and was able to stay out of the frigate's range. As night fell and the frigate became no longer visible, Captain Jack called Thomas Henry to his side. "Thomas, go below and tell Joe to switch from the Welsh anthracite coal to the reserve North Carolina coal."

Thomas Henry replied, "The North Carolina coal burns much dirtier than the Welsh and is going to produce a thick black smoke."

"Exactly. Also instruct Joe to close the dampers. I want the black smoke to stream astern across the deck and hang low over the water rather than billowing from the *Wisp's* smokestacks."

Thomas Henry grinned with the eventual understanding of his father's plan. "Will do, Captain."

Obscured by the continuing storm and a wafting self-made smokescreen, Jack instructed Bennett to make a hard-starboard turn changing course perpendicularly to his previous line. Hidden behind a blanket of dark clouds and thick black smoke, the *Wisp* churned away while the Union frigate flew past in the heated pursuit of what again proved to be an apparition.

By the following morning, the nor'easter had blown itself out and sunshine shimmered across the top of a calmer deep blue ocean. Schools of flying fish darted like silver arrows from wave to wave. The course changes of the night before had confused their exact location. Jack corrected their course back toward Nassau by taking observations on the sun and the horizon with his sextant. Fearing reappearance of their fanatical pursuer, the *Will O' the Wisp* continued to push for all she was worth. The turtleback bow now cleaved the smaller waves like a knife and her flying speed of over fourteen knots was exhilarating.

Copper Joe informed Jack that the pressure of their pursuit had nearly exhausted the coal supply. "Captain, the next twelve hours to Nassau is going to be tricky."

"Joe, have your crew keep the boilers going with the free timber from the decks and wood scavenged from damaged bulwarks and cabins."

"That might still not be enough. I don't think we want to power down again," Joe warned.

"No, we certainly don't. If push comes to shove, take some of the cotton, soak it in turpentine, and feed the bales into the boilers. Better to lose some than all."

The *Will O' the Wisp* limped into Provincetown harbor on its last breath of steam pressure.

Captain Bulloch promised Jack that the C.S.A., or he personally, would reimburse him for the cotton that was cannibalized getting them to Nassau. Bulloch congratulated Jack on what he considered the finest display of seamanship he had ever witnessed. He offered Jack command of the next C.S.A. warship he commissioned in Liverpool. Jack thanked him, but respectably declined the offer.

Belle Boyd gave Captain Jack a kiss on the cheek and patted the satchel of confidential communiques hanging from her shoulder.

"I thought you threw those into the firebox."

"I was standing next to it and ready to, but I had a feeling you hadn't yet played all your cards. I wanted to see what you had up your sleeve before I burned my papers."

"I appreciate your faith in me, bit in all honesty, I was certain we were done for. Drawing down on the Union marines grappled to our side was only a bluff. The captain of their frigate could have raked our decks above the heads of the men lashed to our side. Most of the time, when an ace falls out of your sleeve you get a bullet between the eyes. It was a gamble that could've, and probably should've, gone awry."

Belle took Captain Jack's hands in hers and stared up into his eyes. "I'd push all my chips in on your cards every time. I have not known many men I could say that about. There's something about you that smells special."

"That's probably a combination of engine oil, coal smoke and bilge water."

"Well that too, but this is different. Something only a woman can discern."

Captain Jack blushed for the first time in twenty years. "That is exceedingly kind of you to say, Miss Boyd. There is no doubt that sooner or later, the cards will bust me. But, we ain't busted yet and that's something."

Belle Boyd smiled, knowing that Captain Jack had politely declined her offer. "If you're ever in Richmond please come by for a drink." Belle smiled again, winked and then turned to descend the gangplank.

At the foot of the gangplank Belle stopped and patted a member of the crew on the cheek with a gloved hand. She looked back up to the deck and addressed the assembled crew who had enjoyed her desent down the gangplank. "That was quite a run, boys. Not one I'll soon forget. I'm indebted to each of you for getting me here safely."

With a brief wave and a blown kiss, Belle Boyd collected the hearts of another three dozen men.

Chapter 11

May 5, 1862

Nassau

The Lowcountry's ties to Nassau go back almost two hundred years and has deep piratical roots. The pirates, privateers, and slave traders of the South Atlantic coast recognized the uninhabited island of New Providence as a perfect base for operations. New Providence's harbor was large but shallow, easily sheltering dozens of small pirate ships but not accommodating the large warships of the British Royal Navy. More importantly, New Providence was close to the busy shipping lanes of the Florida Strait.

With nothing else on the island, the port of Nassau was built as a lawless haven and capital of the "pirates' republic." As pirate ships filled the harbor, Nassau flourished without any government or purpose other than to provide unquestioned trade, respite from harassment, and debauchery. Nearly a thousand pirates called Nassau home along with another roughly three hundred permanent residents who made their livings as thieves, saloon keepers, whores, and bankers. When bankers rule, there are few rules indeed.

Woodes Rogers, a one-time privateer himself, arrived in 1718 as the governor of New Providence backed by the might of the British Empire. The pirates found themselves outnumbered and outgunned by the powerful ships of the Royal Navy. Without a haven, fewer merchant ships to plunder, and a dwindling number of cities willing to trade for stolen goods, piracy began its terminal decline. Nassau's once thriving pirate harbor declined to a precarious subsistence economy based on fishing, sponging, turtling, and wrecking. The war between the North and the South, however, awakened the ghosts of the dead.

Nassau became a transshipment hub between the Confederacy and Europe. Gold poured onto the island just as it had one hundred and fifty years earlier. Small sleek blockade runners darted like dragonflies into and out of New Providence harbor. On any given day, the harbor was dotted with long, rakish looking steamers, the *Will O' the Wisp* prominent among them.

The big English and French merchantmen had no interest in tempting the Union blockade of Southern ports. Instead, they anchored outside the harbors of neutral colonies like Bermuda and Nassau, shuttling ashore their cargoes of guns, cannons, mercantile supplies, and specially requested luxury goods. These European goods were exchanged at wharf side warehouses for cotton and other Southern commodities. Charleston financier, George Alfred Trenholm brokered virtually all these transactions on behalf of the Confederate government.

Captain Jack preferred Nassau to Bermuda as a transshipment destination. Bermuda was 650 miles east of Wilmington and a good bit farther from Charleston. Nassau was south and only about 500 miles from Charleston. More significant to an experienced blockade runner, the islands that formed the Bahamian chain extended almost two hundred miles toward the Southeastern coast. At night, blockade runners could steam imperceptibly in the shadow of these Bahamian isles. If challenged by a Union frigate, a blockade runner could also find sanctuary in the waters adjacent to these islands, protected by British neutrality laws. With these advantages and the *Wisp's* speed, Jack had never been chased into open sea by a Union warship. Jack attributed the recent change in tactics to the special passengers he had carried on this run.

In Nassau, Jack met with Harry McLaughlin, George Trenholm's commercial agent on New Providence island. McLaughlin toured the cargo hold and assimilated a detailed manifest. Other than a couple dozen cotton bales used to keep the boiler fired, the *Will O' the Wisp* had again delivered. The cotton bales would be transferred to an anxious English steamer while the *Will O' the Wisp* would be reloaded with crates from one of George Trenholm's warehouses. Jack warned McLaughlin that reloading would need to be delayed.

The *Will O' the Wisp* required significant repairs and the crew desperately needed to decompress. Three crewmembers were dead, and several others had been injured. Memories needed to fade and emotions cool. An angry crew more focused on revenge than stealth was a dangerous thing for a blockade runner.

The *Wisp* was also due a careening for hull scraping. Nassau was a superior port for heaving down than Charleston. Jack estimated that the *Wisp's* top speed was down at least two knots indicating a hull probably fouled by a six-inch lawn of seagrass. Facing newer and faster Federal warships, Jack wanted all the speed his ship had been designed to give.

"Best case scenario, Harry, it will be six weeks before we can complete the necessary repairs and careening. It might be longer before the crew is seaworthy."

"I understand, Jack. Your ship and crew need to be in top form. Over the past three months almost one in six runners have been intercepted."

"Well, the Yankee frigates are certainly faster. One of them dogged me all the way across the South Atlantic and I was lucky to elude them. She was closing the distance on me at top speed. My bigger concern though are the Union spies. I'm convinced they knew we had Captain Bulloch and Belle

Boyd aboard. They knew when we were leaving Charleston and the route we were taking."

McLaughlin shook his head. "I hope you're wrong, Jack, because if you're right, that means it is someone close."

"I know, Harry. I know."

McLaughlin completed the paperwork with Captain Jack. The *Will O' the Wisp* was credited with the value of the delivered cotton bales and McLaughlin parceled out the British sterling necessary to pay the officers and crew. Captain Jack took several thousand more in sterling to pay for repairs, inevitable bail, and shore expenses. The remaining profit was divided between the English accounts of Jack Whitesides Holmes and George Alfred Trenholm. For the first time, however, the ledger required a tally of measurable and immeasurable loss beneath the profit line.

Jack staggered shore leave to make sure the *Wisp* was never left without crew on board. He gave each departing group the same speech. Jack reminded them that their pound sterling represented their futures. A future that extended beyond whisky and women. That portion of his speech had long ago lost its conviction. It went in one ear and out the other. Whisky and women were exactly what his crew needed. With considerably more passion, he reminded his crew to be careful and stay together. Pirates still roamed the backstreets of Nassau where he had little influence. He looked at Copper Joe as he made that last statement.

Jack did not share his crew's fondness for Nassau. Like all boom towns, its dusty streets were swollen by sailors, refugees, rum sellers, cotton brokers, grifters and con men, all making and dissipating fortunes they would never see again. Slewed sailors stumbled from groggery to groggery while ladies of light virtue offered their company in the scores of brothels and wicked public houses that lined the town's narrow lust-filled streets. The cheap bust head sold in the ale houses enabled poor judgement and bad decisions.

Every crewman left the ship a daring El Dorado adventurer. Most returned a befouled and beaten cur.

It was especially hard for Jack to watch his son, Thomas Henry, leaving with the crew for town. His instinct was to restrict him to the ship but knew he could not. The dark alleys of Nassau were far more dangerous than a Union bow chaser.

While in Nassau, the captains and executive officers of the Confederate blockade runners and European merchantmen would socialize together. Occasionally, they would be joined by Royal Navy officers from the British men-of-war. The British officers were convivial, and their brandy first rate, however, Captain Jack struggled to tolerate the invariably large ration of British naval arrogance. He put up with it to talk news and strategy with the Royal Navy officers.

Worse was interacting with the fraternity of English blockade runners. Speculators from across Europe, but particularly Britain, had come to the Bahamas to do well and most did. Early in the war, certain commodities like cut nails and salt fell into the hands of just a few English entrepreneurs who came to control the inbound supply on English blockade runners. The cost of these commodities skyrocketed. The only things that limited their profit making were the lesser familiarity of the English captains with the Southern coast and their recklessness.

Most of the English blockade running captains were obnoxious braggarts with more family money than they deserved or knew what to do with. They rented the finest houses in town, even though Nassau's best left much to be desired. They preferred ostentatious para-military dress and indulged in libertine behavior that turned heads even in the sybaritic paradise of filthy Nassau. They whored and gambled incessantly on cockfighting and cards. Their extravagance eschewed every Victorian value and soured relationships with their families, sponsors and nearly everyone else in Nassau who did not already despise them. In Jack's opinion, their only redeeming feature was that they disappeared quickly. They were endowed with far more pomposity than seamanship.

It was in one of these houses that Captain Jack made the acquaintance of Captain Casimir Brisbin of Boston and the *Titan*, a Yankee whaler. Despite sailing out of Boston, Captain Brisbin had no regional allegiance. He sailed frequently to Nassau to engage in passions that Jack did not care to know more about. Brisbin was a repulsive troll of a man with heavily bearded jowls, a bulbous rum-soaked nose, and eyebrows so thick they partially obscured his dark beady eyes. Jack could not imagine how this man had become a captain and leader of men. Casimir raked his pudgy hands through greasy hair and smacked his lips when Captain Jack placed a shot glass of rum on the table in front of him.

Despite finding him odious, Jack was interested in discovering how the Northern papers viewed the war's progress. "Mind if I sit?" Jack asked.

Captain Brisbin gave him a crooked half-smile revealing irregular, tobacco-stained teeth. "The rum bought you any seat you want."

Jack sat, and they clicked glasses. "I'm Captain Jack Holmes of the *Will O' the Wisp* out of Charleston."

"Heard of you. I'm told that you captain a real fine ship. Can really sprint when she wants to. Must drive those Yankee steam pots crazy."

"Thank you. She can and she does. I heard you're the captain of the *Titan* out of Boston."

"I am. But I ain't lookin' for any trouble. I'm a whaler and I don't give a shit who wins. Ain't got a dog in the fight if you know what I mean. Just waitin' for it all to be over. The cannon balls splashin' into the brine is scaring the whales away."

"I'm not looking for any trouble either, Captain Brisbin. I'm just interested in what the papers up North are saying about the war. Any pressure on Lincoln to negotiate an armistice?"

"Call me Casimir. Papers all say it's just a matter of time. Don't think Lincoln's interested in calling it a draw. They say that big ol' rail-splitter is pretty hardheaded, and it seems like he's got a made-up mind. Can't see it myself. Why would anyone want to put the Union back together? Everyone down here hates everyone up there and I can tell ya that the feeling is mutual." With that, Captain Brisbin clicked glasses with Jack again and downed the rest of his shot.

Jack whistled at the barkeeper and raised two fingers.

"Much obliged, Captain. Whaling is thirsty work."

"My pleasure, Casimir. I appreciate the information. Sadly, it's what I expected."

"You might also be interested in knowing that the last thing I heard before leaving port was that the Union navy had taken New Orleans. Probably makes a difference in your line of work."

"That it does," Jack replied, rattled by the news. New Orleans was the South's most important port in the Gulf and the destination for all traffic on the Mississippi River. Jack was shocked because it must have been taken by naval action alone. There were not any Union ground forces in the region. How the hell had the Union Navy been able to take the port of New Orleans? If the Union navy could take New Orleans, could Charleston be far behind? What had the Northern papers said? "It's just a matter of time," Jack mumbled to himself.

By the time they finished their bottle of rum, Captain Jack and Casimir Brisbin were laughing at each other's stories and no longer concerned with the fate of New Orleans. A thousand dollars in gold sovereigns had also crossed the table. Captain Brisbin's whaler carried several unique cargo items that interested Jack.

Among those were two small crates of baleen whale bone. Corset and dress stays, umbrella stays, fishing rods, and carriage whips were all made from baleen whale bone. It was hard to get and the type of luxury item that would draw top dollar from people with money and perceived need. Appreciative of the rum and the friendly conversation, Captain Brisbin threw in a five-pound sack of dried cinnamon sticks and a goat skin jacket. After splitting a bottle of rum, Captain Brisbin could not remember where he had gotten either the cinnamon sticks or the goat skin jacket.

Jack was most interested in Brisbin's final offering. Brisbin called it ambergrease, but Jack knew it as ambergris. Ambergris is a lard-like lump of material produced in the digestive system of certain whales. Freshly produced, it appears dull white or grey and has a fecal odor. Lumps of ambergris can sometimes be found floating on the sea or washed up on shore, however, Brisbin had harvested his directly from the stomach of a harpooned sperm whale. Eventually, ambergris hardens and develops a dark grey or black coloration. Over time, the odor evolves into a peculiar sweet, earthy, and musty aroma.

Ancient Egyptians burned it as royal incense and considered it an aphrodisiac. During the Black Death, people believed ambergris could ward off the plague. Its fragrance masked the stench of death in the air which was believed to be the illness' vector. Jack knew ambergris as a product used to enhance perfumes. The ladies of Charleston would pay sizably for a fragrance that could mask the stench of war.

Captain Brisbin also knew the value of his ambergris and seemed to sober dramatically when they began to negotiate a price. Casimir knew that Captain Jack was a fortunate encounter. The *Titan* would not be visiting an appropriate port-o-call where he could demand what his treasure was worth. Charleston was just such a port. Jack ended up paying a bit more than he wanted for what was essentially a can of hardened whale vomit. Still, it would turn an impressive profit when he got back to the Lowcountry.

The following morning was one of the more difficult ones that Jack could remember. Nassau rum was known to bite back. He crawled out of bed early to bid farewell to his new friend, James Bulloch. Captain Bulloch had rendezvoused with the new Confederate officers who had arrived three days previously from Richmond. Jack wished them Godspeed. The *C.S.S. Alabama* would put to sea as a hunter instead of the hunted. When Union merchantmen heading to or from Northern ports started being taken as prizes or burned at sea, the pressure on Lincoln would mount. Northern financial and business leaders would howl with each lost cargo. Interruption of Northern free trade might result in diversion of the Union blockading fleet from Southern ports, if not prod Lincoln to the bargaining table.

Coming onto deck, Captain Jack saw Caleb instructing Ezekiel on casting the lead. The irony was striking. Leadsman is the most physically demanding task on the *Will O' the Wisp,* or any ship, demanding exceptional endurance. Caleb was a massive, heavily muscled mulatto who had served with Captain Jack for years. Ezekiel was a thin, spindly-legged teenage boy who had been rescued from a whipping post just a couple of months earlier. Caleb must have seen the same toughness in Ezekiel that Jack had seen.

The leadsman's station was a small platform at the bow of the *Wisp.* Caleb coiled the sounding line in his hand and fed out a length with a heavy lead plummet swinging freely from the end. The sounding line was flung out ahead of the *Wisp* as it navigated shoal water searching for entrance channels. The lead would sink to the bottom and then be quickly hauled back on deck, the fathoms read, and the sounding reported back to Captain Jack. The tip of the lead was covered with sticky tallow that picked up bottom sand. Caleb could read the ocean floor as well as other men could read signs along a trail. This was particularly important in the coastal waters surrounding Charleston were a puzzle of twisting rivers, creeks and bayous conspired daily to remodel the harbor's sandy floor.

Without a capable leadsman, a successful run could easily end up being delivered into the sand or onto the rocks. Captain Jack had the luxury of negotiating the Charleston bar with Caleb showing him the way. Caleb would holler from the bow, "You let her go, sir. I'll give you the bottom." Jack could not remember Caleb ever making an incorrect cast of the lead.

Caleb could stand in the forechains for hours on end in bitter weather, flying spray cutting against him, throwing the lead into a howling wind until the *Wisp* was securely back to the safety of the inner harbor. Such an effort would exhaust any other two men. Caleb lacked for nothing in courage or strength.

"Caleb, you think he can learn to cast the lead?"

"Maybe so, Cap. He's a tough little guy. Smart too."

"Keep working with him, Caleb. It's a good skill for him to learn. However, do you mind if I speak with him privately for a couple of minutes?"

"No problem, boss. I heard there's some good stew down in the galley."

Ezekiel was still a tiny fellow, but under Caleb's tutelage he was beginning to develop some muscular definition that he did not have at the Sugar House. There was also a spark in his eyes that Jack had not seen before.

"You like working with Caleb?"

"Yes suh. He real good to me. I like knowin' how to read the sea bottom. Caleb also showed me how to tie a monkey's fist."

"How's your back?"

"Healed up good. Mr. Joe puts a cream on it that takes out the burn. What can I do for ya, suh?"

"I wanted to keep my promise."

Captain Jack pointed toward Nassau town. "Every black man on that island is free to do as they please. You will be too if you want to get off this ship. You can work the land, or I'll give you a letter that will get you on with an English crew. There's no slavery in England."

"Am I free on this ship?" Ezekiel asked.

"You are. But you've already met the people dedicated to blowing us to kingdom come and drowning you in dark, cold water. After our last run, the Yankees will never offer us quarter again. You won't have that problem on an English ship."

Ezekiel didn't hesitate or take his gaze off Captain Jack's eyes before responding. "If it's just the same to you, Cap'n, I'd prefer to stay on the *Wisp*."

"You'll have a place on my crew for as long as you want."

Ezekiel was like Caleb in another way. Neither lacked for courage.

A rancid odor assaulted Captain Jack wafting over from the adjacent docks. The smell was coming from a dozen crates marked as bacon. Sometimes meat destined for the South was allowed to spoil on the docks. Blockade runner captains preferred less bulky, more profitable cargo.

Nothing was more immediate or demoralizing to either soldier or citizen than a lack of food. Hunger held your attention far better than anger. That hunger was going to become worse with the fall of New Orleans. Texas cattle provided most of the meat for the South. Getting cattle across the Mississippi River was going to be nearly impossible without control of the port of New Orleans.

Jack found himself overwhelmed by his loathing of the captain who had left the bacon to spoil on the wharf and at himself for filling his cabin with whale bone, ambergris, cinnamon sticks, and a goat skin jacket.

Chapter 12

July 16, 1862

Septic Vapors

Jack's plan was to return to Charleston by mid-June. Summer was a good time to pass the blockade. Union soldiers and sailors were unaccustomed to the miserably hot and steamy languor of a South Atlantic summer. It was unbearable to work above deck under the scorching mid-day sun and rest was equally impossible in the sweltering quarters below deck. Morale and alertness were at their lowest ebb as men battled sleep deprivation, dehydration, and sunburn. As a result, Federal crews did their heavy work at night. The lanterns required to guide nighttime ship maintenance illuminated the Union vessels for miles.

Captain Jack had even pulled off an astonishing daylight run back into Charleston harbor the previous summer. Slowed by a mechanical problem, the *Will O' the Wisp* didn't arrive back to the South Carolina coast until well after sunrise. With a furious sun blazing overhead, the sea as flat as glass, and two Union blockaders sitting motionless on the horizon, Captain Jack shocked his crew by casually ordering a full speed run to the bar. As expected, the Union blockaders were sluggish in pulling up their anchors and stoking their boilers. Slow to start and outmatched in terms of speed the Union frigates never had a chance. Frantically fired long-range shells came down well behind the *Wisp*.

Soldiers watching from the batteries on Sullivan's Island wildly cheered Captain Jack's audacious thumbing of his nose at the blockade in broad daylight. The *Wisp's* sprint back to the Charleston harbor only furthered her reputation as being untouchable. Jack knew untouchability was a myth, but a good one to perpetuate.

Taking advantage of the summer doldrums depended on Nassau functioning as a real port-o-call. Nothing happened in Nassau when scheduled or without coin changing hands. Just as in its piratical heyday, pay-offs were required to facilitate every transaction. Even then, you could not make things happen fast. The repairs to the *Will O' the Wisp* were lagging well into July. Prospects for a July departure were scuttled when a merchant ship from Cuba arrived in Nassau harbor flying the yellow jack.

Seamen are a courageous breed of man, but they are uniformly terrified by the prospect of a yellow fever outbreak. Once the yellow jack was seen, everything in Nassau came to a halt. Sailors and workers retired to their houses and bars to wait out the gloomy melancholy of yellow jack's passing over. Yellow fever took down people like a scythe through wheat. In her presence, no one knew when it would be their turn, but all could feel the coldness of the grave as they helplessly waited.

Despite the quarantine of the Cuban merchantman, yellow jack began to appear in the streets of Nassau within a week. The bars and brothels closed, and tar barrels were set afire in the streets to purify the air. Many retreated to farms and plantations in the countryside. No one ventured out to assess the conditions aboard the Cuban trader. Yellow fever brought death in its most appalling form and everyone knew that the Cuban ship was nothing more than a floating charnel-house.

Jack had encountered yellow fever before and knew how to handle the scourge. Crewman were awakened at sunrise and received a small dose of quinine from Jack's

personal stock. Jack forbade any work during the hottest
hours of the day. Each crewman also received a half cup of
whisky at noon and were advised to avoid intemperance or
exercise which Jack believed fostered yellow jack's
selection.

Yellow jack always appeared first in the ports and it
was accepted fact that ships bred the pestilence. Enlightened
physicians attributed the disease to septic vapors collecting
in the holds of cargo ships arising from rotting green timbers,
decaying vegetable or animal matter amongst the ballast
stones, spoiled salt-cured meats or a toxic combination of all
three. The tinder of these vessels' filthy lower decks was
then ignited by the constant high humidity and heat of
summer when yellow jack always made her arrival.

Thwarting the decomposition of organic matter and
the accumulation of infectious effluvium in neglected holds
was the key to preventing yellow fever's propagation.
Captain Jack used a Wynkoop ventilator to circulate air
below decks and pump putrefied air out of the ship. He
regularly flushed a chemical mixture of chloride of lime and
water through the chain lockers and insisted that all surfaces
below decks be whitewashed and bedding aired. The
clothing and personal effects of any victim were burned.
Twice a day the bilge pumps were activated to empty the
ship of seeping water.

Every third day Jack sealed all the vessel's hatches
and fired up the boilers. The sealed in heat created a kiln-like
environment that dried out the moisture below decks. Jack
had seen enough yellow fever in his lifetime to know that it
thrived on filth and standing water. A clean, dry, well-
ventilated ship was the best he could do to protect his crew.

Regardless, more than half of the *Wisp's* crew
became ill over the next two weeks, including Thomas
Henry, and the ship's sawbones, Morgan Southworth. The
jack's arrival was typically sudden and violent. The early
phase was characterized by high fevers, rigors, severe

headaches, and crippling muscle aches. Soon thereafter, the afflicted lost their appetite, began vomiting, and developed characteristic red eyes, face, and tongue. Those were the lucky ones. The unlucky slipped into a toxic phase where the skin turned yellow with purple hemorrhagic blotches. The skin discoloration accounted for several of yellow fever's more feared nicknames including "Bronze John" and the "Saffron Scourge." The yellow skin was soon followed by a ceasing of urination, delirium, seizures, coma, and death in rapid succession.

Dr. Southgate was selfless and heroic in the care he provided to Thomas Henry and the other stricken crew. He ministered to them until he was too peaked to stand. Shortly after using a hand cloth to dampen Thomas Henry's brow, Dr. Southgate bent at the waist as if to cough. Instead, he retched up an enormous amount of black vomit, a sure sign of lethal outcome.

The death of Dr. Southgate turned out to be the peak of the outbreak. Over the subsequent two weeks fewer and fewer crew members fell ill and most who were ill began to recover. White crew members were tended to by the black crew members who seemed uniquely resistant to yellow jack. By mid-August, the yellow jack had disappeared as suddenly as it had arrived. By the end of its run, twenty-four crew members and officers had fallen victim and fifteen had died including the ship's surgeon. Captain Jack thanked God for sparing his son.

Chapter 13

September 21, 1862

Superheated Steam

Jack decided that the *Will O' the Wisp* was finally ready for sea in early September. He had replaced his lost crew and was satisfied with their work. Weakened, Thomas Henry returned as an officer of the deck on a limited basis. There were no murmurs about Thomas Henry's lighter duty. Despite being the Captain's son, the crew respected Thomas Henry. He never shirked, claimed privilege, or asked favor. More importantly, the crew knew Captain Jack would do the same for them under similar circumstances.

The yellow jack and the delays in repairing the *Wisp* had created a new problem. August and September were peak months for hurricanes rolling through the eastern Caribbean onto the southeastern coast of the Confederacy. It had been a quiet season so far, but that meant nothing about what might appear on the horizon tomorrow. Jack considered waiting another month, but truth be known, he could not stand another day in Nassau. He had privately come to view Nassau as his own personal Jonah.

"Bennett, it's time to go. Plot me a course for Charleston."

"We will be taking a bit of a chance with the African storms," his old friend Gibbons replied.

"I know. I've talked to arriving captains who report only calm water. The sky is sapphire blue with only a light breeze blowing from the southeast. I don't think it is going to get much better than this."

"Just another week or two and we can put most of the season behind us."

"To be completely honest with you, Bennett, I'd prefer to match skills with Mother Nature's fiercest tempest rather than spend another day as helpless witness to the debauchery, incompetence, thievery, and septic vapors of Nassau."

Bennett smiled, "Aye, Aye, Captain."

There was no dissent when he announced it was time to go. Even the crew could not stand any more of Nassau's hospitality. As in Charleston, the departure decision was held close. Federal spies were even more common in Nassau than in Charleston. Small packet ships carrying information on anticipated blockade runner departures left almost daily to supply the South Atlantic Blockading Squadron. Jack remained convinced that the *Wisp's* interception beyond the Charleston bar had been the work of Union secret agents.

As was his practice, Captain Jack timed his departure from Nassau so that a high tide and moonless night would welcome the *Wisp* back to Charleston. The coal bins were brimming, and the cargo hold was filled with nine thousand Austrian rifles, three hundred thousand cartridges, and a variety of desperately needed metals: copper, tin, antimony, and lead. The *Wisp* also bellied essentials for the troops including twenty-five hundred army blankets, six hundred sides of leather, eight thousand yards of grey and red flannel, fifty cases of shoes, shovels, and woolens. Jack also made room for thirty boxes of bacon. Observers from the shore could easily tell that the *Wisp* was heavy, riding low in the water.

A modest storm swept through on the second day from Nassau with long marching swells forcing the *Wisp* to labor her way forward. The *Wisp's* dual paddle wheels churned up a broad wake of yeasty foam as she pitched from side to side. By the next day, the ocean had settled allowing the *Wisp* to slice through longer, more sedate, rollers. With clear skies, Captain Jack used his sextant to shoot the sun and realized they had made excellent time. He called down the engine room speaking tube and told Copper Joe to reduce speed. They would conserve some energy before approaching the Carolina coast.

The Federal blockade of Charleston was a double crescent extending north and south of its harbor. The outer cordon included the larger men-o-war and frigates who cruised up and down the gulf stream. Smaller, faster gunboats made up an inner cordon patrolling closer to the bars and coastline. Blockade runners discovered by the big warships of the outer cordon were driven into the snare of the inner squadron gunboats.

The Federals knew that most of the blockade runners preferred an end run around their crescent arc. The Federals extended the horns of the crescent as close to shore as the shoals would allow, leaving only a narrow passage between the endmost cruiser and the shore. If a blockade runner attempted to slip past, the end vessel would send up a calcium rocket and begin pursuit. Alerted by the signal rockets, the smaller gunboats and picket barges would arrive to hem in the blockade runner. Surrounded and pressed up against the shoreline, the runner either had to surrender or run aground in hopes of saving a fraction of his cargo. Captain Jack worried little about the outer cordon. Given the distance between the Federal cruisers in the outer crescent, passing them unobserved in the dark was not a challenge. Passing by the inner cordon required some stealth.

Knowing the *Wisp* to be several miles beyond the Federal outer cordon, Captain Jack ordered an all stop. The *Wisp* would remain unobserved at a distance until nightfall. Standing at the helm, Bennett Gibbons pointed toward the southeast. The optimistic blue sky that had been in such abundance that morning was now being squeezed into thin blue slices by an unseen but certain force. The southern sky was now quilted by puffening white clouds whose feet were gradually turning a more ominous blue grey.

"We've got a nasty night ahead, Captain," Bennett offered.

"Yeah, I've been watching it gather."

"There's not much to like about that sky. Want to pull out and head northwest till it blows through?"

"No. Doesn't look like a hurricane to me. If it's just a bad blow the Union ships will button down, and the storm will drown out our paddles. We could scrape hulls with the blue-bellies and they'd never see us. I like the idea of going in tonight."

"Sounds good to me boss."

At nightfall, Captain Jack ordered the boilers back online. A lookout noted a large Union man-o-war of the outer cordon about a mile and a half to the east. It was brightly lit, cruising slowly and clearly unaware of the *Wisp*. Captain Jack spoke to Bennett Gibbons at the wheel. "Steady as you go. We'll slip past that tub without a care."

The words were no sooner out of Jack's mouth than the Union frigate turned abruptly and pointed herself directly at the *Will O' the Wisp*. Any question as to her intention was answered when she fired two calcium flares over the *Wisp's* position. The rockets illuminated not only the *Wisp*, but also two faster frigates closing in from the west out of the darkness. Jack was dumbfounded that his approach had been marked by, not one, but three Union frigates.

Jack, turned to Bennett Gibbons, "No option but to turn tail and run back out to sea."

The slower frigates soon gave up the chase, but the third stubbornly followed and closed with surprising pace. Jack was doing thumbnail estimations as to how quickly the Union frigate was making up the distance between them and the math was not reassuring. Those concern grew when several shells splashed just one hundred yards astern.

Just then, the black squall Jack had been expecting for the past few hours swept in, obscuring the *Wisp* from the trailing frigate. The rising wind sliced off the tops of the waves and blew them sideways across the deck in sheets of biting spray. Captain Jack altered course eastward and then, after about a half-mile, called for an all-quiet stop. Enveloped by blackness and dense rain, expectation was strained as taut as a boarding rope. The Yankee frigate raced past the *Wisp* in the tempest, firing blindly ahead at the specter of the *Wisp*. The muzzle flashes from the Yankee warship were not more than two hundred yards to port. Dead in the water as they were, the *Wisp* would have been quickly dispatched if discovered. Jack walked calmly to the wheelhouse and Bennett Gibbons. No man on the *Wisp* ever questioned Captain Jack's nerve.

"Close one, Captain. We're lucky that squall blew up. When we get back to Charleston remind me that I'm long overdue at church."

"I wouldn't do that to any self-respecting church. What priest has enough time to take your confession? Moreover, I'm not sure how much of God's work was involved."

"What'cha mean?"

"How'd that frigate see us from a mile and a half away in pitch blackness? And, when have you ever seen three frigates this close together, especially one with that kind of speed?"

"Not sure I ever have, Jack. Maybe the blue-bellies are hunting in packs now."

"Maybe so, but that still doesn't explain how they saw us. It felt like a trap to me."

"Don't know how they could set a trap for us without knowing our location. I think they just got lucky. Even a blind hog can root an acorn every once in a while."

Jack considered Bennett's supposition then shook his head. "Not buyin' it, Bennett. I don't like attributing things to luck. Tends to end up biting you in the ass. Tell Joe to wait another 5 minutes then re-fire the boilers. We're turning around and heading into Charleston tonight. I'm tired of these damn Yankee frigates."

"Yes sir. Will be nice to be home."

"Bennett, I think we should approach the bar from the north. We'll skirt the shore down Long Island and use the salt-pots for guidance. We'll enter the harbor around the Sullivan's Island side."

"Sounds like a good plan. North side it is."

Two hours later, Bennett Gibbons had passed the outer cordon and had the *Will O' the Wisp* moving quickly in the shadows of Long Island. They saw no sign of the inner cordon gunboats. That quietude ended suddenly with the jarring impact of a large shell which staggered everyone both above and below decks. Ragged shards of deck planking flew high into the night and pinwheeled into the sea.

A crewman asleep in his hammock was awakened to a shocking view of open sky. Amidst the smoke and haze of his destroyed quarters, the crewman patted himself up and down for blood, amazed to still be alive. Looking from the annihilation of his sleeping berth to the open sky, the crewman laughed manically and exclaimed, "Message received, God. My days of swearing and whoring are over for as long as I live."

The crewman was true to his word. Moments later, another shell exploded directly over the gaping hole in the deck. When the smoke cleared, both the crewman and his bunkmate were missing. Fragments of flesh and bone smeared on the walls of their compartment was the only evidence of their habitation.

"Union gunboat closing rapidly from the port side," a lookout shouted.

Trapped against the shoreline, there was no place to hide. The *Wisp* would have to outrun her to the bar. Captain

Jack hollered down the engine room tube to Copper Joe, "I need it all and more, Joe. This one's life and death."

"Already coming, Captain," was Joe's response.

With the first explosion, Joe had boosted power. The fireman was throwing kerosene-soaked cotton waste into the boiler, building pressure higher than the gauge could track. Splintered wood, tar-smeared oakum, casts of turpentine, and anything else that burned hotter or faster than coal was being thrown into the furnace. Jack's voice told Copper Joe all he needed to know. "Too much doesn't exit, boys," Joe shouted at his heavers.

The Union gunboat mauled the *Will O' the Wisp* at close range. Shell after shell ripped apart her fine live-oak and cedar timbers. The gunboat was close enough that Jack's crew could see its fire monkeys bringing up buckets of glowing red-hot shot. As the *Wisp* attempted to speed away, the Union deck guns were loaded with woolen cartridges containing ten pounds of powder, wadding, and then the red-hot shot poured from a special cradle tipped into the cannon's maw. More wadding was placed and everything rammed home.

Captain Jack yelled for his men to hit the deck seconds before a hideous tongue of flame belched toward his ship. Another Union gun fired chain shot, two cannon balls linked by a length of chain. Chain shot was usually reserved for taking down rigging and masts at long range. This salvo was designed to kill and maim up close. The deck of the *Wisp* became a slaughter pen. The hot-shot and chains mowed men down, littering the deck with severed extremities and mutilated bits. The gutters along the bulwarks now ran red with blood which flowed from the scuppers as if the ship herself were hemorrhaging. The cacophony was deafening with the roar of cannon, the crashing of spars and rigging, and the screams of mortally wounded men.

Captain Jack rose from the deck uninjured, but he had seen Thomas Henry go down in the face of the hot shot. Jack ordered Caleb to get him a sounding and then ran to where he had last seen his son. Thomas Henry was unconscious, but Jack found no head wound. A fist-sized piece of flesh was missing from his left upper thigh. It was not bleeding as much as Jack expected because the wound had been seared by the sizzling shot. Jack tore a strip of linen from his shirt and tied it tightly around Thomas Henry's wound. He ordered a still able-bodied crewman to take Thomas Henry below decks.

Believing he had sent Caleb on a suicide mission, Captain Jack was surprised when his leadsman returned with a report. "She sounds to ten fathoms with sand and mud adhered to the tallow."

"Thank you, Caleb. Take cover but stay nearby. May need another sounding soon."

"Right here when you need me."

The *Wisp's* burst of speed created some life-saving distance between itself and the Union gunboat. If Caleb was correct, the bar was not far away, and Caleb was always correct. Jack ran to the bow looking for tidal rips from churning water flowing over the bar. Jack spied the agitated water less than one hundred yards ahead and to starboard. Far beyond that was the shadowy outline of Fort Sumter with a single beckoning light. Jack ran back to the wheelhouse as another salvo fell just short of the now sprinting *Wisp*.

"Tell Joe to keep pouring it on. On my mark, I want hard a starboard. We're almost at the bar."

"Just give me the word, Jack," Bennett Gibbons shouted back over the din.

Jack stared ahead at the dark water, imaging the ocean bottom in his mind's eye. No other captain would dare taking the bar at top speed, fully loaded, in the middle of the night with no landmarks except for a tidal rip. It was a gamble that required nerve and long experience. It was also a gamble that reflected a lack of other options.

After counting off the estimated time in his head, Jack shouted, "Now!" to his old friend Bennett Gibbons.

The *Will O' the Wisp* heeled abruptly in a blizzard of foam with the paddle wheels beating ineffectually in the middle of the turn. The *Wisp's* nose dropped into the ocean then lifted herself powerfully like a rising dolphin, throwing the seawater aside. Bennett spun the helm in the opposite direction to bring the rudders into line with the new course.

Jack screamed, "Hold fast," to warn the crew of the sudden change in direction. The few remaining men on deck scrambled to grab onto ropes or rails to keep from being washed into the sea. The *Wisp* pitched forward, then righted herself and charged ahead.

The entire crew froze in place awaiting the next sound or shudder. If Captain Jack had miscalculated, they would run aground and all die at the hands of the pursuing cruiser. The crew knew they weren't yet at flood tide. The *Will O' the Wisp* scraped bottom several times but under Jack's spur and Copper Joe's whip, the *Wisp* safely bumped across the shallows with no more than a foot of free board.

While the heavy Union gunboat could not follow them over the bar, the change of direction would again bring the *Wisp* within range. The crew hunkered down expecting another barrage. Captain Jack strode to the stern to judge their risk from the pursuing Union cruiser.

At the stern of the ship he found a crewman crouching behind a stack of rifle cases with a lantern hidden inside his sea coat. He was a new crewman Jack had added in Nassau. The man claimed to be Dutch, but Jack was impressed with his English. The entire night was now clear. Without a word, Captain Jack drew his revolver and executed him on the spot with a bullet to the temple.

Despite time lost on the turn, the *Wisp* was again racing forward. The gunboat would get only one more chance. Without the signal lamp as a range finder, the *Wisp* would be harder to hit. Jack heard the roar of the gunboat's cannons. Most of the shells fell wide exploding against the sandy bottom, but a single thirty-two pounder smashed through an interior bulkhead and exploded the left-sided boiler. A lethal brew of gaseous fire, boiling water, and a wall of superheated steam blasted through the forward section killing six men and then ascending the hatchway to the pilot house. Bennett Gibbons' clothing and skin were instantly vaporized, transforming him into a seared apparition, still holding a wheel spoke with his left hand and his right reaching for an alarm bell rope which had already disappeared.

Copper Joe hurled himself through a hatch to avoid being scalded. The men in the other engine room were saved because of good training. Despite unbearable heat, the engine rooms were instructed to keep their hatches shut. The brief respite of an open hatch would have killed everyone in the second engine room as well. It was a marvel that the boiler room explosion had not taken down the entire ship. The *Will O' the Wisp* proved to be as strong as she was fast.

The assistant helmsman, Jordan Ryan, took over the wheel as others wrapped Bennett's body in a tarp. Jack inventoried the immense damage and the unforgivable loss of life. He had allowed a treacherous Union spy on board which had resulted in all this carnage including Thomas Henry's injury and the death of his best friend. The Austrian rifles, cartridges, shovels, and shoes were not worth the life of any of his men. He would take Thomas Henry home to his mother and then somehow face Bennett's wife. Jack did not know what he would tell either of them. He had never been so ashamed of himself.

Chapter 14

April 3, 1863

Homespun

Charleston wore its distinction as the righteous epicenter of rebellion like a badge of honor. Charleston's street corner fire eaters, its politicians, pastors, newspapermen, and the favored had all demanded the breaking of ties that had knitted the nation together. Citadel cadets waving their red battle flag fired the first hostile shots of rebellion at the *Star of the West*. Charleston had instigated a betrayal that the North would not forget or forgive.

New Orleans had fallen to a Union naval attack and General Lee's efforts to take the war North resulted in a demoralizing defeat at Antietam, Maryland, in September of 1862. An emboldened Abraham Lincoln issued the Emancipation Proclamation on January 1, 1863, freeing all slaves in the rebellious Southern states. The proclamation also allowed freed slaves to serve in the Union army and explicitly made the elimination of slavery a defined objective of the war.

To emancipated slaves, January 1, 1863, was the Day of Jubilee. Few Southerners consider it jubilant, but its symbolic significance was obvious to anyone paying attention. The South was losing and what Lincoln had reluctantly begun as a war of reunification had now become personal and punitive. The ever-reserved Lincoln was now ready to unleash his wrath on the South for their continued and needless shedding of blood. As a financier, George Trenholm understood the need to balance ledgers. He was unhappily confident that Charleston was going to pay a steep price for its disloyalty.

For most of the war, Charleston had been insulated from its mayhem and mauling. Other than a fire that swept across the lower peninsula on a windy December evening in 1861, Charleston's gardenia and magnolia blossoms had not experienced a single bruise. Even that enormous fire was accidental, arising from a cook fire beneath an East Bay Street dock. The fire was rapidly driven west by strong winds down Broad and Queen Streets obliterating everything in its mile a half-mile long path across the peninsula. The Cathedral of St. John and St. Finbar on Broad Street, where Jack Holmes and Mary Ann Gleeson had married, was now a hollow shell. As horrific as that destruction had been, it had not come from the muzzle of a cannon or the barrel of a gun.

By spring 1863, the pinch of the Union blockade was no longer abstract. Despite the blockade runners' best efforts, the shelves and stock rooms of the Charleston mercantile were short on manufactured goods and household necessities. Noncombatants are always the first to recognize a languishing war effort.

The needs of the army had created severe shortages. Families were pulling forgotten spinning wheels down from their grandmother's attics. The hum of the wheel and the clang of the loom producing homespun cloth were new communal sounds. A black matron in Christ Church taught Mary Ann Holmes how clothing dyes could be squeezed from bark, leaves, roots, and berries. In turn, Mary Ann taught her daughter Eliza how to carve buttons from cross-sections of small wood branches and then polish them smooth. Hand cards, indispensable for the spinning of cotton and wool, and the machines for making them, had become priority items for Jack Holmes and the other blockade runners. Working-class women found new employment sewing shirts, pants, and tunics for the army as well as for their families. Field and house slaves with sewing skills were brought into town and leased to local tailors to make coats, quilts, blankets, rucksacks, socks, and caps.

Country families were forced to improvise even more. Few commercial goods reached the interior plantations. Corn meal replaced wheat flour. When corn was unavailable, families took to grinding and roasting peach pits to make peach pit flour. The roasted peach pit flour had a pleasant cherry or sweet almond-like smell, but unfortunate families discovered that the peach pits could poison if incompletely roasted. Peanut oil replaced whale oil for the lamps. A thick sugary syrup from watermelons replaced cane sugar. Plantation slaves tanned the hides of horses, mules, and hogs with red oak bark to make "country leather." Mixing cottonseed oil with soot made for a fine shoe black and everyone dipped their own candles.

Slave women with an understanding of woodland herbs or swamp flora became even more valuable commodities since medical supplies were non-existent. In the slave community there was an herbal medicine remedy for virtually every ailment. Afternoon tea was brewed from dry raspberry and blackberry leaves and, when needed, a passable coffee could be brewed from dried okra seeds and crushed acorns.

Charleston's strident secessionism had splintered. The city's seemingly limitless prosperity was now a memory. The shortages of household goods increased their prices and added to the inflationary spiral of the Confederate dollar. Charleston's confidence was vanishing in the face of vulnerability, want, and dread- feelings which usually presaged rage and violence.

George Trenholm was determined to hold fearfulness at bay. April 3rd was Anna Helen's birthday and he intended to celebrate it with a lavish party. He considered a Quadrille Association dance for Charleston's finest families but decided instead on an event with greater visibility and a much larger guest list. George decided on a gigantic oyster roast on the grounds of Ashley Hall.

Anna Helen had reservations. "George, with all the bad news about the war and so much suffering, it seems inappropriate to be planning such a party. I'm not sure it is how I want to celebrate my birthday. Maybe we should just have a small dinner for family."

"Darling, I think this is really important. For at least one night, people will forget our flagging fortunes in war and be reminded of the grandeur of the lifestyle we're fighting to preserve."

"George, I think you overestimate the influence of one of your parties."

"May be so, dear. But if nothing else, it will be an opportunity for you to wear that beautiful French dress and crinoline that Jack just brought back with him on the *Wisp*. I admit that I might not be able to take our guests thoughts away from the reversals of the past year. However, I am certain of your ability to charm our guests into the best evening they've experienced in quite a while."

Anna Helen stepped forward and waved her finger in front of George's silly smile. "Don't try to butter me up, George Trenholm. I know what you are up to. You want to create an illusion, a seduction. You want to play dress up and pretend that it's still the old South as each white man and woman believe it will always be."

"Is that so bad for just one night? It might help prepare folks for what I believe is going to be a difficult upcoming year. For God's sake, it's difficult right now. Plus, it is your birthday." George once again tried his boyish, hopeful grin.

"George Trenholm, you are one exasperating man," Anna Helen exclaimed as she turned and walked away.

Jack Holmes' preference would have been to not attend. He was eventually shamed into it by Mary Ann. It was his sister's birthday, and she would be bitterly disappointed if her brother did not make an appearance. George would also be disappointed. He had not seen Jack since his last return from Nassau.

Jack was overwhelmed by both his own self-loathing and his anger. He felt consumed by loss. He was distraught over the loss of Bennett Gibbons and by the loss of his belief in himself. Jack was never more certain that the war was also a lost cause. Thomas Henry had almost succumbed to yellow fever and was now bedridden with excruciating pain. The *Will O' the Wisp* lost a third of its men to yellow fever in Nassau and then another eighteen men on the return. Jack blamed himself for hiring on a Union agent and then not recognizing his betrayal during their initial encounter with the outer cordon. He had been overconfident and sloppy which had cost him a dear friend, too many fine crewmen, and almost a son.

Jack retreated to Christ Church and his Shem Creek docks to repair both the heavily damaged *Will O' the Wisp* and his spirit. The *Will O' the Wisp* could be rebuilt as strong and fast as ever. Mary Ann was not as sure about her husband. His distraction was interrupted only by periods of temper. During Thomas Henry's initial hospitalization, Jack had pulled out his Bowie knife and threatened to cut the throat of any surgeon who recommended amputation. There was not one who doubted him.

After watching the doctors pack Thomas Henry's wound with lint and wrap it with already soiled dressings, Jack, Mary Ann, and Eliza decided to take Thomas Henry home. Eliza tended to Thomas Henry's wound every day using clean water, clean linens, and clean hands. She meticulously debrided the dull, beige patches of necrotic tissue so they would not coalesce and spread. The wound periodically gave up small shards of shattered bone and Eliza would pick them out. It was agonizing for Thomas Henry, but Eliza knew that any missed fragments could be a nidus for the septic spread of a life-taking blood infection. Jack was proud of Thomas Henry for his bravery and for Eliza who bit her lip and carried on with the necessary flaying of her brother's upper leg.

Tabitha, the Negro wife of one of his shipwrights, offered a tonic of rainwater, spices and bromine that she insisted would help heal the wound. Eliza was initially skeptical but ultimately acknowledged its anti-septic qualities as the reddish-brown liquid bubbled away dead tissue. Eliza and Tabby then packed the wound with a bromine-soaked gauze. Gradually, Thomas Henry's splintered thigh bone knitted itself back together and the wound filled in with vibrant pink proud flesh. Finally, the skin margins began to reach out towards each other. Mary Ann and others praised God for Thomas Henry's deliverance. Jack Holmes thanked Tabitha and Eliza.

Besides being his sister's birthday, Mary Ann also enticed Jack with the news that George was bringing in Bulls Bay oysters, Jack's favorite. Jack finally agreed on the condition that they wish his sister a fine birthday, enjoy some Bulls Bay oysters and not dawdle. He did not want to socialize, even with George. He did not want to discuss Thomas Henry's recovery, the repairs to the *Wisp* or when he might make another run. Jack's mood was as dark as it had ever been. Mary Ann was unsure how well Jack was going to tolerate George and Anna Helen's preening and posing friends.

Chapter 15

April 3, 1863

Little Creole

Guests arriving for Anna Helen's birthday party entered through Ashley Hall's storied oriental garden which was just coming into a grand spring bloom. The exotic garden was bound by olive and pomegranate trees hung with Chinese lanterns. Multicolored azaleas and erotically fragrant gardenias were in bloom. The walking paths were marked by yellow-blossomed Chinese tobacco plants whose flower was shaped like a trumpet and played an aromatic tune irresistible to hummingbirds.

Fire pits across the Ashley Hall grounds filled the air with the aroma of burning oak, hickory, and pecan wood. Two dozen slave children ran from the fires to tables with heaping trays of sizzling steamed-open Bulls Bay oysters, soda crackers and a peach and pepper hot sauce. George and Anna's guests washed down the oysters with a potent punch made of water, lemons, sugar, and Scotch peat whiskey. The more refined ladies preferred sarsaparilla soda and ginger pop.

The oysters were accompanied by "palmetto cabbage" which was an old family recipe Anna Helen had learned from her grandmother. The heart of a palmetto tree was boiled, mashed, and then heavily seasoned with peppers and spices so it could stand up to the punch and oysters. Anna's version tasted a bit like artichoke which had not been available in Charleston for months. A fiddle band played a lively tune while a background melody was provided by an evening breeze rustling the magnolia leaves.

While Anna Helen deftly directed the party outside, George assembled several men in his upstairs drawing room. George's evening plans included far more than just music, oysters, and Scotch whiskey. Important information needed to be shared and messages sent. Central to his gathering was Confederate General Pierre Gustave Toutant Beauregard. No man was more important to Charleston's survival and morale than General P.G.T. Beauregard.

General Beauregard dominated Trenholm's study. He was a handsome, serious-minded man of French-Creole descent born on the "Contreras" sugar cane plantation in St. Bernard's Parish twenty miles from New Orleans. As a boy, he had learned to hunt, fish, and sail in the swamps and backwaters of the Louisiana bayou with befriended slaves his own age. A West Point graduate, finishing second in his class, Beauregard excelled in artillery and military engineering. After distinguishing himself during the Mexican American War, he was appointed superintendent of the United States Military Academy in 1861. He held the position for only five days before resigning when Louisiana seceded from the Union. Beauregard was immediately appointed as the first Brigadier General in the Confederate States Army. Recognizing the dangerous situation created by a Federal presence in the center of the Charleston harbor, President Jefferson Davis selected Beauregard to take command of her defenses. Davis believed Beauregard to be the perfect combination of experienced military engineer and charismatic leader needed for the vital Southern port of Charleston. Priority number one was taking control of the imposing Union-controlled Fort Sumter in the middle of Charleston's harbor.

Major Robert Anderson, a native Kentuckian, commanded the Union garrison at Fort Sumter. Although a slavery supporter, Anderson had sworn allegiance to the U.S. Army and was a loyal Unionist. Anderson had been one of Beauregard's instructors at West Point. Beauregard took no pleasure in the prospect of firing on his old mentor and tried to entice him with case after case of fine brandy, whiskey, and cigars. All gifts were returned. Eventually, Beauregard's negotiations with Major Anderson broke down. The shelling of Fort Sumter began on April 12, 1861, delighting the festive and overconfident citizenry of Charleston and a brigade of Sunday soldiers. Thirty-four hours later Major Anderson surrendered.

General Beauregard's reputation continued to grow. Three months later he was again the hero of a Confederate victory at the first battle of Bull Run near Manassas, Virginia, and his design was adopted as the official Confederate Battle Flag. Beauregard was promoted to full general making him the fifth most senior officer in the Confederate Army. He was given command of an army in the Western Theater where he played central roles in the Battle of Shiloh and the Siege of Corinth in Northern Mississippi. Despite unquestioned bravery and mastery of military tactics, General Beauregard's outspoken and combative nature led to a strained relationship with President Davis and the other generals in the West. Frustrated with Beauregard's insubordination, President Davis relieved him of command of the Army of Mississippi and ordered him back to Charleston in early 1863. While unhappy over the loss of his battlefield command, General Beauregard's energy and passion for the defense of Charleston had bolstered George Trenholm's confidence and he wanted to share that enthusiasm with everyone he knew. General Beauregard had already reinforced Fort Moultrie, Fort Sumter and the Morris Island forts with daunting earthworks constructed using conscripted slave labor. He exchanged old army siege cannons with more accurate artillery rifles with greater range. General Beauregard now commanded almost four hundred powerful land-based cannons encircling the Charleston harbor. Beauregard's innovative military engineering mind also introduced several novel defense measures for the harbor itself. He deployed naval mines that he called torpedoes. The torpedoes were loaded with one hundred pounds of powder and strung just below the water's surface. Other torpedoes were attached to spars projecting from the underwater bow of small swift boats which could impale advancing ships below the water line. Rows of beer casks and booms of chain and timber pilings were strung across the main harbor channel between Fort Moultrie and Fort Sumter to foul the propellers or paddles of Union vessels. The obstructions left only a narrow channel adjacent to Fort Sumter which allowed blockade runners to safely slip in and out of the inner harbor. Unwanted vessels attempting to enter the harbor through that channel had to pass directly under Sumter's lethal batteries. All these innovations had been planned in close consultation with George Trenholm, Charleston's civilian director of maritime defense.

Beauregard's reputation was that of a serious, if not stern, man who went months without smiling. At the same time, Beauregard enjoyed any opportunity to peacock about. He was partial to frequent and flamboyant parades leading his troop columns and military band through Charleston's streets. It was not lost on George Trenholm how these parades harkened back to the heady days following the Secessionist Convention. High spirits were vital to a city under siege.

George's other assembled guests included Christopher G. Memminger, the Confederate Secretary of the Treasury; Trenholm's business partner Theodore Wagner; his brother Edward Trenholm; and former Charleston Mayor and friend William Porcher Miles who had assisted Beauregard in designing the Confederate Battle Flag. George had looked for Jack to invite but had not been able to locate him among the assembled guests. He particularly wanted Jack to have the opportunity to meet General Beauregard.

Also present was Robert Barnwell Rhett, Jr., editor of the Charleston Mercury. "Barny" Rhett was a short, curious-looking man with a handlebar mustache, bushy muttonchops, and slicked-down hair, neatly parted in the middle, but curling girlishly at his neck. Always a dandy, "Barny" was fashionably dressed in a full black frock coat and gray vest over a white cotton shirt with a stiff starched collar and a blood-red silk cravat. A long thick-chained gold watch fob dangled between the button and pocket of his vest.

Normally animated, the prospect of interviewing General Beauregard had revved "Barny" to the state of a frenzied ferret. Tonight, was an opportunity for the Charleston Mercury to report crucial news, not just the usual shipping schedules, meeting dates, and market prices. George circulated among General Beauregard's eclectic entourage pouring everyone a glass of his best brandy. Trenholm's best was always exceptional.

Rhett pulled his pad and pencil and was closing in on General Beauregard. George waved "Barny" off, and extended his glass towards the general, "General Beauregard, on behalf of everyone here, everyone enjoying the oyster roast outside, and all of Charleston, let me thank you for your service. Having worked with you over the past several months I can attest to how beautifully you have orchestrated the defense of our city. I appreciate that my beloved wife is celebrating her birthday tonight under the protection of your benevolent shield. Salute."

General Beauregard smiled and extended his glass to a chorus of "Here, here."

Beauregard silenced the group with his left hand "We all serve the Confederacy, each in our own way," General Beauregard responded. "All of you gentlemen have contributed your energies, intellect, and gold to support the cause and to ensure the safety of this lovely city. A city I consider the cradle of the Confederacy and one I'm honored to secure."

With that statement, Beauregard lifted his own glass and exclaimed, "To Charleston, the fair queen of the South and the crucible which gave rise to our liberation."

"Here, here."

George Trenholm raised his hand once again waving for quiet. "I'm afraid we must allow Mr. Rhett to ask his questions or I fear he may go rabid on us."

"Barny" Rhett did not miss a beat and stepped forward smartly. The irony of the juxtaposition between the obsequious "Barny" Rhett and the imperial Beauregard could not be mistaken. Although relatively short in stature, Beauregard was notable for his striking and exotic foreign visage. His skin was smooth, unblemished, and olive-colored. His eyes were dark and half-lidded with a Gallic melancholy. His hair was jet-black, and he sported a finely trimmed moustache and goatee. Beauregard designed his own uniforms with bright red sashes and golden chicken guts.

Beauregard's reputation had also been dusted with allegations of immorality. Rumors were that wherever General Beauregard went he was followed by a train of concubines and wagons loaded with champagne and brandy. That, however, was not the man George Trenholm had come to know. Trenholm had come to know a man that could be caustic but also demanding of both himself and others. Despite more than his fair share of enemies, Beauregard projected greatness and accepted nothing short of excellence. Trenholm considered the accusations of Beauregard's personal failings to be baseless and a result of an accumulation of embittered rivals, his exotic looks, and the common belief that infidelity was a Creole characteristic. General Beauregard's favored nickname was "Little Napoleon." Behind his back his detractors referred to him mockingly as the "Little Creole."

As opposed to "Barny's" agitated machinations, General Beauregard was quiet and calm. Beauregard did not suffer fools gladly and could be abrupt with people who displeased him. Beauregard had antipathy for representatives of the press who he felt covered his battlefield exploits both insufficiently and inaccurately. In a private moment, General Beauregard has confessed to George, "There are many unsavory elements of human behavior that I can overlook with an eye toward a greater purpose, but I have no tolerance for mendacity in a man." George had witnessed Beauregard's fits of pique previously and had concern for how "Barny" would be received.

General Beauregard was familiar with "Barny" and the Charleston Mercury. "Barny's" editorials were known for their self-important and combustible rhetoric. However, he was still an editor of an important conduit to the people of Charleston. "Barny" knew what his readers wanted to know. "General Beauregard, how goes the war effort? The citizens of Charleston haven't recently had much good news."

General Beauregard paused, carefully selecting his words, knowing they would appear verbatim in tomorrow's edition of the Mercury. "Indeed, it was a bitter rebuke when the Army of Northern Virginia was repulsed at Antietam. However, General Lee's army escaped intact and rallied to stop Burnside's Army of the Potomac on Marye's Heights behind the city of Fredicksburg. It was a butchery which left the Army of the Potomac in disarray. In the West, Vicksburg continues to be resolute despite tremendous deprivation and we have re-taken Galveston. The North is war weary. The fall elections were unquestionably a referendum on the war and the Northern voters have swung away from Lincoln's repugnant Republican Party. The citizens of Charleston should remain stout-hearted. We are closer to victory than most imagine. A few more demoralizing Confederate victories, coupled with the continued successful defense of Charleston, will break the Union's spirit. This war is both a military and political conflict. If we remain mentally stronger than our Northern adversaries, they will eventually seek a negotiated partitioning of our two countries."

It was the argument that every man in the room had heard many times before. However, Beauregard proffered it eloquently and with invigorating confidence. Everyone except "Barny" Rhett recognized it as more of a hope than a plan. It was a hope that George Trenholm feared was dispersing like chimney smoke before a harsh winter wind.

"Barny" was writing furiously knowing that he had the next day's headline. His second question was just as provocative. "General, what are the Yankees' intentions towards Charleston and are we prepared?"

"I see you get right to the point, Mr. Rhett."

"First time we've ever heard "Barny" accused of getting straight to a point," Christopher Memminger chimed in with a laugh that was joined by the others in the room. There was no love lost between Christopher Memminger and Barnwell Rhett. Prior to the war, Memminger had angered many in Charleston by arguing in court against the breaking up of families at slave auctions and Rhett had unceasingly lampooned him for being a cooperationist.

"Barny" gave Memminger the stink-eye but did not divert his attention from General Beauregard.

Beauregard held the room's rapt attention. "To be honest, I was surprised the Yankees failed to press their advantage once they took Port Royal. At that time, a serious advance on Charleston would not have faced much opposition. Now, I believe they'll find a much different reception."

"To your credit, sir," George added.

Beauregard continued, "The heavy cannon and Whitworth rifles we have surrounding our harbor makes any attempt to enter a virtual suicide mission. Charleston harbor has the most fearsome fortifications in the world. Union gunboats will never steam into Charleston like they did into my hometown of New Orleans."

William Porcher Miles asked the general if he believed Charleston would be spared attack. Miles, the former mayor, had represented Charleston at the Secessionist Convention. Miles appealed to George Trenholm as an academic who owned no slaves, but vigorously defended the institution as a matter of principle given his belief in the Constitution's unambiguous support of private property ownership.

"No, Charleston will be attacked. It is only a matter of time. There is no southern city more despised than Charleston. Our symbolic significance to the North is far greater than either our strategic or military importance. Fort Sumter is viewed in the North as a thumb in their eye, the physical incarnation of our rebellion, and a citadel that must be re-taken. The first cannon fire of insurrection occurred here at my order. The Union is eager to revisit that sin of betrayal on us in spades."

"When might that happen?" George asked quietly.

"Hard to say. Probably when that old wet-nurse, Admiral DuPont, down in Port Royal can't think of any more excuses."

"Barny" Rhett continued to press his interview. "General, my sources tell me there's a significant build-up in the Union forces around Port Royal. Could this be a sign of an impending attack?"

William Miles added, "Yes, I have family down in Edisto and they tell me the same thing."

General Beauregard calmly sipped his brandy. "Our spies in Beaufort keep us well informed on the situation. It appears to be almost entirely a naval build-up. We do not know exactly what he's planning, but DuPont knows he can't take Charleston by naval assault alone. Lincoln hasn't put sufficient ground troops at DuPont's disposal to launch a combined sea and ground attack."

"Can I tell my readers that they should anticipate Union aggression?" "Barny" asked.

General Beauregard initially glowered at "Barny", but then composed himself when an aide touched his forearm. "It would be premature and inappropriate to suggest an impending attack on the city. You can tell the Mercury readers that while a build-up of Union forces has been reported in Port Royal, it is currently no threat to Charleston. We're well prepared and the Federals know that any attack on Charleston would be foolhardy."

"Thank you, general. Charleston is fortunate to be in your determined and experienced hands." The others in the room responded with polite applause.

George then asked General Beauregard a question that was a bit more nuanced. "When, not if, such an attack occurs, how far have you been authorized to go in the defense of Charleston?"

Beauregard nodded slightly at Trenholm acknowledging his thoughtful question. "Besides being the birthplace of the Confederacy, the port of Charleston is vital to ensuring a continuous supply of European goods. My orders, sir, are to protect it at all costs and to the last extremity. We will defend the city street by street if necessary. We will protect all its citizenry, regardless of the color of their skin or their political leanings."

Former mayor Miles responded, "Well said, sir. I think we all know what will happen to Charleston if the Union army marches down Broad Street. The city will be burned to the ground."

"My boys will never allow that to happen," Beauregard responded.

"Will never happen!" "Barny" Rhett echoed.

"Absolutely," thundered Theodore Wagner.

George wished it were true.

George circulated again, refilling each man's brandy snifter. "I think it's time to let General Beauregard rejoin the party, enjoy some oysters and share his wonderful news with our other guests. I am sure we all want General Beauregard to know we remain steadfast and will serve however is required to defend our city. General, please make Charleston's spirit known to General Lee and ask that after he is done kicking Yankee butts up North, that he come back to Charleston and help us push DuPont out of Port Royal."

"A fine sounding strategy, Mr. Trenholm. I will certainly pass it along. A fine tasting French brandy as well. Thank you all, gentlemen."

As the group made its way down Ashley Hall's splendid spiral staircase, George took hold of Memminger's arm and asked, "Christopher, may I have a moment of your time?"

The two men returned to George Trenholm's study. "The general seems to be a brave and honorable man, does he not."

Memminger responded promptly, "Most assuredly, and highly capable. He is held in high regard by the cabinet. Unfortunately, he's not one of President Davis' favorites. General Beauregard has a penchant for questioning orders which Davis cannot abide."

"How about General Lee and the other high command? What is their opinion of General Beauregard?"

"Hard to say. His military knowledge is well respected, and his courage unquestioned. Most complain about Beauregard's preference for grandiose and self-aggrandizing military proposals. Other generals criticize his lack of a pragmatic logistics, recognition of on the ground intelligence, and an inability to honestly assess relative military strengths or weaknesses. My opinion, almost all generals could be painted with that same brush, including Lee. Beauregard's biggest liability is his utter inability to function within a political hierarchy. He isn't able to take no for an answer."

Memminger continued, "The fact of the matter is that General Beauregard is in Charleston because President Davis couldn't find anywhere else to put him after relieving him of command."

"That's disappointing to hear. Is President Davis doing anything to negotiate peace. Our cotton and timber stores are dwindling. You cannot fight a war without gold, and I know the treasury must be nearly empty. Militarily, the war is, at best, a standoff. Seems like this is the time, if not past time, to seek terms that might preserve the Confederacy and stop the slaughter."

"I don't disagree, George. I have argued the same, as have several others in the Cabinet including Secretary of War Breckinridge and Secretary of State Benjamin. The Army of Northern Virginia's defeat at Antietam was a major set-back, but it also stunned the North that Lee had the audacity and capability to invade. Many of us saw this as an opportunity to discuss an armistice with Lincoln. The problem is that President Davis refuses to negotiate. His is a combination of arrogance and indecision that I have frankly never seen before. He's over-reliant on the resourcefulness of General Lee and can dither endlessly over the most obvious of decisions."

George nodded his understanding. "I've met Jefferson several times, even before secession, and I have no doubt about his dedication to the cause. However, I never believed him to be a man capable of leadership. He lacks the ability to inspire."

"I welcome you to sit at the table with him. He fluctuates widely between being aloof and quarrelsome. He is as aware of the facts regarding the war as the rest of us but lacks empathy for the suffering of our people. He's preoccupied by his musings regarding the legal and moral justifications for the war and is decidedly oblivious to the tragedy that awaits us all if we fail."

"Thanks, but no thanks," George responded with a forced laugh. "However, what else can I do. We must address the inflation. Confederate paper will soon become worthless without an infusion of gold to support it."

"That's my millstone. I've proposed a central bank for the Confederacy, war taxes to support that bank, nationalization of both the cotton and timber trade, and even the potential sale of portions of Texas and Louisiana back to Mexico and France."

"And?"

"My proposals go nowhere. Davis is so deeply entrenched in states' rights that almost any discussion involving central administration elicits screams of Federalism which is anathema to his entire belief system. So, we're left with paper dollars from the Bank of South Carolina, the Bank of Florida, the Bank of Louisiana, and every other state, most of which have nothing but chickens and a silver serving tray in their vaults."

"I am so sorry, Christopher. I promise I will keep the Bank of South Carolina strong. I will also write to President Davis and the Cabinet endorsing the vital importance of your proposals. Wars are not won by the lead in bullets. They're won by the gold in the bank."

"I'd appreciate that. It's been an uphill slog to get President Davis to realize the consequences of our current fiscal intransigence."

"Together we can make President Davis understand."

"I hope so, George, but Davis is a hard man to reach. He's lost in the smoke of war and his heart has been captured by a dark fatalistic spirit. I fear that with Davis, reason no longer holds much sway. I've heard several Cabinet members opine that the only pragmatism left in the Gray House is with Jeff's wife, Varina."

"We must make sure that Davis' pessimistic resignation doesn't bring us and everyone else down with him."

Christopher Memminger's spirits were always buoyed by George Trenholm's incessantly positive attitude. Memminger nodded, smiled, and touched brandy glasses with Trenholm.

"Thank you, my friend. Let us return to Anna's fabulous birthday party. She looks magnificent tonight in that aubergine dress."

The party was exactly as Jack had imagined. The elite of Charleston fiddling while Rome burned. Forced reverie and false bravado. Everything was too high-falutin in Jack's opinion: a reflecting pool with floating flowers, fluted pillars and verandas festooned with bougainvillea and orange trumpet vines. He could not stand to hear one more hallelujah for the blessed South or one more clueless assurance to "trust in God's will."

Of course, God was on the side of the cause. His embrace was praised from the pulpits every Sunday. When had God not been on the side of any cause? Like all wars, this one was a God-sanctioned and then God-forsaken bloody mess. God never went all-in. He was a shrewd card player who always hedged his bets. The inherent nature of any cause is that there is righteousness on both sides. Somehow, God always managed to go home with a nice pile of chips regardless of which side won.

Belief in the sanctified pursuit of God's will to justify the destruction and despair wrought upon the South seemed like a perversion of thought to Jack. Personally, Jack saw little evidence of God's divine intervention on behalf of the *Wisp*, her crew, or the South in general. The great cause was not a crusade in defense of Biblical righteousness. It was not about "God's will" or a struggle for the "soul of the South." It had the same prosaic explanation as all other wars. Thousands lay dead or maimed as the requisite human investment in a cataclysmic battle for economic power. Southern soil and his decks had been soaked in blood to ensure that the wealthy remained wealthy. Causes demand a blood sacrifice and Gods who demand a blood sacrifice are cruel, maintaining obedience only through the indiscriminate dispensation of suffering.

Jack had seen his fill of blood sacrifice. Cotton bandages crisscrossed over the faces of the blinded, soiled crimson and yellow. Violaceous amputated stumps trussed and stitched like a Virginia ham. Wooden masks covering the faces of the horribly marred creating an imagination that Jack prayed was worse than reality. Stained bed linens from quivering bowels released at the moment of demise. The stench of blood sacrifice was overwhelming, and Jack could no longer make any sense of it. He could not perceive a good reason to line up and walk into a withering wall of sizzling lead. He could no longer believe that the war was being waged on behalf of inherent goodness versus existential evil. In retrospect, maybe he never did. He could no longer see the difference between blue and gray. Both their respective flags had faded, were tattered, and heavily spattered with mud and blood.

Jack began agitating to leave soon after his and Mary Ann's arrival. The only conversation Jack desired was with his sister whom he had not seen for months. They hugged and held each other. Anna Helen insisted on knowing the progress of Thomas Henry's recovery. Jack would not share Thomas Henry's misery with anyone else. Anna Helen told Jack that George had been looking for him. Jack assured her that he would seek George out before the end of the party. He felt bad for lying to his sister, especially on her birthday.

Two black children in rags and no shoes ran across his path with trays of oysters for men and women in silk and brocade. Jack realized that the true nature of existential evil had never been less clear. Walking the flower-lined pathways of Ashley Hall with Mary Ann, Jack acknowledged to himself that the only "great cause" left was survival.

As Jack and Mary Ann made their way towards the gate they were hailed by the distinctive voice of George Trenholm.

"Jack, Mary Ann, a moment if you will. There is someone I'd very much like you to meet."

Jack and Mary Ann stopped and turned. George was approaching quickly covering yards of lush green grass at a time with his long-legged loping gait. He was accompanied by another man in a resplendent gray uniform with a crimson sash. Jack recognized the officer as the distinctive General Pierre G.T. Beauregard.

"I thought you might like to meet General Beauregard, commander of the Confederate forces here in Charleston. The general is the man responsible for our harbor defenses which are the most imposing in the world."

"A pleasure to meet you, General," Jack responded. "I've heard much about you and it's all complimentary."

"Obviously, you haven't spoken to any of my men," General Beauregard answered with a laugh. "Madam, a true honor to make your acquaintance," Beauregard added, bowing politely.

"The honor is all mine," Mary Ann responded. "George, simply the grandest of parties. I'm sure that Anna Helen is overjoyed with her birthday festivities. We are sorry to be leaving so early, but Thomas Henry still needs our attention."

"No need for apology, Mary Ann. I know that Thomas Henry has had a difficult recovery. I also know that Anna Helen deeply appreciates your coming and was most pleased with seeing you both. I can't thank you enough."

"He is getting better slowly. Thank you for asking after him," Mary Ann replied. "Jack and I would not have missed Anna Helen's birthday. I must apologize for Jack, however. He's had far more than his share of your Bulls Bay finest."

"I ordered an extra bushel as soon as I heard that Jack was coming," George responded with a smile.

General Beauregard spoke next. "Captain Holmes, I've heard a lot about you as well. Your friend George, as well as everyone else I encounter, count you as the finest corsair on the Atlantic coast."

"That is kind, General, but I don't believe my recent work would support that description."

"As I hear it, you were betrayed, and despite being ambushed you saved the ship and the cargo."

"We were betrayed, sir, and the ship and cargo were saved, but I didn't save my crew. I lost my oldest friend and almost lost my son."

"Yes, and I am sorry for your loss. However, if I may, I would suggest that were it not for your heroic actions the accounting of forfeiture would have been far greater. It is unfair for you to take this burden of guilt all upon yourself. Loss is inevitable in war and your service to the Confederacy is incalculable."

"Respectfully sir, I disagree and there is no patriotic hooey that will bring my men back."

"Your sense of responsibility is admirable. I suspect that is a large part of the explanation for your exceptional record. I hope that sense of responsibility extends to more of us than just your crew."

"I'm not sure we understand your meaning," Mary Ann testily interjected.

"My meaning, ma'am, is that Charleston depends on blockade runners like your husband to bring in necessary food and supplies."

"And munitions, General?" Mary Ann added.

"Of course, munitions as well," General Beauregard replied. "Military supplies are as important to the defense of Charleston as are household necessities. The *Will O' the Wisp* has an unmatched record of providing both. We hope that once the *Will O' the Wisp* is fully repaired we can count on Captain Holmes to again flummox the Union blockade."

"General, I haven't flummoxed anyone. I sailed quietly through the large gaps that the South Atlantic Squadron left in its line. Those gaps have almost disappeared. The noose around Charleston gets tighter with every passing day."

George clasped his hand on Jack's shoulder. "Jack, we still have runners who make it through the blockade every day, and you're a better captain than any of them."

"Don't blow smoke, George. You and I both know that a successful run in and out of Charleston is now a fifty-fifty proposition at best. I may be a good captain, but there are many other good captains who have sailed out and haven't come back. They are blown-up, drowned or in a Yankee prison. I don't intend to count myself or any more of my crew among them."

"Captain Holmes, the Confederacy, and all of Charleston, need your skills and the services of your ship," General Beauregard countered. "You know better than anyone how important the lifeline is that you provide. You were betrayed by a Yankee spy on your last run. I will assign my intelligence officers to personally vet your next crew. From what I'm told, with a good crew, there isn't a Union ship afloat that can catch the *Will O' the Wisp*."

"General, it would be easy to become intoxicated by your flattering comments, but I know what's out there beyond the bar. I will not sail my men into that maelstrom again. It's asking too much, especially if it's just so George and his friends can keep making money off the backs of slaves and so their slave children can serve steamed oysters at their parties."

Everyone was silent. Jack looked at the ground, disappointed in himself and regretting his words.

Mary Ann finally spoke. "George, General Beauregard, let me apologize for Jack's outburst. Thomas

Henry's injury has shaken us all and Jack has been humbled by a great sense of responsibility for Bennett Gibbons and the other crew he lost. I don't think Jack is prepared to consider another run at the present time."

"Yes, please accept my apology," Jack added. "My comments were out of line and I am ashamed to have tarnished Anna Helen's lovey birthday celebration. I must have had more of that punch than I realized. My behavior is mortifying, and we will excuse ourselves before I embarrass our family further."

"Nonsense Jack," George responded. "This was too early to talk with you about another run. I was insensitive to the issues that you and Mary Ann are dealing with. *Mea culpa*, and I ask for your forgiveness. This is a bad time and we can talk again when you're ready."

"George, you are more than gracious. What I can promise you is this. When the *Wisp* is repaired, I will look for a back door out of Charleston that will by-pass the blockading squadron. If I can be sure that I am not leading my crew to their death, I'll make another run to Nassau, Bermuda or Cuba or wherever else you want me to go. But I won't unless I can honestly tell my crew that I've upped the odds in their favor."

"Jack, that's more than fair," George Trenholm responded somberly. "If there is anything I can do to help, or anything General Beauregard can do, just ask. If there is a back door that the Yankees have overlooked, I am confident that you will be the one to find it."

"Thank you, George. It was a pleasure meeting you General Beauregard. I look forward to talking with you again, but for now, Mary Ann and I must take our leave. George, please thank Anna Helen for such a wonderful party and tell her I appreciated her making mom's "palmetto cabbage." It brought back wonderful childhood memories. Give her our best birthday wishes. I would also be in your debt if you did not share with her my inelegant behavior."

Chapter 16

August 20, 1863

Kiawah River

General Beauregard's words proved prophetic. On April 7th, within a week of Anna Helen's extravagant birthday party, Union Rear Admiral Samuel Francis DuPont sailed into Charleston harbor in command of the most powerful naval force ever assembled. DuPont's armada consisted of nine ironclads including seven new Passaic class warships, improved versions of the original *USS Monitor*, and an experimental ironclad called the *Keokuk*. Admiral DuPont, and more so, his superior, Assistant Secretary of the Navy Gustavus Fox, fervently believed in the independent power of the U.S. Navy. Fox and DuPont believed that the heavy guns of these armored vessels could reduce Charleston's harbor defenses and bring the city to its knees without ground support.

On the morning of the 7th the harbor was dead calm with an early morning blanket of haze nestled on the glassy surface. Trusting in the impregnability of the thick iron plating on the new monitors, Du Pont gave the order to advance. However, because of their unusual design and heavy armor, the new monitors moved slowly and maneuvered poorly. Communication between the Union ironclads was also poor, and they ultimately pulled up short of their planned salvo line. That mistake spared Fort

Sumter's weaker northwest facing wall from what might have been a more accurate and devastating assault.

In addition to overestimating the ironclad's capability, Admiral DuPont also underestimated General Beauregard's defenses. DuPont's flagship, the *New Ironsides*, carried sixteen heavy guns, arranged to deliver broadsides so that only eight could be brought to bear at any one time. The Passaic class monitors carried one 15-inch and one 11-inch gun, and the *Keokuk* carried two 11-inch guns. DuPont's 34 big guns were matched against hundreds of Confederate cannons. Cannons precisely placed around the harbor entrance by Beauregard to guarantee a withering salvo from every direction. The design of the monitors made it difficult to swab, reload and aim its cannons, resulting in a rate of fire of only one shell every seven minutes.

During the ensuing two-hour battle, Union monitors fired only one hundred and fifty-four shots. Meanwhile, the Confederates rained down more than 2000 armor piercing rifle bolts and exploding shells, raking the Union monitors like a dog pissing on a boxwood. The thick armor plates protected the crews with only a single Union casualty, but several of the monitors were disabled by damage to their hulls, rudders and gun turrets. The *Keokuk* was hit more than ninety times and eventually sank. The Union Navy limped back to Port Royal with its tail between its legs. Charleston cheered and gloated as their hero, General Beauregard, preened and paraded. Unlike New Orleans, Charleston would not be taken by naval action alone.

Captain Jack saw none of the Charleston harbor battle. He was busy far from the deep water of the harbor in much smaller channels. Jack was furious with himself for the mistakes he had made on his recent return from Nassau. He had relied on the new moon, mist, and fog. He had relied on the speed of the *Wisp* and the ineptitude of the Union blockaders. He had relied on luck. He had not relied on his knowledge of the Lowcountry coast and the waterways he had been sailing since he was a boy. It was not a mistake that he would make again.

Ever since Anna Helen's birthday party, Jack, Copper Joe, Jordan Ryan, Caleb, Ezekiel, and a few other crewmen had been taking the *Sarah Belle*, an eighty-foot sailing sloop, out from the family shipyard on Shem Creek while repairs continued on the *Will O' the Wisp.* The *Sarah Belle* was half the length of the *Wisp* but had a similar width and draft. Captain Jack sailed the *Sarah Belle* across the Charleston harbor, up the Ashley River, through the Wappoo Cut into Wappoo Creek. The *Sarah Belle* sailed unobserved along Wappoo Creek behind James Island to the Stono River.

The broad Stono River flowed south between James and John's Island and emptied into the Stono Inlet. The Stono Inlet was deep water and the southernmost end of the Charleston blockade crescent. Egress from the Stono Inlet was always bottled up by two or three Union gunboats. Entry or exit through the Stono Inlet was rarely attempted by Charleston blockade runners.

On their first reconnaissance, Captain Jack surprised his men by turning west out of the Stono River into the Kiawah River. The Kiawah River ran behind both Kiawah and Seabrook Islands but was neither as wide nor as deep as the Stono. The Kiawah River flowed farther south into the Edisto River which emptied into the Atlantic at the Edisto Inlet. The Edisto Inlet was also deep water and regularly patrolled by gunboats out of Port Royal. Captain Jack surprised the crew again when he guided the *Sarah Belle* into an even smaller tributary of the Kiawah River that split Kiawah and Seabrook Islands and reached the Atlantic just beyond Captain Sam's Spit. Captain Jack ordered Caleb to throw out the anchor.

Copper Joe scratched his head and looked at Jack quizzically. "What's up, Captain? Where you plan on sailin'?"

"I'm taking the *Wisp* out by Captain Sam's Spit. Ain't nobody watching that way out," Captain Jack replied with a mischievous grin.

"Yeah, there's a reason for that. Nothin' down that creek but oyster shells, mud flats, and mosquitoes that carry away small children. It will be a miracle if this little sloop makes it down that creek. No way the *Wisp* is getting out through this glorified drainage ditch."

Captain Jack just kept smiling. "Maybe, maybe not. Gonna be exciting finding out."

"You thinkin' about putting wheels on the *Wisp* and rolling her down river like a wagon?"

"Not a bad idea, Joe, but I've got a better one. Still, I'm gonna keep yours on the back burner just in case mine doesn't work out."

"Jesus, Cap. I'm not likin' the sound of this. It's a long walk home from here."

"We ain't walking anywhere, Joe. We're on our way to Nassau." Jack turned and looked downriver, wiping his forehead with his forearm sleeve, clearly seeing something different than Copper Joe and the rest of his crew.

"Jordan, go below and bring up the maps. Caleb and Ezekiel, start sounding for depth and report your findings to Jordan. The rest of you guys get the poles and spread out around the boat. Shout out and mark any shallows or oyster banks you feel off to our sides. I want a river bottom map that's better than anything we've got in hand. If a single oyster scrapes one barnacle off our bottom I'm going to take it out of your hides. Any questions?"

Each day, Captain Jack and the *Sarah Belle* returned to this narrow, shallow branch of the Kiawah River with the rising tide. Copper Joe, Jordan Ryan, and Captain Jack mapped literally every foot of the waterway. They meticulously recorded the width and depth of the river at high, low, and in-between tide, every mud bank, sand bar, and mound of oyster shells.

Calling it miserable work was not giving it due credit. A slight breeze carried the fetid, briny scent of the marsh across the slowly flowing creek. When the tide fell and the breeze subsided, the mosquitoes came in droves. The crew slathered creek mud over exposed skin, but the mosquitoes were so thick they flew in open mouths, into ears and up their nostrils. The heat was oppressive. Brain-sapping, muscle-wasting, spirit-killing heat and humidity of a type found only in the Lowcountry. A heat God had designed to drive out all mammalian life, preserving a refuge for cold-blooded reptiles and no-blooded insects.

Creek banks scurried with fiddler crabs and the mud banks were tangled with shrubs, fallen trees and root balls. Woodpeckers hammered ceaselessly at the stripped tree trunks of scrub oaks and slash pines scattered across untended fields. Snowy egrets, herons, hawks, and magnificent golden eagles filled the sky. Every half mile or so there were collections of primitive cabins with groups of slaves turning the soil and spreading manure. Chickens squawked, pigs squealed, and goats bleated in small pens next to the slave huts. The white planters had long since left, fearful of both the inevitable arrival of the Yankees and the reprisals which would follow liberation of their field slaves.

The *Sarah Belle's* progress eventually came to a halt as the riverbanks narrowed and mud flats approached. Captain Jack's war elephant trek across the Alps was going to require more than sounding and mapping. Jack was stymied by the fact that no man could be paid enough to work the banks of the Kiawah River during God-forsaken summer.

With the next arrival of the *Sarah Belle* at the dwindling extreme of the Kiawah River, the crew was met by almost four hundred slaves with picks, shovels, mules, and their overseers. The slaves belonged to George Trenholm or had been leased from local planters. Only then did Copper Joe and the others fully comprehend Jack's intentions.

"Captain, are we really going to dig a canal all the way to the ocean?" Joe asked.

"Not unless we have to. We are going to excavate those banks, strip out the marsh grass and roots, dredge the sand bars, and clear those giant oyster heads. If that doesn't work, then we'll dig a canal. One way or another, water is going to flow through here down to Captain Sam's Spit."

"Captain, with all due respect, clearing this branch of the Kiawah River to allow passage of a ship like the *Will O' the Wisp* is going to be something out of the Old Testament."

"Don't fret, Joe. This won't be nearly as hard as building the pyramids and, thanks to Mr. Trenholm, we now have the army needed to do it."

Joe shook his head and walked away mumbling under his breath, "Well, the people building the pyramids didn't have to put up with these God-damned mosquitoes."

The idea of using slaves to clear the river sickened Jack and he had struggled with George's recommendation. He had opposed slavery his entire life. He murdered a man for torturing Ezekiel at the Sugar House. Jack found every justification for slavery self-serving and unacceptable. Yet now he was the overseer of an army of slaves and his justification was every bit as shameful and tormenting as all those others he had decried. It was a devil's bargain and Jack knew he had lost a part of his soul. For all his guilt, he also realized it was nothing compared to the misery about to be experienced by his enslaved engineers. It made his stomach churn to think of them as his slaves.

The ebb and flow of the tides marked the time. The *Sarah Belle* arrived each day at the extreme of the Kiawah River just behind high tide. The crew and the slaves worked through the receding tide until returning high water made further work on the river bottom and banks impossible. Some days the tides allowed the *Sarah Belle* to return across the inner harbor to Shem Creek. Some days they were not so lucky, and the *Sarah Belle* remained plugged into the river bottom. Those nights were stifling and rest impossible. Energy that failed to dissipate in the heat was sucked away by the mosquitoes. Slaves and crew alike were periodically incapacitated by a high bilious country fever and all were terrified by the possibility of yellow fever or malaria.

Low tide exposed the oyster crowns. Oyster crowns were voracious, capable of tearing skin from a bone or the hull from a boat. Given the shallowness of the Kiawah River, and limited room for maneuvering a large ship, Captain Jack needed all the oyster beds dug out. It was treacherous work but would give him another five feet of depth at high tide. The slaves tasked with removing the oyster crowns stood thigh deep in muddy water and were anchored calf deep in the pluff. Pickaxes and iron bars chipped away at the steep shell banks and oyster mounds. Slaves tied ropes and chains around large oyster clusters and dragged them out of the river using mules on the bank. The slaves formed a bucket brigade to haul huge wicker baskets of mud and shells out of the river. As sections of the river were cleared, the channel was marked with poles reflecting the depth at high and low tide, respectively.

The oyster work made the slaves long for the cotton fields. The razor-sharp oyster shells sliced deep, slow-healing rents in feet, shins, calves and hands. At dead low tide, the river bottom was a viscous gelatin of black, mud-filled creek water which quivered more than flowed. Small streams of blood from oyster lacerations could be seen coursing over the top of the pluff mud's surface rather than dissolving into it.

Jack brought shoes, food and clothing to the slaves working on the river. He began bringing his daughter Eliza to the excavation to clean the wounds with Tabitha's bromine solution and dress the filthy oyster cuts. Caleb and Ezekiel began a dialog with Horace, one of the elders of the slave community. Older than most of the other field slaves, Horace was dark black, like onyx, with a shock of graying wooly hair and exceptionally bright white teeth. Horace commanded respect and carried himself erect, despite a lifetime of stooping. At Jack's direction, Caleb and Ezekiel extended an offer to Horace to take selected families to the Caribbean once the river was cleared.

There was tremendous fear of this offer among the slaves. They had been told all manner of tales to keep them on the plantations as civil order broke down. One of those tales was being shanghaied and sold to Cuban sugar plantations where the heat and work would be even more punishing. Even though almost all the owners and overseers had fled, most slaves chose to stay on the plantations. They tended their animals and worked their gardens for crops that would sustain them. They remained, however, deeply distrustful, and fearful of the white masters' return. After a lifetime of subjugation, that seemed far more likely than a day of jubilation. That fear included Captain Jack and his offer to take slave families to freedom.

The leaden summer heat intensified as the river excavation carried on. The harder that the *Sarah Belle* and the slave army pushed, the more aggressively antagonistic the Kiawah River became. The daily hope for a breakthrough became more remote with each passing week. In addition to the pitiless heat and carnivorous pests, the river threw new obstacles in their path each day. In addition to the recalcitrant oyster beds, the slaves struggled to clear fallen pine, scrub oaks, and cypress trees from choke points along the narrow river.

The hull was smeared with mud and bottom slime to help the boat slip through water thick with green scum and vegetation. The *Sarah Belle* frequently became snarled in tangles of marsh grass and willow switches. Crew members took long knives and machetes into the water in an exhausting effort to free the boat. As one switch was cut, another would be exposed. Water work was detested by the crew, unwelcome in the habitat of moccasins, river rats, leeches, and lizards. They worked on, however, motivated by the fact that the *Sarah Belle* could not return upriver at the end of the day unless freed from the entangling river vegetation.

On those nights when the *Sarah Belle* either remained entangled in the switches or dug helplessly into the mud, Jack lowered the sails and he and the crew slept on deck to avoid the oppressive heat below. Captain Jack frequently found himself talking with Ezekiel who also slept little awaiting the dawn and the tide.

Ezekiel had been delivered by an unattended mother on the dirt floor of a one room slave cabin with a tabby chimney. The cabin stood among a line of nine identical huts beside an elegant two-story brick home of a wealthy James Island planter. The cabin was shaded by majestic live oaks which lined the approach to the plantation house. His mother had borne the burden of slavery bravely but sobbed as she held her newborn Ezekiel. She knew he would eventually be taken from her.

Slave owners deconstructed families according to their financial needs or desires. A convenient dogma preached from Christian pulpits was that the African did not have the same regard for family as did whites. Slave fathers were sold for misbehavior or profit if the slave's reputation as a worker or a buck preceded him. Slave mothers were taken from their children to wet nurse the babies of the woman of the house so she could promptly return to her privileged antebellum life. When a master's child needed a playmate, or an older son or daughter married, they were often gifted a young slave. When a slave owner died, his slaves where property distributed by will. Once slave families were broken up, they rarely saw each other again. The image of a benevolent Christian master made for an uplifting Sunday sermon. However, the appearance of contentment with enslavement was achieved only by the willingness to exert relentless indignity and remorseless suffering the other six days of the week.

Ezekiel's plantation straddled a piece of land between a river and a tidal marsh. As a child, Ezekiel was responsible for gathering firewood, tending garden, and picking berries. Like all other slaves, Ezekiel wasn't allowed to learn to read or write. Whatever Ezekiel knew, he'd learned from stories shared by elders at night or at the end of a lash. Plantation slaves received a ration of corn and pork each day. Small slave gardens supplemented those rations with sweet potatoes, cucumbers, and string beans. Ezekiel also tended several chickens and a pig and learned to mold and dry clay, fish and crab in the creeks.

Ezekiel impressed his master with his cleverness and how rapidly he assimilated skills. As an older boy, Ezekiel was brought into the master's home to be trained as a household slave. House slaves learned to clean boots, tend the fireplace, bring water from the well and empty chamber pots. His mother was happy that Ezekiel would have better clothes, better food, and an opportunity to overhear at the white man's table. Mostly, she was happy that Ezekiel would not die in the cotton fields of malarial shakes or dysentery. She did not allow herself to think about the fact she would probably never see Ezekiel again.

After a year and a half of working in the plantation house, Ezekiel was given as a wedding gift to a son who lived in downtown Charleston. One year after that, Captain Jack discovered him being beaten to death for an offense that Ezekiel could not describe.

Ezekiel was fascinated by the lights he saw dancing deep in the swampland on both sides of the Kiawah River. "What's they, Cap'n Jack?"

"That's the Will O' the Wisp," Jack explained.

"Like our ship?"

"Exactly. The Will O' the Wisp are ghost lights that rise from the swamps and marshes. At night, at the right time of year, you can see them. Most times they look like a flickering lamp, but sometimes, they can be so bright as to resemble a lighthouse or signal fire. Some sailors call it "fool's fire" because it can induce captains to change course and ground themselves in shallow water."

"Is somebody out there, Cap'n?"

"That's what it looks like, doesn't it, Zeke. But no, there ain't nobody there. Backward folks attribute it to ghosts and fairies. My grandmother used to call it "pixy light." The snake handlers claim it's the spirits of unbaptized or stillborn children flittering between heaven and hell."

"What you think it is, Cap'n?"

"Well, people who supposedly know, claim that the light is the result of exhalations arising out of the earth from decaying plants buried under the bog and water. For some reason, the gases ignite when they contact the air. Me, I'm not so scientifically oriented. I think the Will O' the Wisp represents one of God's miracles that he saves just for sailors. Once when I was younger and very lost, the Will O' the Wisp guided me home. If your faith is strong enough the Will O' the Wisp will lead you to safety. It has always been a good omen for me."

"So, you name your ship for the lights," Ezekiel surmised.

"Yes, I did. Whenever I see the Will O' the Wisp I'm comforted that they are signaling me the right way. It's a good thing that we've seen them tonight."

"I hope so, Captain. I tired of this river."

"Me too, Zeke. I have brought a lot of suffering to a lot of people just to get some high water. This river may yet prove me a fool."

The following morning, August 20th, the *Sarah Belle* rose from the mud bar and moved forward unentangled and unobstructed. Caleb and Ezekiel confirmed deepening and faster water. More poles were placed indicating water depth. Within an hour, the *Sarah Belle* approached Captain Sam's Spit and the Kiawah River's exit into the Atlantic. Some of the astounded crew cheered the open path to sea. Others cried.

Captain Jack scanned the horizon for a Union presence, but there was none. He ordered the *Sarah Belle* out into the Atlantic to test the depth of the offshore bar. Once he had passed it, Captain Jack turned the *Sarah Belle* around and rode the in-coming tide back up the Kiawah River the way he had come.

Captain Jack caught Ezekiel's eye, nodded and smiled.

Ezekiel smiled back and mouthed the words, "Will O' the Wisp. Good omen."

Chapter 17

September 3, 1863

Swamp Angel

It was more difficult for the larger *Will O' the Wisp* to negotiate the Kiawah River than it had been for *Sarah Belle*, but Jack and his army of slave engineers made the necessary modifications. Their first run encountered some shifting sand and oyster banks that needed further excavation. Still, taking the Kiawah River at high tide was far easier than any of the crew had imagined, a testament to the careful calculations and fine mapping they had done during those miserable mid-summer visits on the *Sarah Belle*. The Kiawah River proved to be the loose seam between the Charleston and Port Royal detachments of the South Atlantic Blockade. Over the ensuing months, Jack repeatedly pulled at that seam, tearing apart what the Union had believed to be a well woven blockade.

The repeated undetected arrival of the *Will O' the Wisp* in the Charleston inner harbor stunned the blockading squadron. On both sides of the Charleston bar the *Will O' the Wisp* was considered a phantasm that appeared and disappeared at the will of its captain. Jack Holmes had obviously struck a deal with the devil.

Jack knew better. The *Wisp's* success continued only as long as his back door remained undiscovered by the ever-growing cadre of Union spies. A couple of times each week, Captain Jack steamed the *Wisp* across the harbor from the

Ashley River to his Shem Creek dock or on longer steams along Long Island to Bull's Bay or down the Stono River to the Stono Inlet. Misdirection designed to confuse prying eyes seeking to discern the *Wisp's* secret to exiting Charleston unseen. George and Jack decided together not to tell the other Charleston blockade runners. The decision troubled Jack, but he understood that one slip-up in security or a single inexperienced captain running their ship aground in the narrow Kiawah River would close this door. The Yankees could shut down the skinny exit at Captain Sam's Spit with a single gunboat. Crew member were sworn to secrecy. Their lives depended on being clandestine. Literal rather than figurative threats were always more effective.

Jack kept his word to the slaves who had carved a shipping channel out of muck and razor-sharp oyster shells. Each trip down the Kiawah River, Caleb and Ezekiel rendezvoused with Horace who delivered a slave family to the *Wisp* in a pirogue he kept hidden in the high marsh. The men and boys worked as coal heavers in the boiler room. The women and children helped in the galley. On arrival in Nassau, they were paid the same as the other crewmembers which was more than enough to get them settled. They were paid in coins they had never seen before, but Caleb educated them regarding their worth and use. Whether any of the crew minded Jack's illegal slave smuggling was unknown. No one questioned the captain. A man in league with the devil was not to be trifled with.

The *Will O' the Wisp's* repeated success was more than just a thumb in the eye of the Union blockade. Fewer and fewer blockade runners leaving Charleston ever returned. The *Wisp* and a handful of other resourceful runners were the lifeline preventing Charleston from becoming Vicksburg where the fine citizens on the bluff were living in caves and eating rats, weasels, and possums. Fear filled the eyes of people on the street. It was the people on the street who recognized the changing direction of the wind well before their leaders.

The "Swamp Angel" now reigned over the city. The "Swamp Angel" was a long-range, two hundred-pound Parrott rifle hidden in the marshes on Morris Island. It could hurl ten-pound shells into Charleston from more than a mile away. With downtown Charleston within range, the Union demanded an immediate surrender of the city which General Beauregard summarily refused. After Beauregard's rejection of surrender terms, Lincoln authorized a daily bombardment of Charleston using the steeples of St. Michael's and St. Philip's as range finders. In defiant response, the bells of St. Philip's were melted down and recast into cannon. That defiance would gradually fade in the face of daily shelling.

The "Swamp Angel" had far more psychological impact than military effect. The lower peninsula was the only part of the city that the "Swamp Angel" could reach. Residents and businesses relocated north of Calhoun Street and the "Swamp Angel" shells fell harmlessly into the burnt-out district. In the face of incessant Union shelling, Jefferson Davis pronounced it was better that Charleston be reduced to a "heap of ruin" rather than be left as "prey for Yankee spoils." President Davis' malignant wish was realized. Never in any war had an American president authorized a sustained bombardment of a civilian population. The North had not forgotten Charleston's responsibility for firing the first traitorous shots on its own countrymen. Day upon day, month upon month, the Union singled out the city of Charleston for holocaustic revenge.

Deserted, the grand houses south of Broad Street could no longer maintain the pretense of aged elegance. The toll of war had been far greater than ever envisioned from their galleries overlooking the Battery just a few years earlier. The self-congratulatory speeches and brass bands which had previously resounded up and down Broad Street had been replaced by silence. A silence interrupted only by the now familiar banshee's scream of the "Swamp Angel's" calling.

Jack barely recognized some of the once proud homes he had previously known well. Shattered roofs and crumbling walls stood like broken teeth along formerly fashionable streets. Stylish horse drawn carriages were no longer parked by large granite step-stones. Gates had been stripped for their iron. Ramshackle window shutters hung at angles from rusted hinges, and the eaves were pockmarked by rot or cannon blast. Paint had been curled into chicken feathers by summer heat and explosions blackened their edges with soot. Any color which may dare show itself was obscured by gray dust and dirt.

Trees were shredded and the landscaped hedges neglected or destroyed. A dilapidated, vine-threaded gazebo stood lost amidst an overgrown and rubble-strewn garden. Jack's mind flashed back to the lovely side garden and the innocent girl who had overseen it. It was a tragic ruination. Jack feared that the perpetual season of mud, blood, and cannon blast might never end.

Jack rode across the peninsula, past Ryan's Mart, a slave parlor on Chalmers Street. The bidding area behind its arched brick entrance was destroyed and the holding pens were empty. One block south at #4 Broad Street, the offices of the Charleston Mercury were shattered and shuttered. Lower East Bay Street was nothing more than rotting wharves, demolished warehouses, and deserted homes. Charleston's most celebrated streets were now traveled only by the desperate, the sinister, or the lost.

The war had been brought to Charleston by ambitious men seeking profit and prestige. They stirred passionate prejudices, defiant in their defense of slavery behind the mantra of states' rights, racial superiority, and selected Biblical passages. They feasted on the less informed and less invested countrymen. They anointed themselves with sanctity and virtue and took their chances on a grab for power and personal reward. The possibility of failure, and the immense suffering it could bring, was dismissed with thoughtless bravado. The elite Southern nationalists comforted themselves with the certainty that any failure would be cushioned by wealth and connections. Secession was a gamble, and as every gambler knew, it was always best to play with someone else's money.

Charleston's aristocracy would resist succumbing to the realities of war until the bitter end, if not beyond. George persisted in throwing extravagant dinner parties at his Ashley Hall home. Jack wondered if George understood the stark contrast between his lavish parties and the dinner tables being set by everyone else in Charleston. A blood debt had been paid by virtually every home. Empty chairs belonging to fathers and sons who had died at Shiloh or on some other God-forsaken field, to brothers who were dying more slowly, but just as certainly, in rancid Yankee prison camps, to a grandfather dead from pneumonia, an uncle who fell to yellow fever, a sister who wasted away with consumption or a child dead from typhus.

Confederate money bought less and less. Families, whose menfolk were missing, were faced an inability to feed, clothe or shelter their children. Shattered families unable to flee turned to begging, thieving and prostitution to stay alive. Those family members now stared back at Jack and his fine stallion from the street with sunken eyes and lifeless expressions. Whatever hope they had held expired long ago. Widowed wives struggled down broken sidewalks shouldering their own bags while orphaned, emaciated, and feral children foraged for food in the piles of debris.

The city had experienced huge successive waves of whooping cough, smallpox, and yellow fever. The tar barrels Jack had seen in Nassau now burned in the streets of Charleston. Meanwhile, the wealthy planters and bankers retreated to their summer homes in the North Carolina mountains to escape the pestilence and ugliness.

Refugees, both white and black, poured into Charleston and were deposited into uninhibited buildings south of Calhoun. The overflow of sick and injured filled makeshift infirmaries in still standing public buildings, churches, and hotels. Others lay on the ground under pitched tents in parks and open fields. Courageous nurses, including Eliza Holmes, struggled, and failed to meet the medical needs of so many. Erysipelas spread at will and gangrene chose at random. Charleston's fine ladies tried to help but could do little more than read the Bible to the wounded and write last letters to loved ones when the Bible no longer brought solace. Pitiful maimed and broken soldiers laid silently on their cots with unrecognizing eyes; their hair crusted with dried blood and thick with flies. Powder-burned faces from musket flashes and swollen, split purplish lips from gunpowder in the bitten-off cartridges made them unrecognizable even to family.

Besides pitiful, the conditions were also combustible. Charleston had sent more than five thousand men to fight. More than a third had died and many of the rest had limped home- aimless, limbless, armed, and angry. Former slaves collected on street corners with all their worldly possessions on their backs. No provisions had been made for their care or shelter. Their presence created an elemental fear among the remaining white citizens. There was no semblance of civil order as the Charleston constabulary had been conscripted long ago.

In the distance, Jack heard an explosion he estimated was near South Battery. Others on the street barely turned their heads. The frequency of shelling had fallen off dramatically in recent months. The "Swamp Angel" now only roared a couple of times each day. Its purposeful irregularity and inaccuracy achieving a constricting and draining terror that only random violence can accomplish.

With each explosion, no matter how far away, moods darkened. Charleston had finally bent to Union will. There would be no preservation of its antebellum past. With each explosion, the great cause, and all its justifications, became harder to remember. Each night as the light died on the western edge of the Ashley River and the evening breeze carried the dense metallic smell of cordite over the city, people no longer dreamed of victory or glory.

Riding farther up Broad Street, Jack again heard the distinctive whistle of an in-bound shell. This one was closer. The shell exploded beside a home immediately to his left. Jack's stallion reared but did not bolt. Dirt and dust from the explosion covered Jack's face and filled his nostrils. The concussive wave confused his thoughts and sucked the air from his lungs. His vision blurred and his ears rang. Jack instinctively calmed his horse and gradually regained his senses. A quick inventory confirmed he was still alive, and neither he nor his animal were injured. The message, however, was received. The end days were near.

Chapter 18

September 7, 1863

Battery Wagner

Jack Holmes was running to Nassau on the exact date the fate of Charleston was irrevocably sealed. Jack's daughter, Eliza, had been asked by a nursing friend, Janie O'Shea, to accompany her on a trip to Battery Wagner across the Ashley River. They would work a few days in the Battery's infirmary, meet some young boys, have lunch on the beach and, best of all, get away from the squalid downtown hospital. Eliza was thrilled to have a brief adventure. On the day after Eliza and Janie's arrival, Union soldiers under Brigadier General Quincy Gillmore stormed across Light House Inlet on the southern tip of Morris Island. Confederate soldiers retreated up the beach to the sanctuary of Battery Wagner and dug in like ticks.

After several futile ground assaults, the frustrated Gillmore settled on a siege strategy, trapping the Confederate defenders of the Morris Island fort. Also trapping Eliza Holmes and Janie O'Shea.

Eliza arose on the morning of September 7th to a terrible sight. Smoke from dozens of Union ships drifted toward Battery Wagner like a darkening storm cloud. The gray and baby blue-uniformed gunners in Wagner's traverses stood by their cannons watching the huge flotilla while others brought up powder from the fort's magazine. Eliza and Janie held hands and prayed before putting on their white dresses and hurrying to the infirmary. An overcast morning, the only color against the grim sky and drifting smoke was the red and blue of the Stars and Bars flying over Battery Wagner. Deep ditches and palisades of sharpened logs encircled the high embankment of the fort to deter any advancing infantry. Even Eliza could tell that the fort's defenses would be inadequate to repel the force steaming toward them. An ear-splitting broadside erupted simultaneously from the Union men-of-war and iron-clad monitors breaking the anxious silence. Fifteen-inch shells exploded in the air spewing deadly shrapnel along the fort's parapets. Other shells tore massive clumps of sod and buckets of sand from the sloping walls of the fort. The air shrilled with iron as the large Brooke guns from Battery Wagner responded. Both the fort and the fleet poured furious and murderous anger on the other. Men hurried through the sheltered traverses under the drifting haze of acrid powder smoke carrying wounded soldiers in one direction to the infirmary and shells to the gun emplacements in the other.

Eliza, Janie, and the Confederate surgeon were overwhelmed. For the surgeon it was by the number of wounded, for Eliza and Janie it was the severity. At the downtown hospital, they provided post-operative wound care, packed abscesses, soothed the feverish, and quieted the delirious. Charleston, however, was far removed from the battlefield and the most hideously wounded were culled out long before Eliza and Janie's arrival at their bedside. Neither Eliza or Janie had ever dealt with traumatically severed limbs, massive head injuries, or body cavities torn asunder. It was human violence on an unimaginable scale. Eliza rapidly became numb to the carnage and assisted the surgeon operating on instinct alone. She kissed each soldier on the forehead before placing a sooty X-mark indicating a lethal triage assessment. Janie, however, was reduced to cowering in the corner, tears rolling from unblinking eyes, hands covering her ears and shrieking with each explosion of a Union shell.

The Union naval cannons targeted the fort's twenty-five-foot embankment with an intent to hammer it down into a smaller slope that could be breeched by Union marines. At the same time, the shelling would destroy the traverses, scatter the palisades and silence the Confederate cannons. Nine-inch sphericals crashed into Battery Wagner's forward slope, ricocheted through the wooden parapets, and bounced down behind the gun pits before exploding with an eruption of grass, dirt, flesh, and blood.

Within two hours, Battery Wagner was reduced to a shapeless pile of sand and rubble by the Federal bombardment. Several Confederate gun batteries had taken direct hits and were either no longer functional or without a crew. Brooke number one overheated and exploded with such ferocity that it tore the enormous cannon from the jaws of its cascabel and trunnions. The heavy iron bands securing the breech slashed through the gun crew like a giant scythe. The captain of Brooke number two ordered the powder charge cut in half, but the reduced range rendered them ineffectual. Despite the reduced powder charge, Brooke number two also exploded a short time later. One by one, the Confederate guns fell silent.

Ultimately, Battery Wagner was only able to answer with a single eight-inch Blakely. With a dwindling response from Battery Wagner, Federal transports began landing Union ground troops. The Union infantry formed up into long skirmish lines preparing to assault the diminished fort.

Rather than hopelessly firing at distant Union transport ships, the captain of the remaining Blakely gun turned his attention to the ground troops amassing directly in front of him. The Confederate captain depressed the Blakely's gun barrel as far as it could go, and crammed canisters of case shot into the muzzle. "Let'er rip," the captain screamed. As the Union marines advanced, blue flame erupted from the maw of the eight-inch Blakely and hundreds of deadly musket balls sawed through a twenty-yard-wide column of marines leaving only a hazy mist of smoke and blood. The marines pitched headlong into the sand screaming and writhing before laying still. Another pull of the lanyard sowed a second wave of death.

Most of the marines were new Irish recruits without any experience under fire. Not surprisingly, men broke ranks and ran backwards up the beach succumbing to fear. Others remained flat on their bellies with faces buried in the bloodstained sand. Some of the dying men lay quietly, swallowing their pain as brave men do. Others cried for their mothers or for water as the thirst brought on by blood loss became more than they could bear. A small group of Union marines circumvented the carnage and made it up the forward slope to the parapet only to find themselves facing a line of Confederate musketeers who cut them down where they stood.

The effectiveness of the eight-inch Blakely battery in stymying the Union advance came with a price. The Blakely battery was now the sole remaining target for the amassed Union naval firepower. Within another half hour of concentrated shelling, Battery Wagner's final gun was silenced. A second wave of Union marines met far less resistance.

The Confederate defenders of Battery Wagner understood that the fate of Charleston depended on their perseverance and they fought like men possessed. Vicious hand-to-hand combat played out in the traverses and gun pits with the grays and blues savaging each other with musket shot to each other's faces, pig stickers to the belly, and then clubbing each other with gun butts when too close to reload. It was courageous, but hopeless. Grit would not be enough to even the odds against the relentless onslaught of new Union troops who kept pouring into the battle.

It was a horrifying slaughter. The Union ships pummeled Battery Wagner with more than 30,000 shells. More than twenty-five shells were in the air at any point in time throughout the battle. There was not a square foot of ground within the fort itself that had not been turned by a Union shell or stained by the blood of a good man in a bad place.

Eliza Holmes was returned to Charleston along with the few surviving Confederate wounded after the fall of Battery Wagner. Eliza was in a state of shock and it was several weeks before she was able to venture out of her Christ Church home. Eliza had lost her girlhood on Morris Island. She had seen terrible things that no person should ever see. Her wounds were far more profound than the gash to Thomas Henry's thigh.

Many nights, Eliza awoke crying and screaming from nightmare images of mangled boys that she hoped might have asked her to lunch on the Morris Island beach. Helpless, Jack Holmes cursed the war and all the men responsible, including himself.

Janie O'Shea never recovered. She never spoke again but was not mute. She also awoke at night, shrieking in horror, her face contorted in fear, and screaming incomprehensible words. Whenever an artillery shell exploded in the distance, Janie cowered in a fetal position in the corner of her room and scratched at the walls until her fingernails bled. Eliza visited Janie many times but there was never a hint of recognition. Janie's family finally took her to a convent outside of Asheville known for their work with the insane and war weary.

The fall of Battery Wagner marked the end of successful blockade running out of Charleston. With a Union garrison and heavy cannon occupying Battery Wagner on the western edge of the inner harbor no one could safely enter or escape the port. The single exception was the *Will O' the Wisp* and its backdoor on the Kiawah River. Jack Holmes knew that would never be enough. Charleston's reign as the antebellum and spiritual capital of the Confederacy was over.

Chapter 19

June 4, 1864

Abbapoola Creek

George's message had been obscure. He needed an urgent meeting but gave no indication of what was on his mind. Jack had seen plenty of men who had lost their nerve or been broken. He did not believe George Trenholm was such a man. He would know by the end of the day. Jack loaded two revolvers for his ride from the docks to Ashley Hall. Since Gettysburg, desertion was taking a greater toll on the army than Union lead. Deserters hid among the wounded and in the abandoned homes of the lawless lower peninsula. Random "Swamp Angel" shells were far smaller risk than either being returned to the front or retribution from the brutal home guard. Jack made a point of locking eyes with the displaced men along his route who appeared capable of taking what they needed in the new barter economy.

"Good day, sir," Jack would say as he made a point of resting his hand on the butt of his pistol. He rarely received more than an appraising nod. Blockade runner officers and crew were favored targets to waylay as they were known to be paid in gold or English pound sterling. On the streets of the lower peninsula, life was as cheap, and violence as routine, as it had been on the battlefield. Captain Jack warned his men to travel together and only visit saloons or brothels in groups. Two unkempt men were standing to either side of Jack's path along Wentworth Street. Jack slowed his ride as he approached them, but they did not move. Despite their disheveled appearance, they were both young, had aggressive bearings, and could not hide the nastiness in their eyes. Jack recognized there was no place for pleasantries. Pulling on the reins Jack came to a stop five feet from the two men. "Anyone going to miss you when you don't come home tonight?" Jack asked the former C.S.A. private standing closer.

"Not a soul," was the deadpan reply. "You?"

"Enough that I know I can't be late." Although his gaze never left the deserter standing before him, Jack caught a glimpse of movement to both his left and right. "You boys hunting in packs now?"

The deserter in front of Jack only shrugged and pressed the conversation, "Nice horse. You cavalry?"

"Nope, just a fortunate citizen," Jack replied as another man appeared from a derelict storefront. Jack pulled his revolver from his right hip and shot the new man in the knee. The would-be robber collapsed screaming into a heap as the others ran away. "See ya boys," Jack yelled after them as he rode on toward Ashley Hall.

Anna Helen invited Jack into the kitchen for lunch as George was busy with some other bankers. His sister set out some boned turkey, field peas, plum pudding, and a glass of sauterne that Jack recognized as coming off the last steam of the *Will O' the Wisp.*

As Jack ate and waited for George, he noticed the subtle signs of a certain turn in fortune. Looking around the Trenholm kitchen, Jack saw shelves of preserved pickles, okra, and tomatoes in the cupboard along with bottles of homemade gooseberry syrup and blackberry wine. Handmade soap was on the counter. Anna Helen was sewing a torn seam on one of George's formal jackets. The needles, pins and threads were from a Union sewing kit stolen off a dead Yankee. Sewing and canning were both things Anna Helen had learned as a girl. However, she had not done any of them in a decade. Nor had she imagined she ever would again.

Jack looked at his sister and smiled. "Save me a bottle of that blackberry wine. It'll smooth out some of the lonely nights on the *Wisp*."

Anna Helen smiled back. "I'll do you one better. I am working on a large batch of Momma's peach brandy in the basement. Makes this blackberry wine seem like fruit juice. If you drink Momma's peach brandy on the *Wisp*, you'll sleep clean past Nassau and wake up when you bump into Africa."

Anna Helen's smile was simultaneously heart-warming and heartbreaking.

"Warning acknowledged. I look forward to trying it," Jack said. Both turned as George walked into the kitchen.

It was impossible not to see the toll the war had taken on George. Gone was the expansive and gregarious George. His anxieties multiplied by the day and they wore on George as unceasingly as rushing water over river stones. The fading sense of Southern aristocracy was a bitter pill for George. Resentment among the working-class for men like George Trenholm was growing. It grew in direct proportion to the decreasing purchasing power of Confederate paper. It was ironic that the war had created the redistribution of wealth and power that it had been specifically intended to prevent. Anna Helen confided that George was more hurt by the loss of respect than any other consequence of the war.

Anna Helen also confided that George was purchasing glassine packets of morphine and kept a brown glass bottle of laudanum on his bedside table to settle his bilious and burning stomach. The opium's initial laudatory affects were now lessening, and Anna Helen was tracking his ever-greater need. George was also taking a daily tincture of magnesium sulfate to deal with his relentless constipation.

Jack took as a positive sign that George still stood erect with shoulders square and his luxurious silver hair swept back. However, a substantial weight loss was obvious. He looked a bit lost in his signature black suit, collared shirt bleached a brilliant white, and blood red silk tie. A cinched black and gray striped waistcoat helped disguise George's thinning middle. Handsome, high-shined black riding boots suggested a vitality that was exaggerated.

"Jack, sorry to have made you wait."

"Glad to have waited. Got to catch up with Anna Helen and have some wonderful plum pudding."

"One of my favorites. Thank you, dear, for taking care of Jack. I hope you two left some pudding."

"Of course, I saved a little for you," Anna Helen replied. "But later, or else you'll get your acid stomach and be grousing around the house all day."

George grunted his disapproval but did not argue. He invited Jack to follow him to his study.

"What's the big mystery, George? It had better be something good to bring me all the way over from Christ Church. Mary Ann doesn't like it when I come downtown. I don't really like it either. I had to shoot a man in the knee on Wentworth Street."

"Oh, Jack, I am so sorry."

"No need to be concerned for me George. I'm fine."

"Well, then, I guess I'm sorry for the man you met on Wentworth."

"No need for that either. He showed some extremely poor judgement and now understands his mistake. Let's talk about your news."

"Well, I'm not sure if you're going to like it, but it's important. When are you planning your next run?"

"The *Will O' the Wisp* is already loaded. We'll be departing in a couple of days."

"Jack, I hope you know how much I appreciate all you've accomplished over the past year. Clearing the Kiawah River was brilliant. I know how horrid an undertaking it was. Without your successful blockade running, our city would be in even more trouble than it already is."

"Thank you for saying that, but I consider it a duty. Remember, I am also well compensated for the work. You know how much I hated using the slaves to clear the river. I pray that the benefits have been worth the cost."

"Absolutely. What the *Wisp* has been able to smuggle back into the city has sustained many. You should be proud of your success."

"George, we've had this conversation before. I don't think it's why you summoned me."

"True. I wanted you to know that next week I will be introduced as the new Secretary of the Treasury for the Confederacy. Christopher Memminger has resigned under pressure."

Memminger had issued millions of dollars in Confederate bank notes in an effort to reverse the Confederacy's souring economy. Those notes were now worth, at best, a tenth of their original value and, at worst, only useful for wiping your ass. Public outcry over the worthless bank notes had finally forced Memminger's resignation. Only George Trenholm, and a few other highly placed Confederate officials, knew how hard Christopher Memminger had worked to maintain the solvency of the C.S.A. and, more importantly, how badly he had been undermined by the meddlesome, ill-informed, and dithering Jefferson Davis.

Jack settled quietly into an overstuffed leather chair and ran his hands through his shoulder length hair before responding. "Jesus Christ, George, you can't do that. You haven't had an idea this bad since you decided to partner with me."

"Now, we are talking about my duty, Jack."

"That is bullshit, George, if you'll pardon my saying so. People are starving and what little food is available can't be afforded. They will forget Memminger and blame you as things get worse. And, if we lose the war, you'll go from a man who can walk away with a solvent business to a man the Union will hang for treason."

"When we lose the war," George corrected.

"Exactly, when we lose the war. So, why invite a noose when there isn't anything you can do to alter the fact that the war is lost?"

"Our impending defeat is precisely why I must take this position. Christopher Memminger is my friend and one of my most trusted advisors, but he can't handle what needs to be done."

"What can you do to stop the collapse of the Confederate dollar that Mr. Memminger hasn't already tried?"

"Nothing. Mistakes were made that can't be unmade. The last chance was a large loan floated with the French, but that has fallen through. I know that our economy cannot be resurrected. I didn't take the position as a fool's errand."

"Then why, George?"

"Two reasons. The first is to help negotiate an end to this ruination that does not end up with my head, or Christopher's, in a noose. Jeff Davis is a sad, bitter old man who can't see beyond his own personal legacy. No one's ever accused our President of having any personal graces or social skills. What we didn't know was his massive failing as a strategist. Everyone knows we're about to be checkmated and President Davis keeps offering a draw."

"What do you mean?"

"Opportunities to end this war have been missed. There are few options left, and Lincoln knows it. Davis sent Lincoln a proposal to trade the abolition of slavery in the South for the preservation of the Confederacy. He promised gradual emancipation in exchange for the Union's recognition of the Confederate States of America."

"Would Lincoln even consider that?"

"Hell no! Lincoln did not spend all those lives and treasure to leave the Union asunder. Davis threatened

Lincoln with arming the slaves if he didn't agree. I'm sure
Lincoln laughed out loud. Maybe Jeff Davis doesn't know
what would happen if we armed the slaves, but Lincoln
does."

"Everyone does."

"Not everyone, and that's why I need to join the
Cabinet. There are too many simple-minded or self-serving
sycophants in Richmond that have blindly hitched their
wagons to Jefferson Davis' fatalistic determination. Davis no
longer listens to Memminger's counsel. I might not fare any
better, but I'm going to use whatever debating skills I have
to persuade President Davis that we must negotiate the best
possible terms before we lose all our leverage. He needs to
understand what unconditional surrender looks like."

"Not to be a wet blanket, but what can you do that
Christopher Memminger hasn't tried?"

"I can communicate with my business and trading
contacts in the North and convince them that it's in their
financial interest to leave the South with the means to
support itself. Northern industrialists need to endorse the
advantages of resuming trade with the South. Our natural
resources fuel their factories. Together, we can make the
politicians in both Richmond and Washington understand
that a post-war, economically healthy South can be both a
supplier of raw materials and a consumer of Northern
industrial products. Businessmen understand win-win
propositions. Politicians need more explanation."

"George, you're taking a huge risk. The North will
want to satisfy their blood lust and still take whatever
resources they want."

"I don't think that's what Lincoln wants. What is the
point of reunifying the nation if his plan is to decimate half
the country? Does he want to be president of filth and
rubble? If he allows the end of this war to only be about
retribution, everything of value in the South will be

destroyed, we will starve, and eventually turn our violence on each other."

"Do you think there is any time left for those entreaties and negotiations?"

"Even though the Confederacy is crumbling, there's a great deal of blood that can still be spilled. Jefferson has pledged to fight to the last drop of Southern blood, which I assume excludes himself. If we can avoid pointless loss of life on both sides of the Potomac, then there is an opportunity to negotiate. I can be a new voice to help convince President Davis of the hopelessness of our situation and to parley with the Republicans."

Jack shook his head with skepticism. "There're a lot of maybe in that plan. The Union may be willing to negotiate a surrender with reasonably favorable conditions, but they're going to want somebody to swing. We can dress it up with all the indignant anti-Federalism and virtuous states-righteousness we want, but at the end of the day we're all just traitors. Unless they've changed the Constitution while we were away, the penalty for treason is death."

"Be that as it may, I've got a second reason for taking the job which is even more important."

"And what might that be?"

"The treasury. It is in Richmond and I need to save it. Once hostilities have ceased, that gold and silver will be the only wealth left in the South. The Union will take it, and without it, we'll never be able to rebuild."

"George, you've got less chance of safeguarding the Confederate treasury than you do of not ending up on the Yankee gallows."

"Ah!" George interrupted, "I have a plan, and you're a big part of it."

"Oh, Jesus, that's not good."

"Don't be negative, my friend. You're going to love this plan."

"I'll be the judge of that."

Trenholm continued undaunted, "That's fair, but before I give you the details, I need to know a couple of things. When Charleston succumbs, will you be able to keep the *Will O' the Wisp* from falling into Union hands?"

"Are you talking about taking it to the islands or Mexico?"

"No. Is there anywhere it can be berthed near Charleston where it'll be safe?"

"It will depend on how Charleston is taken and how large the occupying force is. Once the Yankees control the city, I imagine that all the blockade runners, and their captains, will be rounded up."

"No doubt. The Federals know your name and finding the *Will O' the Wisp* will be a high priority. They will burn you out, both home and shipyard. It is not too early to start arranging to get your family to safety. I can help you with their evacuation."

Jack could hear the resignation in the voice of his ever- optimistic brother-in-law. "Any idea how long we have?"

"I don't know anything for certain. The defense of Charleston is becoming more untenable by the day. General Beauregard's troops and cannons are needed on multiple other fronts. Losing Charleston is no longer as emotional an issue as it used to be. What I do know is that when the end does come, it will happen fast.

"I have a cousin with deep-water over on Abbapoola Creek. It's off the Stono River and not much traveled because the waterway is tricky. Too easy to get grounded on shifting sand bars. It's not a guarantee, but the Abbapoola isn't patrolled and there really isn't anything up there that would be worth the Federals marching up to see. There are some secluded spots where the *Wisp* could hide."

"Speak to your cousin as soon as you can. We're going to need the *Wisp* if this plan's going to work."

"What else," Jack asked.

"Would you be willing to let Thomas Henry and George Chapman come with me to Richmond?"

"Why do you need my boys?"

"With your permission, I have arranged for Thomas Henry and George Chapman, my son, Alfred, my protegee, James Morgan Morris, along with a few other nephews to receive appointments to the Confederate Naval Academy outside Richmond. The appointments will come directly from the Secretary of the Navy, Stephen Mallory. They'll be assigned as cadets and personal aides-de-camp to Lt. William Parker."

"Who's Lt. Parker?"

"William is an old friend and Superintendent of the Academy. He and I went to sea together when we were teenagers. I was smart enough to get my feet back on dry land. William never left the salt. He was on the *CSS Virginia* when she did battle with the *USS Monitor*. He has forgotten more about seamanship than most other captains know. I can promise you that between William and myself, your boys will be well taken care of. It will also get them out of Charleston."

"There's more to this than just my boys becoming Confederate naval cadets."

"Yes, much more. Let's get some of Anna Helen's peach brandy, and I'll tell you what I've got planned. I'll ask Anna Helen to put a sprig of mint on top for you."

"If you're trying to get me liquored up, I don't think it's going to work. That peach brandy is a Holmes family recipe. We called it Christ Church Cognac," Jack added with a laugh. "I've been drinking it since before I could walk."

"I'd never consider trying such a low-down trick. Plus, I'm pretty sure you're going to hate my plan, drunk or sober."

Chapter 20

February 18, 1865

Quaker Guns

No one was surprised by the wire from General Beauregard regretfully announcing the necessity of abandoning Charleston. No one believed it had been his decision. The General had promised to defend Charleston with all he had to give, and he was an honorable man.

There proved to be more important considerations. The trained and disciplined soldiers who served the guns surrounding the city were coveted. The Charleston garrison was the last substantial force that could be mustered to prevent Sherman from marching north to join Grant in front of Lee at Petersburg. Neither surrender, capture or annihilation of the Charleston garrison were tenable military options.

In the spring of 1864, General William Tecumseh Sherman led his 100,000-man Union army east from Tennessee into Georgia. By the end of August, Atlanta had been burned. From Atlanta, the merciless Sherman began his march to the sea. Never accused of hesitating or intellectualizing, Sherman was General Grant's street bully whose simple military mantra was that when you had a man by his balls, his heart and mind would follow.

Sherman's intent was to show the South the consequences of sedition. He ransacked plantations, plundered farms, killed livestock, twisted railroad ties, and burned bridges. Public buildings and the homes of any identifiable Confederate leader were reduced to smoldering ruins. The cause, for which so much blood had been spilled, sacrifices made, and desolation endured, had finally been put to the torch and reduced to cinders. It was payment come due for Southern rebellion.

As much as Sherman terrified those Southerners in his army's path, they were even more afraid of what they would encounter in his wake. By the time he reached Savannah, Sherman's caissons were being followed by a second army of more than 10,000 contrabands. They had learned from Sherman's example how to take what they needed as they marched.

Sherman's antipathy for the Negro was well-known and rivaled anyone in the South. However, personal prejudices did not dissuade him from taking military advantage. Able-bodied slaves were incorporated into his corps as servants, cooks, transporters, and engineers. Sherman was willfully ignorant as to the fate of sick and wounded Confederate soldiers or civilians who were stripped, savaged, and butchered in retribution by their former slaves.

To deal with his growing entourage of displaced slaves, Sherman issued Special Field Order No. 15 setting aside the islands south of Charleston, all the rice fields along the coastal rivers for thirty miles inland, and all the land bordering the St. John's River in Florida for settlement by Negroes. Sherman gave each family possessory title to a plot of not more than forty acres of tillable land and a mule. Northern abolitionists hailed Special Order No. 15 as a long overdue and progressive step. They celebrated Sherman, unaware of the red-haired general's vile racial hatred and solemn bigotry.

Sherman arrived in Savannah in mid-December and most assumed that Charleston would be next to feel Sherman's black hearted wrath. Instead, Sherman turned north towards Columbia intent on sweeping aside any remaining rebel forces between himself and General Grant in Virginia. General Beauregard recognized the consequences of Sherman's maneuver. With Union troops already north and south of Charleston and Sherman marching west toward Columbia, Beauregard was being encircled and his garrison trapped. Jefferson Davis personally ordered the evacuation of Charleston.

On the night of February 17th, 1865, Charleston was abandoned. Beauregard's 15,000-man Charleston detachment retreated to Columbia where they would establish a line of defense along the Congaree River. General Beauregard believed that he could make Columbia the sea wall against which Sherman's wave would finally crash. Beauregard was ashamed to be deserting the city he had come to consider a jewel in the crown of the Confederacy. However, survival of the C.S.A. was now the only important objective.

Jack Holmes had taken George's advice. As rumors spread of Sherman's advance, Jack shuttered the family home in Christ Church. Valuables were placed on trains leaving Charleston for the North Carolina mountains. Pickled foods, salted hams, grains, coffee, and other household items not worthy of transport were distributed to the carpenters and shipwrights at the family shipyard. A neighboring freedman took the Holmes' livestock into the swamp for hiding with the agreement they would become his if the Holmes family never returned.

Jack and his family, along with Copper Joe, Jordan Ryan, Caleb, Ezekiel, and a few other tenured crewmembers evacuated the Shem Creek shipyard. Supplies and family treasures were loaded onto the *Sarah Belle* which they sailed up the Ashley River to Abbapoola Creek where Jack had arranged for the family to stay with some Legare cousins on John's Island. The Legare cousins on Abbapoola Creek lived near a narrow tributary where a re-painted, mud slicked,

Spanish moss and tree-branch covered *Will O' the Wisp* waited derelict.

Jack and Copper Joe scuttled a one-hundred-and-forty-foot side paddle-wheel schooner under construction at the shipyard. They watched the *Will O' the Wisp's* beautiful sister sink into Shem Creek, groan, shudder and then roll onto her side on the shallow bottom. An older black man silently watched their every move from a straight-back chair leaning precariously against the wall on the deck above the dock. Curls of smoke rose from his pipe as he impassively watched the lovely ship go to her premature grave. He had a large forehead, oversized ears, and receding curly grey hair. Years of dock work had given the man a proud, muscular build. Jack was ashamed he did not know the man's name.

Jack walked up onto the upper deck to engage him in conversation.

"Sir, my name is Jack Holmes and I'm sorry you had to witness such a waste of a fine ship. I apologize for not knowing your name."

"I know who you are, Mr. Holmes. I've worked for you pert near all my life. No real need for you to know my name, but it's Samuel just the same."

"Samuel, my family and I are clearing out before the Yankees get here. I'd be willing to pay you twenty gold pieces, a 5-pound sack of rice, and two hams if you'd be willing to watch over the dock in our absence."

The modest offer was more wealth than Samuel had ever seen. "Why you want to give me so much to just be here when we both know that the Yankees are going to do as they please whether I'm here or not?"

Jack nodded his approval of Samuel's insight. "When the Union troops inevitably arrive, I'd like you to identify that sunken ship as the blockade runner, *Will O' the Wisp*. When they ask about me, tell the Yankees that Captain Jack left for Cuba two weeks ago on a sailing yacht out of Florida."

"You know they'll kill me if they catch me lyin' to them."

Jack nodded again. "I'd be trusting you."

Neither man spoke for the next minute. Smoke curled from each man's pipe bowl. Jack Holmes studied the black man's eyes to gage his trustworthiness. Samuel studied the white man's eyes to gage his worthiness. After a few more tense seconds, they both extended their hands.

When the Union army arrived in Charleston it would not find the one-time gem of Southern civility. Charleston's antebellum beauty and commercial might was now reduced to cinders and heaps of rubble. The streets were largely deserted except for starving slaves and wounded soldiers in mud and blood-stained greatcoats all scavenging amidst the debris. The Southern elite who had pressed for secession had fled the harsh reality of failed insurgency.

With Confederate currency not worth the paper it was printed on and all men between the ages of ten and sixty evacuated, the only Charlestonians happily awaiting the arrival of Union troops were the whores. Their business model was fluid and they anxiously anticipated the arrival of new customers with wallets full of Federal dollars. Charleston's prostitutes would send the blue bellies home to their wives and sweethearts wounded and crippled by rampant gonorrhea and syphilis, scoring a victory over the Union army that the Confederate regulars never could.

On the morning of February 18th, Union soldiers on Morris Island awoke to an unusual quiet. Confederate flags flew from all the usual staffs around Charleston harbor, but the tattered garrison flag at Fort Sumter was missing. Lt. Col. Augustus G. Bennett, commander of the 21st U.S. Colored Troops noticed and suspected that the fort might be abandoned. He instructed Capt. Samuel Cuskaden to take some men over to Fort Sumter in a boat and reconnoiter the situation.

Cuskaden rounded up a squad of Rhode Island artillerymen and piled in a boat headed for Fort Sumter. As they approached the degraded, but still formidable fort, they met another boat heaving in the opposite direction. The evacuating C.S.A. forces had abandoned the Confederate band from Sullivan's Island. The unhappy bandsmen gladly told all they knew about the Confederate evacuation. Capt. Cuskaden took the band as prisoners and returned with them to Morris Island.

Upon hearing the band's story, Lt. Col. Bennett grabbed his own boat and ordered the men to pull for Fort Sumter. Halfway across the harbor they were caught by a second boat captained by Major John A. Hennessey of the Pennsylvania Volunteers. The two boats raced for Fort Sumter with Major Hennessey first ashore. Hennessey hoisted the first Union flag over Fort Sumter in five years.

Disappointed, Bennett pulled his boat back into the harbor and boldly decided to make for Charleston. Halfway between Fort Sumter and the Battery they landed at Fort Ripley built on pilings in the inner harbor. They discovered that Fort Ripley's imposing battery were only Quaker guns carved from palmetto logs and painted black. They hauled down the Confederate flag and hoisted the Stars and Stripes. Even more convinced that the rebels had completely pulled out of Charleston, Bennett decided to row on. At approximately ten a.m. Lt. Col. Bennett, four other officers, and twenty-two black soldiers reached Mill's Wharf on the Cooper River behind the Exchange Building. Many of Bennett's men were former Lowcountry slaves. Tears of joy streamed down their faces entering Charleston as liberators. They were greeted by a cheering crowd of Negroes experiencing their own day of Jubilee.

Overstating his military strength, Lt. Col. Bennett hurriedly wrote a letter which he brashly headed, "Headquarters, U.S. Forces, Charleston, S.C.," calling on the city's mayor to surrender Charleston without delay. Mayor

Charles Macbeth and a small delegation soon appeared to meet with Lt. Col. Bennett. Charleston was formally surrendered to Lt. Col. Bennett in a brief hand-written note:

"To the General Commanding the Army of the United States at Morris Island:

Sir- The military authorities of the Confederate States have evacuated the city. I have remained to enforce law and preserve order until you take such steps as you may think best. Very respectfully, your obedient servant.

Charles Macbeth, Mayor. Charleston, S.C., February 17, 1865"

Mayor Macbeth asked Lt. Col. Bennett for assistance in fighting the fires that were spreading across the city, to help control the looting, and for protection against the throngs of former slaves now roaming the city. The retreating C.S.A. cavalry had set fire to the cotton at the Northeastern Railroad depot. That fire had gotten out of control and ignited the immense powder magazine at the Half-Moon Battery. Several hundred men, women and children who had been foraging for provisions were killed when the entire depot blew up. That fire, as well as several others, threatened to reduce the city to ashes. Mayor Macbeth recognized that this request to Lt. Col Bennett may be the most crucial moment of the war in terms of Charleston's future.

The disordered state of affairs in the city was obvious and Lt. Col. Bennett agreed to aid in extinguishing the fires and restoring civic order. Within hours, Union transport ships filled Charleston harbor delivering troops from the Third Rhode Island Volunteer Artillery and the 55th Massachusetts Colored Regiment.

With this hastily assembled force, Lt. Col. Bennett marched uptown to the Citadel where he established his headquarters.

Bennett's immediate actions were affirmed by General Sherman who personally decided that Charleston would not be put to the torch. Negroes were rounded up and put to work on fire engines and water brigades. Pickets and patrols were established to control looting and protect the few remaining large mills and warehouses where provisions had been stored. Rice was distributed to the hungry, both black and white. A recruiting office was established to sign up eager former slaves who wished to join the Union army.

By nightfall, the liquor had been found and celebratory songs and rifle shots pierced the darkness. Charlestonians who remained and remembered the earlier celebration of secession, closed their shutters, and locked their doors. After a siege of 567 days and the mounting bitterness of a lost cause, there was no more defiance left in the city.

Chapter 21

March 16, 1865

Capital Square

George Trenholm found Richmond vastly different from his native Charleston. Despite its imperial perch high on the north bank of the James River, Trenholm failed to understand, and sometimes resented, the selection of Richmond as capital of the Confederacy.

Richmond had never been a hotbed of secessionist fever nor had it done any of the heavy lifting of upheaval. Virginia was ambivalent about rebellion and was the last Southern state to vote for dissolution of the Union. Virginia prided itself on its American revolutionary history and multiple native sons who had served as President of the United States. Richmond stood to lose more manufacturing trade with the North than any other city in the South. Only after Lincoln called for the raising of an army in the wake of the Fort Sumter shelling did Virginia belatedly secede.

Richmond had prospered differently than Charleston. Compared to Charleston's relatively one-dimensional international cotton trade, Richmond enjoyed a more diverse trading portfolio. The James River was lined by large mills converting grain into flour. Richmond traded her flour for South American coffee and cacao. Richmond also boasted dozens of tobacco mills, satisfying a worldwide demand as well as filling the evening air with a rich, golden aroma. Richmond's greatest strength, however, was its strong industrial base. The Tredegar Iron Works, which sat upriver on the western edge of Richmond, was the only foundry in the South with forges sufficient to produce large caliber artillery or the iron plates needed to replace wooden ships with ironclads. Richmond's factories also included some of the South's few textile mills, lumberyards, and brick kilns. As in Charleston, successful business drew bankers, factors, lawyers, speculators, and commission merchants like bees to honey. Ultimately, it drew politicians.

Richmond's wealth had financed a regal collection of public buildings on the bluffs above the river. The Capital Building dominated Richmond's Capital Square. Thomas Jefferson designed the Capital Building based on a Roman temple he had seen while serving as Ambassador to France. The grandeur of these public buildings factored into the selection of Richmond as home for the Confederate government.

Secretary Trenholm's Office of the Treasury was on the second floor of the Capital Building. Each day, Trenholm walked past Jean-Antoine Houdon's iconic marble statue of George Washington which stood in the building's rotunda. From his north-facing window, Trenholm could also see Thomas Crawford's majestic equestrian statue of George Washington in the north corner of Capital Square. The irony was not subtle.

In the opposite corner of Capital Square stood the thicker-walled, fireproof and far less grand Custom House which contained Jefferson Davis' Office of the President. The blandness of the building matched its occupant. Visitors to Richmond much preferred the hubbub of the Capital Building to the relentlessly stern Custom House.

The charming Secretary Trenholm enjoyed tremendous popularity in Richmond. Anna Helen's Saturday night dinner parties were a must have invite for Richmond's political elite. The sumptuous Trenholm dinner table and seemingly endless supply of fine Madeira allowed a few hours respite from the scarcities of a failing war effort. The mercurial Varina Davis found George Trenholm to be one of the few witty and interesting men among her husband's dour circle of political and military lickspittles. Varina was a regular at George and Anna's chic gatherings while Jefferson Davis fretted away his time alone back at the Gray House. George also burnished his reputation among the decidedly non-elite by personally financing a Christmas Day pork barbecue for the entire Army of Northern Virginia. For at least one day, Lee's bedeviled legion must have felt like victory was still possible.

George was not so successful politically. George had no better luck than Memminger in convincing the Confederate Congress to levy the necessary taxes on the wealthy to support the war. It infuriated George that the agricultural interests who had fomented the war resisted paying the taxes their war demanded. Frustrated, he turned his charm on the people of Richmond, imploring them to part with their hard currency, jewels, silver plates and gold watches. The nightmare of the Confederate economy coupled with the escalating toll of military reversals sapped even George's irrepressible optimism. He had already begun planning for the evacuation of the Confederate treasury.

Secretary Trenholm spent the morning preparing for a series of important meetings. The first was with General Richard Stoddert Ewell who oversaw Richmond's defense and commanded about 5,000 Confederate regulars. An insufficient number for anyone who cared to consider it. Trenholm knew he could not be of any help to Ewell with whatever he might need, but he was desperate for an unfiltered military appraisal.

General Ewell arrived precisely on time as is typical of men in need. He looked unkempt, muddy and harried. General Ewell apologized for his appearance which George assured him was unnecessary. Ewell's appearance was all the military appraisal that Secretary Trenholm needed.

"Welcome, General Ewell. I appreciate your taking time to come in person. What can the Treasury Department do for you?"

"Thank you, Mr. Secretary. I'm sorry to say that we're facing an imminent military crisis."

"I've been told as much. Still, I'd certainly appreciate whatever insights you might be able to share with me." It was a rhetorical question. Trenholm already knew from Cabinet briefings that Union armies roamed the Southern states at will, the Western states were cut-off, and both Charleston and Wilmington, the last two open Atlantic ports, had fallen. George was hoping for detailed eyes-on intelligence regarding the countryside surrounding Richmond.

For the past eight months, General Grant had been battering Lee's Army of Northern Virginia. Bloody battles at Fredricksburg, Chancellorsville, Spotsylvania, and the Wilderness had inflicted heavy losses on Lee's army and pushed him relentlessly back toward Richmond. Grant and Lee now found themselves staring at each other across the no-man's land surrounding the Confederate capital.

"We've constructed a ring of defenses running in a forty-mile arc from northeast of Richmond down to Petersburg, twenty miles south. We have extended those fortifications farther southwest in case an evacuation from Richmond be required. Our ramparts are stout and studded with abatis shorn of all foliage and sharpened to a point. Our artillery batteries are deeply entrenched all along the forty-mile line of defense."

"Will it hold Grant back? We hear that his Army of the Potomac grows by the day. It is believed his campaign will begin as soon as the warmer weather dries out the muddy roads but before the heat of summer arrives."

"Yes, sir. I believe we can. It took a colossal effort of impressed slaves, but we laid bare the ground for more than two hundred yards in front of our earthworks and trenches.

There is not a single tree, bush, clump of grass, or road apple to provide the blue bellies cover. Any living thing which tries to cross those open fields will surely be sent to meet his maker. With our defensive positions and clear fields of fire, I believe our men can heroically resist a numerically superior foe."

"Are they up to another brave stand?"

"That is why I'm here, Secretary Trenholm. This is where I need your help."

"Please explain."

"The men's spirits are flagging. They are sleeping in mud-filled trenches. They're cold, wet, and underfed. They are beset with Bragg's bodyguard and constantly battling the eruptions and formication that come from sharing their blankets with vermin. The boys have been through the mill and it concerns me that they have moved past bellyaching. As you can imagine, there's nothing more miserable than prolonged trench warfare."

"I'm not sure that I can imagine it, General, but I certainly don't doubt it."

"The never-ending rumors of our battlefield reversals also magnifies their misery. The most dangerous contagion is the loss of hope. That contagion is now spreading at the exact same time the men are recognizing the lengthening spring days. It is planting season and the men worry for their families this coming winter if they don't get crops into the ground. Lee's lost more than a thousand men to French leave over the past two weeks. I'm experiencing the same desertion rates in the diggings surrounding Richmond."

"What can I do about the coming of spring?"

"Sir, I need more men, food, and supplies. For those, I'll see the Secretary of War. What I need from the Treasury is gold and silver. Gold and silver are the only currency that will keep their families fed when winter comes. It's all they will fight for. They are patriotic Southerners and have fought with grit for years, but I'm sure you can understand their fear."

"Can we not find replacements or reinforcements for these men?" George already knew the answer to that question.

"No stone has been left unturned. We have conscripted virtually all the government clerks, hospital rats from Chimborazo, teamsters, dockworkers and even refugees coming into town from the countryside. I've invoked martial law which has allowed me round up deserters and malingerers and put them back on the line. Unfortunately, between disease and desertion, I'm losing men faster than they can be found."

"General Ewell, I understand your predicament, however, there's nothing the Treasury can do to help retain your men. With the closure of our ports, we can no longer trade cotton for specie. Our treasury is empty. You've probably seen the pitiful notices I've been placing in the newspapers asking for donations to the Confederacy."

"I have, sir. Have they been successful?"

"Our people have honored us with all they have to spare. The wealthy businessmen of Richmond have the same concerns as do your troops for the safety and security of their families come winter."

"I can promise that the winter will be colder and more dangerous for everyone if the Yankees collapse our lines and take Richmond."

"I have no doubt of that, General. As Secretary of the Treasury though, I have learned that the well only goes so deep. We missed the opportunity to place Confederate currency on solid footing. I understand, however, that President Davis has endorsed General Lee's call to enlist every black male, slave or free, of fighting age."

"Indeed, I've raised two companies of Negroes myself. We drill every afternoon on Capital Square. They wear their uniforms with pride and comport themselves with military bearing. However, I fear it's too little, too late. President Davis did not make the conscription compulsory as General Lee requested. Davis preferred we take volunteers. He's offered emancipation to any slave who fights for the Confederacy."

"Sounds politically motivated. I am sure you know that many members of our government find the idea of arming slaves abhorrent. I imagine that few wealthy Virginians are willing to give up their slaves regardless of General Lee's implorations."

"Well, that I wouldn't know, but we have not had the number of volunteers necessary to make a difference. Worse, my officers in the trenches don't trust the black regiments. They grumble that the slaves volunteer just to get a rifle. My officers believe the blacks will fight at first, but as soon as they see their chance, they'll turn their rifles on us and switch sides. Who knows, maybe they will."

Both Trenholm and Ewell looked at each other silently. They both understood the inevitability of defeat, but neither man could speak the words. There was nothing either could do to help the other.

"General, I fear that arming the slaves does nothing more than create an illusory hope of prolonging the war."

"So, it seems, Mister Secretary. I fear for us all."

"General Ewell, I'm truly sorry. I wish there was more I could offer. I promise to bring your concerns to the attention of the full Cabinet when we meet later this afternoon. Our every discussion involves the survival of the Confederacy. I will also commend you to the Secretary of War for your valor and ardor."

"I thank you for that Secretary Trenholm but be assured it's an unnecessary commendation unless the Cabinet can come up with a way to refit and reinforce my men." General Ewell saluted smartly and turned to leave.

George had approximately an hour to prepare for his next meeting. It was a meeting that had become a highlighted event on his calendar. Since his arrival in Richmond, Secretary Trenholm had hosted a small retinue of Cabinet officers just before the full Cabinet meetings. The group included the Secretary of War John Cabell Breckinridge, his Assistant Secretary John Archibald Campbell, Secretary of the Navy Stephen Mallory, Secretary of State Judah Benjamin and himself.

The men had more in common than their love of the lovely brandy and warm ham biscuits with peach jam laid out by Anna Helen. The men in Trenholm's office shared the immense responsibility of negotiating surrender terms with the Union that spared the South years of vindictive retribution. They were all men clear on the difference between reality and fantasy. The earthworks and trenches around Richmond were impressive but each of them knew Richmond could not be defended. Evacuation of the capital was inevitable. Self-deluding hope was an intolerable negotiating option. George quietly repeated to himself his father's words. "Wish in one hand and spit in the other and see which one fills up first."

Assistant Secretary of War John Campbell, Senator Robert M.T. Hunter, and Vice President Alexander H. Stephens of Georgia had been previously sent by President Davis to meet with Lincoln to negotiate possible armistice. They had met on February 3rd on the steamboat *River Queen,* near Hampton Roads.

President Davis was convinced that Lincoln would be willing to suspend hostilities and forge a military alliance with the South against the French-installed Emperor Maximilian in Mexico. President Davis wrote Lincoln a letter proposing negotiations to secure peace between the North and the South. Unfortunately, when Campbell, Hunter and Vice President Stephens left for Hampton Roads, President Davis told them they could explore all options except renouncing Southern independence. The negotiators knew it was a poison pill.

Discussion of a possible alliance against France were cut off by President Lincoln who wanted an answer on the question of sovereignty. Lincoln demanded that the South disband its armies and submit to Federal authority. Lincoln offered an amnesty resolution with pardons for almost all Southern leaders except President Davis, restoration of all confiscated property except for slaves, and a $200 million dollar cash infusion payable immediately on cessation of resistance and another $200 million dollars if the Thirteenth Amendment was successfully ratified by July 1st, 1865. While President Lincoln opposed the French incursion into Mexico, he was clear in his response to Davis that his only interest was in securing the peace for the people of one common country.

President Davis became livid when he received the debriefing. He denigrated Lincoln's honesty and desire for peace. He railed against Lincoln's demand for what Davis described as "unconditional surrender." Lincoln's demands were an "insult" to the Confederacy. Davis used the collapse of the peace conference to generate new hostility against the North and discredit the Southern croakers for peace.

Trenholm's small gathering of Cabinet members believed differently. President Davis had sent his representatives to the Hampton Roads Conference in bad faith. Davis knew that Southern surrender would be a non-negotiable requirement for peace. The men gathered in Secretary Trenholm's office no longer had confidence in Jefferson Davis' ability to bring the war to anything other than a needlessly punitive conclusion where bloodlust would overwhelm any remaining blood ties.

George believed President Davis to be both intellectually and emotionally incapable of recognizing or dealing with these issues. Davis was almost sixty years old, and the stress of rebellion had aged him beyond his years. He had lost substantial weight and strength from a dyspeptic stomach and had developed a nervous facial twitch and blindness in one eye. Those closest to Davis debated whether these were physical manifestations of the war's burden or a consequence of his all-consuming fear of failure. The men gathered in George's office believed the latter more than the former. Jefferson Davis was a petty, irascible, and self-centered man whose natural inclination was to blame others rather than accept responsibility.

Trenholm and his colleagues were also angry over what they saw as Davis' personal distraction from the immediacy of a crumbling Confederacy. As members of the C.S.A. Cabinet they all feared being fugitives, Federal prison, and the hangman's noose. President Davis, however, perseverated over it incessantly. They feared how long he might drag out hostilities to protect himself as well as his tumultuous and enigmatic marriage to Varina. Varina Howell was an ambitious Mississippi belle twenty years younger than Jefferson. She had been drawn to his wealth and power and fully luxuriated in her role as First Lady of the Confederacy. Her expectation was for the Confederacy's continued protection and for the provision of all her wants and needs. Varina Howell Jefferson was as entitled a lady as there could possibly be and would have no patience for a fall from grace.

George Trenholm was confident that he had assembled the men necessary to help protect, not Lady Varina, but the remaining wives, mothers, sisters, daughters, farmers and soldiers of the Southern states. Most important among the assembled men was Assistant Secretary of War, John Archibald Campbell. Campbell was a brilliant, but unassuming former U.S. Supreme Court Justice. Despite his secession and the failure of the Hampton Roads Conference, he was still well-connected and highly respected in the North. So well respected, in fact, he had always been viewed with suspicion by Jeff Davis.

Campbell had been urging President Davis and the Cabinet to seek terms with Lincoln for almost a year. On more than one occasion, he wondered aloud how responsible men could not be convinced that peace was required. Campbell's ability to foresee eventual defeat was considered unpatriotic by President Davis. The rest of the Cabinet, though, respected his intellect and thoughtful nature. He was not an imposing man like George Trenholm nor was he a particularly strong orator. His speaking voice was nervous and high-pitched, but he had the quiet authority of a learned and serious man.

Campbell believed he had been sent on a fool's errand to Hampton Roads by President Davis as restoration of the Union was Lincoln's only unmalleable condition. His frustration had boiled over into a shouting match at the last Cabinet meeting. Harsh language was exchanged. Trenholm feared that President Davis was going to fire Campbell. Others, who knew Davis better, worried that he might challenge Campbell to a duel and shoot him dead.

He might have, were it not for John Breckinridge. Breckinridge was a vital forty-four-year-old Kentuckian who had served as Vice-President of the United States under Buchanan. Only recently had he been appointed Secretary of War in hopes of reversing a string of military disappointments. He stood and demanded that his Assistant Secretary receive an apology from the President for only doing his job, which was to explore all possible options. Confronted by the powerful voice of his most recent, and vigorous Cabinet appointment, Davis caved and offered an insincere apology for "the misunderstanding."

The groups' only order of business was to determine how best to steer President Davis into accepting the reality of Lincoln's best, and likely last, offer. Lincoln's offer to stop the bloodshed in exchange for the South being re-assimilated into the Union with dignity, a return of confiscated belongings, and generous compensation for the emancipation of Southern slaves was certainly not an "insult." In fact, Lincoln's terms were a far better offer than they had thought possible. Knowing the war to be already lost underscored how much they had to gain in Lincoln's offer and how little there was to lose. Continuation of the misery was simply not a reasonable option.

A still angry John Archibald Campbell started the discussion bluntly. "Jeff Davis is slow of mind and needlessly obstructive. His obsession with Lincoln's insults and his doubtful vacillation makes him unfit to govern. For me, it is not a difficult decision when the choice presented is between yielding and being demolished. Davis must accede to Lincoln's demands."

"I'm not inclined to think President Davis has changed his mind if Lincoln still demands dissolution of the Confederate Republic," Secretary of State Benjamin opined.

"John, do you have any idea how the Union would respond if we were to depose President Davis?" George asked.

"To be honest," Campbell replied, "they'd be nonplussed. Lincoln knows he's holding all the cards. It won't delay their advance on Richmond very long. They'd probably give us some brief time to sort out who's in charge and organize an offer of surrender."

"Hang on just a minute now, gentlemen," Secretary of the Navy Mallory interrupted. "I think we're discussing something I am not comfortable with. I'm already considered a traitor on one side of the Potomac. I'm not interested in making it both." Stephen Mallory was generally regarded as both the timidest and dimmest of the Cabinet members. George Trenholm had included him in the group for other reasons.

John Campbell knew that Mallory could be either bullied or manipulated. He chose the latter. "Stephen, it's an old saying but still appropriate. Desperate times, which these surely are, call for desperate measures. The Union will win this war and will win it soon. They'll decide who is, and who is not, a traitor. I don't see how deposing Davis could do anything but help us when our day of judgement arrives."

"People will feel like we're just trying to save our own skins," Secretary Mallory replied.

Campbell answered, "I don't suggest this to save myself. Like I said, that will be Lincoln's call. This is the only way forward to save countless lives and our Southern states, or at least what is left of them. If it benefits our personal fortunes to be responsible for bringing an earlier end to this accursed war, then so be it. However, we must act now. Those interlacing trenches and redoubts encircling Richmond will soon become a bloody killing field that'll make Gettysburg seem like a family picnic."

"President Davis will certainly see the wisdom of surrender in preference to such a terrible and valueless waste of humanity." Mallory's anxiety caused his voice to crack. "There must be another way." His words more pleading than argumentative.

Secretary of War Breckinridge supported Secretary Mallory. "I understand the need for us to act boldly to protect our countrymen. However, I did not come to Richmond to immediately turn around and betray my commander-in-chief."

Secretary of State Judah Benjamin followed. "I agree with Stephen as well. Before we consider declaring Jefferson unfit, or deposing him in some other way, we must explore all other options. We also need to have Vice-President Stephens with us. I am told he has left the capital."

"Alexander despises President Davis and is already exploring other options," Trenholm added. "I'm told by contacts at home that Vice-President Stephens has returned to Georgia, at General Sherman's invitation, to discuss an independent cessation of hostilities between the State of Georgia and the Union."

"We must get him back to Richmond immediately," Assistant Secretary Campbell responded. Each man agreed that the support of Vice-President Stephens was essential. Trenholm pledged to get a message to Stephens as soon as possible.

Secretary of War Breckinridge spoke next. "Before we go into the Cabinet meeting there is some other information that you need to be aware of. President Davis has approved a plan devised by General Lee to reverse the direction of the war."

"For Christ's sakes. Are we headed back to Gettysburg?" John Campbell asked sarcastically.

"No, but I would remind you that if the Union lines at Gettysburg had faltered in the face of General Pickett's advance, this war may now be over. It's certainly a last gasp, but General Lee wouldn't have proposed it unless he believes there is some chance of success."

Trenholm put his hand on John Campbell's shoulder while asking Breckinridge to continue.

"General Lee is planning an attack on Fort Steadman east of Petersburg. Lee believes that Fort Steadman is a weak spot in the Union lines. If Steadman can be taken, it will split Grant's army in half and allow Lee's Army of Northern Virginia to escape south. Lee's plan is to then meet up with General Joe Johnston's Confederate army in North Carolina and try to trap Sherman between themselves and General Beauregard's army coming up from South Carolina. Lee believes that Sherman is vulnerable having marched across the entire South without adequate supply. Once Sherman is defeated, Lee will return to Virginia re-supplied, re-manned and revitalized with General Grant in his cross-hairs."

"Damn," John Campbell said for everyone present, "no one can ever accuse the esteemed General Lee of not having a vivid imagination and one colossal set of balls."

"Admittedly, it's the longest of shots," Breckinridge continued, "but it's better than waiting for dysentery and desertion to cripple him in the trenches."

"Why do we always believe that General Lee can do the impossible?" Campbell asked.

"Because he already has time and time again," Breckinridge replied.

Trenholm concluded with what the group already knew. "President Davis will unquestionably endorse this plan. What choice does he have? If Davis believes there is a road to victory, or even just a pathway to an upper hand, he'll never consider a negotiated surrender. I pray for Robert's success. However, we must also be prepared for potential failure. I will get Vice-President Stephens back to the capital. I will also speak confidentially with our Attorney General to determine what options are allowed by the C.S.A. Constitution. However, if this attack fails, we'll need to be prepared to act regardless of what the Constitution may or may not allow."

There was a silent nod of approval from everyone in the room apart from Secretary Mallory who still seemed overwhelmed by the entire discussion. As the group dispersed, George Trenholm asked John Campbell if he could have a word.

"John, I know you have a million things pulling at you, but I was hoping you might be able to do me a favor."

"Absolutely, George, if I can."

"I understand that you're responsible for the issuance of rite of passage documents for civilians wishing to travel north."

"I am, but I must warn you those passports are carefully scrutinized by Union authorities. They're on high alert for C.S.A. government officials and military officers trying to escape."

"Not an issue. These are for legitimate civilians, women and children only. They are for family friends of mine back in Charleston who I believe are in danger. The head of the family is our most successful blockade runner, and he has frustrated the Yankees for quite some time. I'm sure they're being hunted as we speak. They have relatives in New York City. I'd like to get them reunited before something untoward befalls them."

"Surely George, get me the necessary information and I will prepare the passage documents."

"Many thanks, my friend."

"I'm happy to be able to help somebody."

"I know what you mean, John. Let's get into the Cabinet meeting before Jefferson decides to invade Mexico."

Chapter 22

April 1, 1865

Naval Cadets

Big dreams die hard. The bigger the dreams the more they must bleed out before they will lie still. General Lee sent word from the front which everyone anticipated, but mythology had not allowed them to expect. General George Pickett and several Confederate brigades attacked a weak spot in the Union lines at Fort Stedman. It was to be redemption for Pickett after his blood-soaked failure at Cemetery Ridge.

The bold early morning assault on Fort Stedman took the Union forces by surprise and was executed magnificently. Confederate troopers breeched the Union breastworks, opening the desired rent in the Union lines. Either misplacing his nerve or satisfied with a success far too inconsequential to alter the course of the war, General Pickett did not press his advantage. Pickett and his other senior officers retired from the field and celebrated their success with a fish fry that evening, dining on grilled shad and drinking brown whiskey.

The following morning, General Grant counterattacked with an overwhelming Union force driving the Confederates back to their trenches. The gamble had failed. Lee had made an inexcusable mistake in trusting the limited bravery and judgment of General Pickett with the last gasp of the once fearsome Army of Northern Virginia.

General Lee's telegram to President Davis on Sunday morning informed him that his lines had been broken. Lee anticipated that Grant would quickly push his counterattack and that the Army of Northern Virginia would not be able to offer any effective resistance. Tactically, he was planning a fighting retreat to the Southwest towards Danville. General Lee recommended that the government evacuate Richmond immediately before they were completely encircled. Although unstated, General Lee knew his position was doomed and that surrender was inevitable. Lee did apprise President Davis that he was relieving General Pickett of command.

From his office window, George Trenholm watched the good folk of Richmond walk to church. It was a warm, breezy chamber of commerce day with church spires reaching out to a crystal-blue sky calling the faithful to worship. No one took notice of the ominous absence of distant cannon rumble or the ever-closer Northern observation balloons floating east of the city. They had not appreciated how the Union campfires grew more numerous and brighter each night.

The citizens of Richmond had also failed to notice the week-long transfer of government crates from Capital Square to the Richmond-Danville railroad depot. The relocation of government documents had been undertaken in a piecemeal fashion specifically to avoid alerting the populace or enraging the few remaining true believers. The former true believers in the C.S.A. Congress had already adjourned and slipped quietly from Richmond concerned only with their petty and personal apprehensions.

Most of the folk walking to church were women. Virtually all were in black mourning dresses, a weekly indirect tally of the killed or missing. So many fathers, sons and husbands had failed to come home that black silk had long ago disappeared from the clothing shops. House slaves taught widowed white women how to blacken their cotton dresses with a dye made of walnut hulls and indigo.

The few men who could be seen had empty sleeves pinned to tattered uniform shoulders, hobbled on crutches, or road in drayage carts. Even for those who survived the battlefield physically intact, their forfeiture of family, friends, and property would leave a dumb sense of vast loss embittering the South for generations to come. Trenholm lowered his head. Each man, woman, and child were the tragic victims of his and other's miscalculation. None of them were aware of General Lee's defeat at Fort Stedman. Nor were they aware of the darkness that would soon envelop them.

The previous day, Trenholm had requested that Secretary Mallory of the Navy summon his old friend Lt. William H. Parker, superintendent of the Confederate Naval Academy, to present himself at the Treasury Department. George impatiently awaited Parker's arrival.

Secretary Mallory established the Naval Academy in 1862 under the command of Lt. Parker. Parker recruited a corps of experienced professors and established a well-organized, professional school for the education of naval midshipmen. Well-connected and high scholarship candidates were selected by congressional appointment from all over the Confederacy. Trenholm's protege James Morgan, several of his nephews, and the Holmes boys had joined the Confederate Naval Cadet Battalion a few months earlier.

Sixty midshipmen were assigned to the school-ship *Patrick Henry* anchored off the shore batteries at Drewry's Bluff, south of Richmond. They studied navigation based on the sun and stars and trigonometry based on the sound of artillery fire. While the dilapidated *Patrick Henry* was past her prime, Commander Parker never let the midshipmen forget her illustrious past. Their school-ship had steamed under the name *Yorktowne* as a tender to the *C.S.S.*

Merrimac during her famous battle with the Union's *Monitor*.

John Hale came into Trenholm's office to announce Lt. Parker's arrival. Hale was the Treasury Department's chief clerk and Trenholm's most trusted aide. At Trenholm's request, Hale had been secretly preparing for the transport of the Confederate treasury for more than a week.

"Thank you, John. Please send him in. Also, John, it's time to implement our evacuation plan for the treasury. We will need to onboard the treasury boxes this evening at the Richmond-Danville station. The government is leaving tonight."

"So soon, Mister Secretary?"

"I'm afraid so. Grant has broken our lines and will be in Richmond by tomorrow morning if not sooner."

"Dear lord. I am sorry to hear that, sir. However, all preparations are in place. I'll see to it that the treasury is safeguarded."

"Thank you, John. I'll see you tonight at the train station. Once things are set in motion, make the necessary plans for your family to leave the city. They shouldn't wait for tonight which might prove to be a long one. Please make sure that your family remains discrete about the evacuation of the government."

"Understood, sir. Desperation and panic will not change what's coming or make it any better."

"Exactly."

Lt. William Parker entered George Trenholm's office after John Hale departed. Parker arrived in his most glorious commander's attire. He stood before Trenholm's desk taking a military posture with hands clasped behind his back and legs spread apart as a naval captain would. A life-long navy man, he had been on sinking ships before. Lt. Parker knew, that as a matter of respect, your ship deserved for you to look your best on her last day.

"Commander, thank you for coming so promptly. It is a matter of great urgency. Please sit."

"I suspected that time might be precious, Mister Secretary."

"Without doubt, William. President Davis has just been advised by General Lee that our back has been broken at Petersburg. The General is in full retreat towards Danville and the government will be following him there tonight. The Yankees will be here as soon as they realize our trenches are defended by only scarecrows and river rats."

"How can the Naval Academy Corps be of assistance?"

"By order of Secretary Mallory, you are to muster your cadets and march them to the Army depot where they'll be armed and equipped as infantry. Your cadets will then join the men and officers of a naval brigade formed from the deactivated iron-clad squadron at Drewry's Bluff."

"My cadets will serve with honor, sir. However, I must let you know that our complement has thinned. Several of my cadets have been taken down by dysentery due to foul bilge water."

"I'd heard that was the case. Please, ask the surgeon to reassess each man's condition. If they're capable of carrying a rifle, I fear they may be better off on the march as opposed to laid up at Chimborazo Hospital waiting for the Yankees to arrive. If truly incapacitated, then so be it."

"Understood, sir."

"Unfortunately, I must reduce your complement of men even further. This is a list of fourteen of your midshipmen that will be transferred to the Treasury Department under my authority. I need for them to report to the Danville rail depot. They are needed for a service of particular danger and delicacy. When the government leaves Richmond tonight, they will be given guardianship of a train containing the invaluable archives of the government as well as its gold, silver, and other treasure."

"These young men are some of my finest, Mister Secretary," Lt. Parker commented as he reviewed Trenholm's list. "It's a great honor, but if I may ask, why did you select my young middies for such an important responsibility?"

"As you can see, many of these men are South Carolinians that I either know personally or recommended for their positions at the Naval Academy. I feel most comfortable exercising leadership over a group of young officers that I know to be gentlemen and of high character. I need a cadre of men I can trust to be honest, brave, and discreet."

"Well again, you've selected well. How would you like the men outfitted?"

"Heavily. Fully uniformed, rifles, dual revolvers and at least three days of rations. It may prove to be a long trip to Danville. Make sure they have plenty of coffee as watchfulness will be at a premium."

"I will have them at the depot by six p.m. and they'll be prepared. I will impress on them the need for utmost vigilance and steadfastness. I feel obliged to warn you, sir, that when the rule of law evaporates, my cadets, for all their virtue, will be a very modest line separating you and your train from anarchy and plunder. A lot of citizens will be looking to join that train on its way out of town."

"That is why I need your best, Commander. Can I trust in their arrival?"

"They'll be there, sir, and will be prepared to serve the Confederacy unto their death if that is required."

"I would expect nothing less from men trained by you, William. Let me also thank you for your service. In another couple of days there won't be anyone left to recognize all that you've done for your country. If you have any valuable personal items left on the *Patrick Henry*, I'd recommend that you retrieve them this afternoon. The engineers are planning to blow her up later tonight to obstruct Union rivercraft."

"I'd appreciate that opportunity. She's a bit long in the tooth, but she was a fine ship."

"William, get yourself and your cadets out of Richmond as soon as you can. Whatever happens, it will be better to be on the move rather than trapped in the city. The Naval corps deserves a better fate than a Federal prison ship."

"They do, sir. If the Confederacy falls, I'll do my best to see that they all get home. I wish the same for you, sir. You must know that every one of Sherman's cavalry units will be hunting for Cabinet members."

"That seedy little man is someone whom I'd prefer not make acquaintances with."

"Nor I. I'll see you on the other side, George."

Lt. Parker excused himself to his many assignments. George poured himself a glass of bourbon and drained it in a single swallow. This was not a day for sipping bourbon. After refilling his glass, Trenholm pulled a ledger from the top drawer of his desk and filled out his final official disbursement from the Confederate States Treasury. He approved a payment of fifteen hundred dollars in gold to the Secretary of State Judah Benjamin for the listed purpose of "Secret Service."

Whatever happened in the coming days, the families of those he cared for and depended on, would be protected.

Chapter 23

April 2, 1865

Danville Platform

John Hale had raided the War Department for all the wooden boxes and barrels they could spare. Hale and Mann Quarles, his most trusted Treasury Department teller, spent the day filling the containers with Confederate gold and silver bars, Liberty Head double eagle gold pieces, silver dollars from Mexico, and Maria Theresa thaler silver bullion coins from Austria. The resulting collection of long rifle boxes, wooden trunks, squat ammunition barrels, and a hodgepodge of other available containers were stacked waist high in the Treasury vault room. Hale estimated that he was standing amidst three to four million dollars in gold and silver specie.

Everyone in the Treasury Department understood the need for complete secrecy. Movement of the Confederate treasure could create unwanted intrusion. The citizens of Richmond had given all they could to the Confederacy. If it had all come to naught, they would want it back. With the collapse of their republic, a coming Union occupation, and only worthless Confederate paper in their pockets, they would insist. Neither Trenholm nor Hale were interested in discovering how insistent they might become.

Hale created a handmade booklet and recorded the contents of each box, barrel, or trunk on folded brown paper. It was the one and only accounting of the remaining Confederate wealth. Hale used an iron poker, heated white hot in the Treasury furnace, to brand obscure markings onto each wooden container. The code marks were replicated on the corresponding pages of Hale's improvised booklet indicating each boxes' content. To a cursory inspection, the burnt lines, slashes, crosses, and hashmarks would look no different than a million other war weary munitions containers.

Hale personally sealed each container and applied a heavy lock. The size and newness of each padlock was the only inconsistent feature of these otherwise nondescript military supply crates. The keys to each padlock and the inventory booklet were placed in a small lockbox that Hale gave to Secretary Trenholm.

Orders were issued for two trains to be prepared. One would carry President Davis and his Cabinet and a second train for the archives and treasure. They were to be assembled at the Richmond to Danville station by early evening. Simultaneously, the C.S.A. regular army would quietly disengage from their defensive trenches. They spiked their cannon barrels and pounded rat-tailed files into the torch holes of the cannons too big to spike. Even the most oblivious civilian would recognize the bad implications of the C.S.A. regular army marching back through Richmond toward the Mayo toll bridge.

The Mayo toll bridge connected the Richmond business district with Manchester, Virginia, to the south. There was an island in the James River where the toll booth stood. The Richmond-Danville railroad line ran next to the Mayo toll bridge. President Davis had ordered the Mayo toll bridge burned after the Confederate rear guard crossed to the south side. The Mayo was the last intact bridge over the James and its burning would trap the remaining populace of Richmond. Davis also ordered the tobacco warehouses and other factories razed to prevent those resources from falling into Yankee hands. Trenholm believed that President Davis' planned arson was needless and the burning of the Mayo bridge irresponsible. It was the citizens of Richmond who would suffer for it, not the Yankees.

The fourteen midshipmen selected by Secretary Trenholm were assembled by Commander Parker and instructed regarding their responsibility for protecting the treasure and archives of their country.

"No group of midshipmen have ever been assigned a more important duty," Commander Parker thundered. "The Naval Cadet Battalion has been entrusted with both the history and future of our country and we will not let our country down."

The cadets cheered and Thomas Henry Holmes exclaimed, "For the honor of the Naval Academy and to the memory of the *Patrick Henry*." The midshipmen cheered again, and Commander Parker smiled recognizing their commitment and his success.

"Men," Commander Parker shouted above the hurrahs. "Have no doubt, this will be a dangerous assignment. You have been selected because of your character and courage, but those virtues will be tested. I am certain that this group will rise to that challenge. I am sorry that I cannot be with you. I am placing midshipman Thomas Holmes in charge as our most experience seaman and also his experience in leading men under fire. He will lead you well and you will serve him magnificently. Godspeed to you all."

"Thank you for the confidence, Commander," Thomas Henry replied. He then turned toward his men. "You heard the Commander. To the Danville platform; double quick time."

As the midshipmen marched to the railroad platform, Thomas Henry's younger brother, George Chapman, stopped briefly to console a young girl left alone in the street. Tears were flowing down her cheeks. Probably ten years old, she was in a thread-bear linen shift worn to an indistinguishable color which could not hide her emaciation. Slack muscles melted against her bones. Her skin was as pale and as near translucent as bone china. Her face haloed by an unkempt tangle of densely curled blond hair. George picked her up and gave her a biscuit from his haversack. She looked at him with reddened, unblinking eyes devoid of light.

Thomas Henry circled back and put his hand on George Chapman's shoulder. "Got to go, George. There's nothing more we can do for her."

George Chapman nodded and put her down. He turned his head so that Thomas Henry would not see the tears welling up in his eyes.

The arrival of Thomas Henry's midshipmen at the Danville depot could not be mistaken. Heads turned as the young, well-groomed, and sharp-dressed middies marched into the railroad terminal. The small squadron of midshipmen cut through the butternut gray gloom in jaunty blue caps, blood red sashes, gleaming gold clasps, and shining silver sabers.

In short order, they fixed bayonets and cleared the terminal building and platform of deadbeats, the curious, and the frantic. Guards were posted at the station doors at each end of the platform to deny entry to panicked citizens hoping to find either fortune or escape. The mood at the depot sobered the cadets of any sense of high adventure. They were all that remained of Confederate order and their line was thin at best. Beyond the platform a growing throng of Richmond's livid citizens were looking for solutions the cadets could not provide. The deadly seriousness of their assignment became more obvious as rumors spread regarding the absconding C.S.A. government and the Confederate gold and silver. Thomas Henry reflected on the most important lesson Commander Parker and his father had ever taught him. That lesson was the importance of will when numbers were against you.

Thomas' midshipmen maintained security as Treasury clerks loaded the coded boxes and other supplies onto the treasure train. The crowd grew rapidly in size and animosity as darkness encroached. The crowd was a mismatched collection of displaced citizens, laborers, deserters, hooligans, the maimed, and widows of the needlessly dead. Their only commonality was having no place else to vent their rage. The crowd howled insults and curses at the naval cadets as the last remaining vestige of Confederate authority. Midshipman Thomas Henry Holmes walked the line and whispered words of steadiness and fortitude to his classmates.

"Remember, words can't hurt us. It's the sticks and stones we need to worry about."

Thomas Henry realized that he was watching over the final moments of the Confederacy. An independent Southern Republic was no longer the dream, but rather a lingering nightmare. Surveying the crowd gathering in front of the platform, Thomas Henry knew he was staring into the abyss of failure. Its depth was unknown but certainly dangerous.

The sound of breaking glass and looting could be heard behind the insults of the crowd. Fearfulness and fearlessness would spiral together into depravity born of demoralization and desperation. The crowds on the streets of Richmond were intent on plunder. Looters rushed frantically from store to store with axes and clubs searching for anything of value. Scalps were split and men and women alike were beaten bloody as hungry citizens scrounged for food and looters brawled over worthless trinkets. Thomas Henry feared that sooner or later that chaos in the street would reach the railroad terminal.

Walking the line, Thomas Henry reminded his classmates that the mob could not be allowed to surge past them. There was no fall back point, no back up plan or reinforcements. The middies numbered only fourteen, but were well-armed with revolvers on both hips, bayonetted rifles in their hands, and long silver swords at their sides. Understanding the unfocused nature of mob rule, both

Thomas Henry and George Chapman had hung sawed-off twelve-gauge shotguns around their necks on a lanyard.

The cursing and jeering increased as a black carriage arrived carrying President Davis. Even at a distance and silhouetted in black by flashing explosions from a nearby munitions depot, the President looked defeated and tragic. Thomas Henry had once seen President Davis speak in Charleston early in the war. He remembered Davis as slim and proud with the perfect posture of an accomplished horseman. Thomas Henry most remembered the President's thick mane of silver-streaked dark hair which swept back dramatically as if he was constantly riding into the wind. That could not be the same man.

Davis quickly climbed up into the passenger car of the Presidential train which remained dark with window shades drawn. Several of Davis' house slaves loaded bags from the carriage into the passenger car before getting into the stock car with two of the President's finest thoroughbreds.

The crowd watching Davis' arrival grew increasingly dark spirited. The crowd's voice had gone from loud, to ugly, and now vicious. Insults gave way to threats. Eventually the anger and whiskey-heated churn of the mob was able to puke forward a leader. He was a broad-faced Scotsman, flushed with alcohol, and sweating profusely in a shoddy woolen winter suit. He was unarmed but clearly possessed brutish strength from years of bucking bales of tobacco along the waterfront. He walked towards Thomas Henry who stepped out in front of tenuous line of midshipmen.

"You boys best move on. We got bidness with the men over yonder on that train."

Thomas Henry initially said nothing as the attention of the crowd focused uneasily on him. "My orders are to stay here and provide security for these trains. The Yankees are coming, and it is going to be a bad night. You and the rest of you friends need to head back home and keep your families safe."

"Stand aside, soldier boy. Ain't no way we're letting Jeff Davis bring us down the way he has and then roll out of here with all our money. Just ain't gonna happen."

"Navy, sir."

"What you say, boy?"

"We're not soldiers. We're cadets from the Confederate Naval Academy and we'll not abandon our post."

More indecencies and epithets were howled at Jeff Davis and the amassed crowd surged forward forcing the Scotsman to within four feet of Thomas Henry. "We ain't got no truck with you boys. Lots of other places where fine looking soldiers like yourselves can go play dress up without getting a beat down."

"I told you once already sir, we're navy, not army. That is an important difference for you to recognize. When you're on a boat, there's no place to retreat to. We'll go down with the ship. Tonight, this railroad platform is our ship."

"Nobody here wants to hurt you boys, whatever you are, but we'll go through you the way Sherman went through Georgia if we have to. You fought for us and we appreciate that, but we're gonna get what we came for."

Cheers went up from the crowd for their unofficial spokesman. Thomas Henry wondered why the hell the trains weren't already rolling. The engine built its steam several times, but then released, and the train stayed still. The engineers and important men in the passenger cars had to know that things were getting dicey. It was time to find out how dicey.

Thomas Henry swung the twelve gauge from behind his back into his hands and stepped forward. He put the twin barrels about six inches from the Scotsman's ruddy face. Simultaneously, George Chapman stepped forward to join his brother with revolvers in each hand. The remaining midshipmen cocked their rifles at a ready position.

"Mister, the most foolish thing I can imagine is being the last man to die in a war. I won't miss at this distance with this scattergun and there won't be nothin' left to show your family. Midshipman Holmes next to me will take out the dozen men around you. The rest of my boys will put mini balls between the eyes of anyone else who steps forward. And you know what, it won't even make my heart rate go up because I'll just be doing my job. I don't have any other options. You still do."

A man from the back of the crowd shouted something about teaching these boys a lesson, but he could not see the look in Thomas Henry's eyes that the Scotsman did. It was a look that Thomas Henry had learned from his father when he had when the time for talking had passed. The crowd surged forward again cursing both the midshipmen and Jeff Davis. The men in the front, however, understood that those in the back wouldn't be taking the first volley of lead.

Thomas Henry pointed his sawed-off shotgun toward the sky and got the crowd's immediate attention with a blast. Then, he re-pointed it at the Scotsman. "I saved a barrel for you. What's it to be?"

Looking again into Thomas Henry's eyes, the Scotsman and several of the other men in the front broke and took off running away from the trains. The mob quickly melted away as it always does once accountability is established. Also awakened by the shotgun blast, the steam engine of the Presidential train finally came alive. It was a small train with a locomotive, a wood car, several worn passenger cars, two baggage cars and four cars for slaves and stock. President Davis, Secretary of State Judah Benjamin, Secretary of the Navy Mallory, Postmaster General John H. Reagan, and Secretary of the Treasury Trenholm sat in the faded red velvet seats along with about twenty other aides and servants. Secretary of War Breckenridge decided to stay in Richmond with General Ewell who was providing the rear-guard action. Anna Helen Trenholm, with a delicate double-shot derringer and a small flask of laudanum in her purse, was the only woman on board among almost thirty men. Her unfailing good spirits were welcomed. Those good spirits were both personal and contained in several oak casks of peach brandy she'd brought on board with her.

Anna Helen had sent her daughters, Helen and Eliza, ahead on a special train with the First Lady Varina Davis the preceding Friday. At George's suggestion, Secretary of the Navy Mallory assigned Midshipman James Morris Morgan to escort Varina and the Trenholm girls on the train south to Charlotte. From Charlotte, Midshipman Morgan was to take Helen and Eliza to a family home in Abbeville, South Carolina.

Trenholm hated splitting up the family but reluctantly agreed with Anna Helen that it was safer to get the girls out of Richmond earlier. He wanted Anna Helen to accompany the girls, but she would not hear of it. George was aware of the romance between Midshipman Morgan and his daughter Helen. He knew that Midshipman Morgan would lay down his life before allowing anyone to violate or take his daughters. He pulled Midshipman Morgan aside to make sure he understood his responsibility. "Helen and Eliza will not fall into the hands of any Yankee guerillas or Southern highwaymen. At no point will you spend more than four of the cartridges in your final revolver in their defense."

James Morgan nodded, "The last two will be for their honor, sir."

President Davis' decision to burn the tobacco warehouses had proven cataclysmic. A brisk wind from the South had fed the fires and blown it back on the city. The firestorm had grown into a living, hungry hunter which was consuming Richmond. The flames from engulfed factories and warehouses rose higher into the darkening sky and tongues of flame protruded from windows and leapt from building to building. Exploding buildings threw up a profusion of sparks and cinders that ignited the trees in which they landed and started secondary fires which incinerated homes and shops spreading the conflagration. Acrid smoke filled the air and reddened eyes. The streets resembled a level from Dante's Inferno as the wind whipped embers, trash, and valueless Confederate paper.

The Presidential train finally lurched forward a few inches as the drive wheels engaged and the steam-driven pistons began to pump. Black smoke belched from the train's stack which stood out in relief against the crimson and orange fire enveloping the city. The steel wheels of the locomotive began to squeal against the iron rails until friction overcame inertia. As the Presidential train began to roll forward, only George Trenholm looked back at the fire enveloping Richmond. His only emotion was a seething hatred of Jefferson Davis. A man whose haplessness and fecklessness had resulted in the immolation of Richmond as surely as if he had struck the first match himself. George prayed that President Davis would never be able to outrun his responsibility for this iniquity.

Chapter 24

April 3, 1865

Water and Wood

After the Presidential train cleared the station, a shrill steam whistle signaled the midshipmen to board the waiting treasure train. Thomas Henry stationed two midshipmen in each of the five cars containing government archives and the boxes or barrels of silver and gold. The other cars carried Treasury Department clerks, their wives, and personal baggage. Two armed midshipmen stayed forward with the locomotive engineers and two others took positions on the roof of the final car.

Thomas Henry and George Chapman took charge of the final treasure car. The brothers stood on the back end as the train crossed the James River. They could see the *Patrick Henry*, afire in the middle of the river, having been exploded in an act both midshipmen found deeply disturbing. Other vessels were burning as well, drifting downriver on the tide. The tobacco warehouses were skeletal infernos filling the sky with smoke and the air with the pungent odor of burnt tobacco. A collapsing flour mill roof created an eruption of burning timber and shingles that soared into the air like a fireworks display. The blaze illuminated the sky from below with lurid orange, yellow, and reddish hues reflecting off the choking black smoke. The ominous crackling of burning wood and the whoosh of blowing flames could be heard over the noise of the locomotive. As the fire spread to the C.S.A.

arsenal, heavy ordinance began to explode, creating further panic among innocents and looters alike who feared Union bombardment.

From their perch on the back of the final car, the Holmes boys could see cans of kerosene, cotton waste and wooden barrels of tar beside the tracks. They were angered by the realization that both the Mayo and railroad bridges would be put to the torch after their train had passed. After they had ridden to safety, the bridges would crack, shudder, and collapse, hissing into the James. Everyone in Richmond would be trapped in a raging inferno. George Chapman teared up again remembering the forsaken little girl he had given a biscuit. Uncle George had always said that empathy was Jefferson Davis' blind spot. George Chapman now understood the power of aloofness to doom men, women, children, and a city. Thomas Henry patted George Chapman on the back and told him to get some sleep. He would stand the first watch.

Thomas Henry had crewed steam ships since before he could remember but had always longed to take a train ride behind a steam engine. As the Confederate treasure train slowed to another stop on the endless roll to Danville, Thomas Henry had officially lost his fascination with the iron horse. No steam ship voyage in any weather had ever been as miserable as this train ride, and that included the time Union shrapnel almost took his leg. If he never set foot on a train again it would be too soon.

Like the rest of the Southern railroad network, the Danville line suffered from neglect and deferred maintenance. Any semblance of luxury was long gone. Benches were without cushions or missing altogether. Carriage lamps were smashed, stoves missing, and windows broken. Cars reeked of unemptied spittoons and chamber pots. Wooden slats on the boxcars were missing in such great number that there was no more cover than an open wagon.

The rails themselves were iron rather than the stronger steel enjoyed by Northern railroads. Expedient repairs during the war years resulted in oak ties being laid directly on the ground instead of on gravel-ballasted roadbeds. The irregularities in terrain forced the train to travel at much slower speeds than the locomotive could otherwise achieve and for the cars to rattle and sway. The roll to Danville would be a deplorable all-night affair at a maximum speed of just ten miles per hour. The *Will O' the Wisp* moved faster floating on the outbound tide.

The South also lacked available coal for their locomotive steam engines. Instead, the train boilers were wood fired which was both less efficient and burned much faster. The Richmond to Danville train was forced to stop every two hours to collect more wood for the coal box and take on water for the steam engine. The black firemen had run off days earlier, so it fell to the midshipmen to take to the surrounding woods with axes and lanterns to collect the pine and scrub oak needed to keep the engine's boiler fired. George Chapman took charge of the cutting crews while Thomas Henry took responsibility for refilling the boiler from the water tanks positioned at intervals of every twenty miles along the tracks.

The glowing sky in the distance remained visible no matter how many miles they put behind them. The reddish blush on the horizon represented the destruction of a city they had come to like. The cadets wondered how much of the mob they had dispersed at the depot had reorganized, found their nerve, and were following them to Danville. The leaderless army of angry, frantic men coming from behind were more fearsome to the midshipmen than any Federal cavalry which may lay ahead.

The trip was made bearable by the ample supply of peach brandy that Anna Helen Trenholm had left with Thomas Henry and George Chapman at the Richmond platform. Once underway, the middies killed the time between stops for water and wood by enjoying the Trenholm brandy and eating the hoe cakes, hardtack, and embalmed beef they had stuffed in their bread bag. They celebrated the nerve they had showed in buffaloing the mob at the station and their youthful indestructability. Mostly, they toasted Anna Helen for her delicious peach brandy.

Having grown up on the family recipe, Thomas Henry and George Chapman were accustomed to, and appropriately fearful of, the peach brandy's alcohol content and addicting flavor. The other cadets were not as circumspect. The toasts became more frequent, boisterous, and slurred as the all-night marathon continued toward Danville.

By four a.m., Thomas Henry and George Chapman, were the only two midshipmen left fully in charge of their senses on the treasure train. They studied the folded brown paper and coded symbols that chief clerk Hale had locked away for Secretary Trenholm. The improvised code book and padlock keys had been included in Anna Helen's hamper of peach brandy. Thomas Henry and George Chapman identified each box or cask containing Confederate gold according to Hale's seared markings.

With the other midshipmen either befuddled or asleep, Thomas Henry and George Chapman had little trouble sequestering each of those boxes and barrels into their storage car. The one midshipman aroused by their activity began to ask a question but was interrupted by the need to lunge for a missing slat on the side of the boxcar. George Chapman rubbed his neck with a wet cloth until he was done and then laid him back down unconscious on the straw. At the final few stops for more water and wood, the engineer and fireman failed to notice that among the oak and pine loaded into their coal box were chopped up wooden boxes with strange symbols branded on their splintered shards. It burned just like all the other wood and the train crept forward again.

Chapter 25

April 4, 1895

Green Potatoes

Danville, Virginia became the final capital of the Confederate States of America when the Presidential and Confederate treasury trains arrived on the morning of April 4th.

The midshipmen bivouacked in a grove of dogwoods and clover approximately fifty yards from the trains. The dogwoods were nearing full bloom boasting the Holy Cross of the Savior with Christ's stigmata on every white petal. They enjoyed the last of the peach brandy complemented by slapjacks with sorghum. One of George Trenholm's nephews toasted their successful arrival. "Lord save us and preserve us; we're drinking brandy for breakfast." Eventually, they fell asleep in the deep grass nursing hangovers and exhaustion.

Admiral Semmes and the men of the James River Squadron arrived later that morning after having blown up their ironclads. Greater in number and experience, Admiral Semmes' men assumed guardianship of the Confederate treasure train. The midshipmen were relieved of duty and the small detachment of naval cadets gradually drifted from camp beginning a long walk home.

Midshipmen Thomas Henry and George Chapman Holmes and the two of George Trenholm's nephews remained behind. They had another assignment. With a sack of twenty-dollar double eagle gold coins the boys found a sturdy wagon and team of able horses. With chaos creeping ever closer, the residents of Danville were eager to sell whatever possessions they had worthy of hard currency. Gold coin could get you fine furniture, silver table ware, well-aged liquors, horses, mules, or Negro slaves who had not already run away.

Thomas Henry and George Chapman purchased an abandoned army ambulance from an apparently able-bodied but shattered young man. He claimed to be the ambulance's driver but he had run off the horses so he would not have to go out into the field again. No other questions were asked. The ambulance was war-worn but had heavy axles and sturdy wheels. A dirty white canvas was stretched over bent oak-splint ribs with only a single tear and a few scattered musket ball holes.

The brothers also found a team of four condemned military horses who had rallied a bit with some fresh air and country hay and without the incessant explosion of nearby mortar rounds. The boys worried that the farmer might have some gypsy in him and knew how to treat the heaves with a kerosene-soaked gauze stuffed up the horses' nostrils.

After purchasing some needed provisions, the brothers and cousins awaited nightfall when they would take off on their own hook. They were heading back up the railroad line towards Richmond. Wary of army stragglers and refugees escaping the bedlam of a burnt-out city, the boys armed themselves with revolvers and shotguns. They folded away their fine midshipmen tunics. If stopped, they would pretend to be farm boys too stupid to know the right direction to flee.

They cautiously picked their way back up the railroad line by lamplight. With the Mayo bridge collapsed, Thomas Henry presumed that the railroad tracks would be deserted, and refugees or military patrols would be on the Danville road approximately one-half mile east of the rail line.

At each water station, Thomas Henry stripped down and climbed into the cistern. He swam to the bottom and retrieved the gold bars, ingots, and sacks of Liberty Head gold coins. Each time the treasure train had stopped for boiler water and firewood, Thomas Henry and George Chapman broke up selected boxes. George Chapman carried the busted wood to the coal box and Thomas Henry dropped the gold into the cistern as he fed the boiler. George Chapman checked off a detailed list of what had been dropped into each water tank. Thomas Henry was a better swimmer and dove into the cold rainwater for sunken treasure.

By sun rise they had recovered the last of the Confederate gold. They had purchased two good-sized metal trunks and had stolen several long Enfield rifle crates. The gold was placed into the metal trunks and four long rifle crates and laid on the floor of the ambulance. Wood planks were stripped from the base of several water towers and nailed together to cover the gold. The ambulance's false bottom would not hold up to close inspection.

Exhausted, Thomas Henry decided it would be best to hide and rest during the day and travel again in the evening. They drove the ambulance deep into the woods until they found an open field just beginning to green with the coming of spring. There was ample grass for the horses and a nearby stream. On the other side of the clearing were the remnants of an abandoned farmhouse now burned to its foundation after the most discontent of all winters.

They parked the ambulance by a thick stand of sweet-scented pine trees. Dawn was rising above the pines in an artist's paint board of colors which would require at least another hour to coalesce into a glowing ball of gold. Thomas Henry and George Chapman found a spot in the thick grass. Thomas Henry stretched out, laced his fingers together behind his head, and surveyed the untended field bravely attempting to resurrect itself. He yawned and then spoke to his brother, "This is a world that deserves better than us."

"Damn straight," George Chapman responded solemnly.

To amped up to sleep, George Chapman went to collect a deadfall of kindling from under a cluster of large pines and then helped the cousins, Billy and Troutman, start a fire. George Chapman placed a few small pieces of roasted mutton, salvaged from a previous meal, into a soup made of water thickened with corn meal along with a mess of fiddleheads and wild scallions that Billy had collected. Thomas Henry went to the creek to refill their canteens.

Returning from the creek, Thomas Henry shocked the others by kicking over a pot of potatoes boiling above the flames.

"Why'd you boot the potatoes, Tom," Billy asked.

"Where'd you get'em?" Thomas Henry shot back.

"I found'em in a box over by the burnt-out farmhouse with a sack of goobers," Billy replied.

"They didn't look funny to you?"

"Well, they had a bunch of sprouts, but we cut them off."

"Are you boys too stupid to know that you can't eat green potatoes?"

"They ain't blighted."

"They're green, Billy! Look at'em! Even after you peeled them, the meat is still green. You can barely see them in the grass. Besides being bitter, they'll give you the bloody flux."

Billy threw up his hands and kicked a couple of potatoes away from the fire. "I bet they'd be okay, but if you don't want to eat them, that's fine. Just thought some potato cakes would've stuck to the ribs."

Thomas Henry smiled. "Probably best not to take any chances being out here on the road. I'll warm up some biscuits and I've got a honey jar in the ambulance. That'll stick to your ribs better than those green taters."

After eating, the boys rested back in the soft, still moist grass with their heads against a pine log. George Chapman asked Thomas Henry if they had been wrong to fight for slavery.

Thomas Henry looked at his brother like he was crazy. "Really, now?"

"Yeah, now. We never owned no slaves, but I never thought it was wrong. Pastor says the Bible is okay with it."

"The Bible can't make up its mind about slavery. The Bible seems to say whatever men need it to say. If you want to understand slavery you have to read the history books, not the Bible."

"What' cha mean?"

"Every powerful nation in history built its fortune on the backs of slaves. The Egyptians used slaves to build the pyramids. The Greek city-states enslaved those they conquered. Rome enslaved most of the world. Britain, France. and Spain all built their empires using slave labor long before we started growing cotton. I ain't sayin' it's right. I'm just sayin' it has always been that way."

"Are we God's chosen race?"

Thomas Henry laughed aloud. "You think Billy and Troutman could be part of anyone's chosen race? They were getting ready to eat green potatoes. My experience is that any man with a bullwhip in his hand considers himself a member of the chosen race."

"Then how did we get into this mess?"

"We've been told all our lives that we're masters and they're slaves because we're white and they're black. But that don't make any sense. We were born white because Mamma and Poppa are white. We didn't have no say in it and didn't earn any privilege. Blacks are born black because their mammies and pappies are black. They didn't have any more say in being black than we had in being white. It cannot be right that skin color determines your entire fate. The way I see it, we're all just different breeds of dog. Some dogs will hunt, others retrieve, some haul carts, some herd animals, others will defend you with their life and some ain't good for nothin' but yappin'. But they are all dogs, and nobody cares a whit about what color they are. People only care about how well they can do what they're supposed to do."

"Poppa don't have any slaves and he treats the blacks on the *Wisp* the same as everyone else."

"That's just his way. Pa's a captain because he deserves to be captain. Caleb is a leadsman because he deserves to be a leadsman. Copper Joe's an engineer because he's the best damn boilerman on the water. With Poppa, you get what is rightfully yours based on your work. Poppa believes that the ownership of another human being is immoral, and I'm of a like mind. A man should get what he deserves based on merit."

"Uncle George owns hundreds of slaves. They pick his cotton and load his ships. They've made Uncle George the richest man in the South. Does Poppa think that Uncle George is immoral?"

"You'd have to ask Pa, but I wouldn't advise it. Me, I think we just got lazy and greedy. Since it has always been around, we just accepted it rather than calling it out as a sin. By accepting it, then becoming dependent on it, we boxed ourselves into fighting a war to keep it."

"It didn't work."

"No, it didn't, and the war has revealed our slave holding to be a mortal sin."

"Why is that?"

"Some slave owners, and I think Uncle George is among them, treat their slaves decently. They think they will be able to accept freed slaves, but I ain't sure. For them, the fissure between white and black may not be very wide, but it is a far deeper chasm than they realize. Slaves ain't ever going to understand white man's law or our behavior. Former slaves are going to learn that the smiling, well-dressed white man with a stack of papers is every bit as dangerous as the overseer with a whip in his hand."

"What about the ones who beat their slaves bloody every day?"

"They're just small angry men with wide streaks of mean who enjoy inflicting pain. For them, erasing the line between free and slave won't mean a thing. Sooner or later they'll get themselves killed. Maybe by Negroes, maybe by whites. Maybe they'll move West where angry men can find enough space to live without infuriating the people around them. Mostly, I don't know how blacks will ever be able to forgive us for how we've treated them. I wish I knew how they did it up North. Maybe they can teach us. I really don't know."

"I think we're going to pay a heavy price for this war," George Chapman concluded.

"You don't think we've already paid a heavy price? Don't you think that farmer who got burnt out paid a heavy price? How about that little girl in Richmond? What about all those people in Richmond whose homes and businesses got burnt up by Jeff Davis. Men like Uncle George should have figured out a bloodless way to end slavery, instead, of choosing this God-forsaken war."

"Are we stealing this gold or protecting it?" George Chapman asked.

"I don't know George. I trust Poppa and he feels like this is important. Plus, Uncle George is the damn Secretary of the Treasury and responsible for the gold. I don't know what they have planned, but I know Pa would never steal anything just for himself."

"You think we're going to get hanged for this?"

Thomas Henry laughed again. "We're far more likely to get shot over this gold than hanged, if that's any comfort."

"Not really. I don't think we've done that much wrong. Neither of us believe in slavery."

"George, we don't have a lot of high ground to stand on. The Yankees don't care that Mamma and Poppa don't own slaves or that you and I have reservations. The only thing that matters are the choices made. We chose sedition and we fought. That's all history will write. No history book chapters chronicle good intentions or honest remorse. Our acquiescence makes us just as responsible as old Jeff Davis himself. And, believe me, it makes me sad to say."

"Makes me sad to hear."

"Well, get some rest. You're givin' me a headache."

It was a warm sunny day and the boys slept well in the deep grass with the comforting trickling of a nearby creek. Thomas Henry awoke earlier than the others and quietly watched the dragonflies swarming the wildflowers. The others were awakened by a refreshing late afternoon sun shower. Stripped to their waists they enjoyed the cool rainwater rolling down their faces and bodies. Thomas Henry could not remember the last time his hair had not been matted to his head.

Thomas Henry passed out some left-over honey biscuits while the cousins re-loaded and hitched up the ambulance. The cloudburst had pooled in the wagon ruts and clogged the cart path with ankle deep mud. For several hours, the horses trudged through the mud with their heads down and nostrils flaring. Thomas Henry and George Chapman sat up front with a lantern while Billy and Troutman tried to sleep in the back on a filthy quilt that smelled of rotten plums and perspiration. Sleeping over a million dollars' worth of salvaged gold bars did not make them any more comfortable.

The moon was at its zenith when a rider approached the ambulance from the rear. Thomas Henry calmly turned up his lamp while listening carefully for other riders as the traveler pulled up alongside the ambulance. The horse was cavalry and far too fine for the raggedy Negro rider in dirty canvas pants. There was no conceivable lawful explanation for this muggins' ownership of such a fine beast, but Thomas Henry figured it was not any of his business.

He was of medium height and had broad shoulders. He was slim but all tense sinew. He sat casually in the saddle with an easy smile and large white teeth that shown brightly in the light of the lamp. He wore a pointed goatee that lengthened his face. His pale blue eyes suggested a Caribbean ancestry, but they were not engaging. His gaze was distant and revealed nothing of his intentions. A shotgun rested across the horn of his saddle.

"What you boys doin' driven this ambulance in the middle of the night? The name's Carson Wolf. A pleasure to meet ya'll."

Thomas Henry and George Chapman were both wearing non-descript gray work shirts, but their naval blue pants with red stripes down the outside of each leg could be easily seen. Both Thomas Henry and George Chapman wore navy-issued revolvers on each hip and a saber laid on the floorboards. The smile never left Carson's lips as he carefully looked over the boys and wondered who else might be in the back of the ambulance. Carson made the instantaneous and accurate calculations of a larcenous heart regarding the risk versus benefits presented by this military ambulance travelling alone on a dark road.

"My name's Thomas and this here's George. We're cadets from the Confederate States Naval Academy on the *Patrick Henry*, recently sunk in the James River. Our commander, Lt. Parker, and the remainder of our squadron evacuated to Danville. We're responsible for bringing our naval records and supplies from our quarters on Drewry's Bluff. We broke down and the rest of our unit moved on."

"From Richmond then, huh."

"Yeah, from Richmond. We're travelling at night to make up some lost ground."

"Good thing. Richmond's just a pile of soot and ashes. Anything still standing is being used by the Yankees to make themselves comfortable. If you see Jeff Davis, be sure to tell him that a Yankee general is livin' in his Gray House. I hear tell that his high-toned quadroon, Varina, is keeping his old bed warm with that new Yankee general."

Carson laughed out loud at his own sick imagination.

"I think you're mistaken, sir. Ms. Varina left Richmond near on a week before President Davis."

"Ain't my President, boys. In case you haven't heard, there's a new sheriff in town goin' by the name of Massa Lincoln."

"Well, Carson, Mr. Lincoln ain't out here on the road with us tonight, so I imagine we're going to do whatever we please. And tonight, what we please is to continue down this road towards Danville. You got any problem with that plan?"

Carson strummed his fingers over the stock of his shot gun and redid his mental calculations. Thomas Henry and George Chapman were also fingering their revolver handles while Carson completed his cipherin'.

The horses looked better than most and these boys were almost certainly lyin' about what was in the back of that ambulance. Rifles probably, and Carson did not have much use for them. That market was flooded. The boys were young but military trained. They looked to be well armed and there were likely more in the back waitin' to jump him. What gave Carson greater pause was that the boy he had been talking to did not seem rattled at all. It was not the faux confidence of assumed racial superiority that Carson had encountered many times. It was the confidence of someone who had killed before and would not hesitate to kill again.

Whatever it was, it tilted the treacherous algebra of anticipated armed robbery. The ambulance and the horses would be a nice prize even if the back of the wagon was empty. However, all things considered, it was best to leave these boys alone.

"I ain't got no problem with that plan at all. In fact, I'd endorse it mightily. I suspect them Yankees will be moving down this road tomorrow. If it ain't bluebellies, it'll be some ugly-ass band of Confederate deserters or outlaws wantin' to get theirs. Rumor along the road is that a lot of real money made it out of Richmond just before the place burnt to a crisp. There are some hard men huntin' up and down this road for that hard currency."

"Well, we ain't carrying nothin' but a little Confederate paper."

"That's too bad. Confederate dollars ain't good for nothin' except tinderin' your campfire. Still, you don't want to be waylaid by either the Yankees or those highwaymen. I picked my way around a rough looking group about twenty miles back. They're not men who'd be interested in a civil conversation like we havin' now."

"Thanks for the heads up. We'll be careful to stay ahead of them boys. Any idea how fast they're movin'."

"Not sure. They stop and fan out into the woods to beat the bushes for wagons a lot like this'un. Even with those diversions, they're still likely to catch ya if you dawdle."

"Like I said, mister, we appreciate the heads up. Why ain't you circlin' back toward Richmond where the Yankees can set you free?"

"Ain't that obvious boys? I'm already free." With that, Carson threw his head back, cackled like a madman, dug his boots into the horse's sides, and disappeared into the darkness.

George Chapman looked at Thomas Henry and asked, "What did he want with us?"

"He wanted to kill us, George."

"For the gold?"

"Probably not."

Billy stuck his head out from behind a canvas flap separating the drivers from the back of the ambulance. "What the hell, Thomas. We're trying to get some shut eye back here. Did Lincoln issue another proclamation that you have to hit every rock and pothole in the road?"

"Sorry, Billy. I'll try to get the nags to roll us a bit smoother. Go back to sleep and we'll switch off in a couple of hours."

Carson's news was not unexpected. Thomas Henry knew they could not afford any more stops if they wanted to stay ahead of whatever was coming up from behind. Thomas Henry informed the others about his intention to push for Danville. "Keep your weapons close by. We won't be able to bluff our way past the next encounter."

Thomas Henry doused the lamp and cracked the reins above the horses' backs. With weary and irritated first steps they lifted their hooves from the mucky road with an audible popping sound of broken suction. The ambulance lurched forward thumping over road stones and pitching left and right from mudhole to mudhole. Thomas Henry heard a clear, "Jesus Christ" from the back.

The dark railroad track unspooled ahead of the awkward slow-moving ambulance illuminated only by bright moonbeams. Thomas Henry prayed that the night would not get any bumpier.

Chapter 26

April 9, 1865

Palm Sunday

The remainder of the slough back to Danville was without incident and they arrived mid-morning the following day. Their bivouac was remarkably empty. The regular army soldiers assigned to Presidential protection had been selected for their loyalty. In the face of a disintegrating Confederacy, however, those fidelities were splintering. Some men shamefully slipped away in the middle of the night while others denounced Jefferson Davis to their officers' face. Discarded uniform tunics at the edges of trampled fields and at the sides of rutted roads were the enlisted men's last comment on the war.

Thomas Henry reported their successful return to Secretary Trenholm. In turn, Trenholm arranged for all the cousins to receive warm baths and a dinner prepared by Trenholm's own cook. Secretary Trenholm was confident in Thomas Henry's leadership of his small squad, but still reminded them of the need for absolute secrecy. Over brandy, they reviewed the plans for the next several days.

On Palm Sunday morning, Thomas Henry and George Chapman decided to go hear President Davis speak at church. At dinner, the night before, Uncle George explained that the C.S.A. Cabinet had known for months that the end was coming. Their desire was to surrender with dignity rather than be mauled like the loser in a cockfight.

Negotiations regarding surrender were consistently frustrated by the single issue on which President Davis would not compromise. Uncle George believed that Davis' noble-sounding insistence on Southern independence was motivated by his fear of culpability. The Union could not hang the leader of another independent country.

Davis' Palm Sunday sermon was going to be fascinating. The President of what everyone now realized was a make-believe country would opine on a future which everyone knew stood no chance of being realized. Thomas Henry likened President Davis' face to that of a predatory raptor. A hawk-like nose, eyes sharp and menacing, his face narrow with sweptback hair as if in flight, constantly searching the ground for snakes or field mice. Early in the war, Davis had moved with the grace of an accomplished rider and carried himself with a formal military bearing. Thomas Henry had never viewed President Davis as inspiring, possibly a little frightening, but today in Danville, it was the first time he had ever appeared pathetic.

Thin to the point of gauntness, Thomas Henry noticed that Davis wore stacked riding boots making him appear taller than he really was. Thomas Henry could not fathom how he had pledged his loyalty to a man so preening and lacking in confidence that he wore elevated riding boots. Seated on the church dais, President Jefferson's cheeks were hollow, and his skin yellowed to the color of old ivory. President Davis sat sideways in his seat, presenting himself in profile to hide his milky useless eye. This morning, even his good eye had a distant and disinterested cast.

Uncle George described President Davis as humor-less, bloodless, and hard to reach on a personal level. He was disengaged unless the topic involved matters of politics which stirred him with ambitious zeal. Even from the rear of the nave, Thomas Henry could tell that zeal had not traveled with the President to Danville. Sitting beside the reverend, the brooding Davis must have finally recognized the futility of continued belligerence.

The days of amassing huge personal fortunes on the backs of slaves were gone and would not be coming back. Did he now understand that his wealthy land-owning and slave-holding friends could no longer protect him? History was rife with ill-fated leaders who failed to realize that their power had slipped away until the barbarians were already at the gate. Davis had to recognize that the sound in the darkness was the circling and snarling of hungry wolves. Both brothers wondered if they might be about to hear President Davis officially surrender and bring the war to an end. Uncle George had also told Thomas Henry that nothing brought Jeff Davis to life more than the opportunity to orate. An excited restlessness gripped the congregation. The old goat did not disappoint, but he surely surprised.

It was a fire and brimstone service that would have made the most fervent Pentecostal blush. Any notion of capitulation was quickly dismissed. President Davis' Palm Sunday sermon was a rallying cry for the true believers, if such persons still breathed. He exhorted the flock in the righteousness of the cause and the continued possibility of victory as we "entered upon a new phase of a struggle." President Davis explained that the prospects for the Confederacy had been enhanced by being "relieved from the necessity of guarding cities and particular points, important but not vital to our defense, with an army free to move from point to point. Nothing is now needed to render our triumph certain but the exhibition of our own unquenchable resolve. Let us will it, and we are free."

The thunderous applause seemed awkwardly out of place in church. For just a moment, Davis' cloudy eye cleared, and he appeared even taller than his one-and-a-half-inch heels allowed. Thomas Henry stared incomprehensively at the cheering crowd. Were the congregants as self-delusional as President Davis or was this a final show of respect to a flawed, but good man, who would soon suffer an ugly fate? Did Jeff Davis even believe in his own sanguinity for the cause or was this a calculated rear-guard action of self-preservation essential to a government on the run?

Certainly, the turning of lemons into lemonade was a sermon all the congregants had heard before. Thomas Henry and George Chapman could not believe that the fine folk of Danville would once again allow their anger and pride to be rallied into censorship of their own good sense. Even Jeff Davis' God-fearing optimism could not restore the sweet smell of magnolia blossoms to a beaten South.

Had they not seen the army? Tired, hungry, and reduced by unsustainable losses and desertions. Traumatized soldiers either sitting quietly at the edge of the woods demoralized to apathy or wandering aimlessly waiting for capture by advancing Union cavalry. Had they not seen the burning wagons and bloated carcasses of dead mules and horses strewn along the road to Richmond? Everything of value between Richmond and Danville stripped clean, burnt out, or stolen. If there was still pride in the cause, the only explanation must be that pride was all people had left. Thomas Henry found it unconscionable that Davis would try to take the people of Danville down that primrose path once again. It had been madness that started the war, and now madness again to not let it end. Doing it inside a church only made it a greater sin.

After services, the parishioners gathered in small groups for conversation in the courtyard under red buds blooming pink and reverent dogwoods blooming white. Animated excitement over President Davis' speech was soon overtaken by a spreading grease fire of breathless rumor. Robert E. Lee had surrendered to the Union General U.S. Grant at the Appomattox Court House. There was no more army to move freely from place to place. The war was over with more than 600,000 dead, a million maimed, and the

South devastated. Fear had finally, and completely, conquered fervor.

In the wake of Lee's surrender, President Davis decided to evacuate farther south to Charlotte, North Carolina. George Trenholm informed President Davis that he was unwell and would no longer be able to carry out his duties as Secretary of the Treasury. Trenholm told Davis that he would continue south in an ambulance with his wife and a few family friends who could provide him safety. If better, he would meet up again with the President in Charlotte.

Since the night of the Richmond evacuation, Trenholm had been intermittently incapacitated by numbness and tingling in his arms and legs along with lower abdominal pain, diarrhea, and vomiting. The Presidential surgeon diagnosed miasma and dysentery and advised President Davis that it might be wise for Trenholm to travel separately. Sometimes dysentery chooses a single victim, other times it spreads quickly. An outbreak of dysentery could compromise the entire Cabinet's evacuation.

President Davis' inclination was to resist anyone leaving the presidential entourage, but in this case he acquiesced. His procession was growing smaller by the day. Davis understood the reason why. No one wanted to be running in the company of the most wanted fugitive in North America. The Confederate Secretary of War, John Breckenridge, and the Secretary of State, Judah Benjamin, had already fled. Secretary of the Treasury Trenholm, was now striking out on his own. President Davis sensed abandonment and he was right.

On the morning of April 10th, George and Anna Helen loaded themselves and some supplies onto the military ambulance along with Thomas Henry and George Chapman Holmes and cousins, Billy O'Dell and Troutman Legare. They were accompanied by Trenholm's personal aide, an imposing freedman named Hampton Riley and his assigned military attaché Lt. Alexander MacBeth. Hampton Riley and

Lt. MacBeth would be the outriders and lookouts for the ambulance.

Anna Helen made sure that the ambulance was loaded with enough food for the journey as well as clean linens, pillows, and patchwork quilts. Riley and Lt. MacBeth added several more rifles and handguns to the back of the ambulance along with the last cask of Anna Helen's peach brandy.

Remarkably, once aboard the military ambulance, George's neurological and gastrointestinal symptoms began to abate. His improvement corresponded with Anna Helen throwing out the tincture of Southern blue monkshood she had gathered in the western Virginia mountains. By the time they reached Greensboro, North Carolina, George Trenholm was again a man in full.

Chapter 27

April 15, 1865

Secret Service

Western North Carolina and Charlotte had been spared much of the war's maelstrom. The trip was uneventful, almost pleasant. The roads were nearly empty and eerily quiet. Spring songbirds had collectively decided to remain silent in protest of the disappearance of the antebellum South.

The roads were in generally good condition, and, on most days, the ambulance covered thirty to forty miles with an early start. On many late afternoons, the clouds walled up, taking on a scornful gray-black coloration before bursting and then dispersing. The brief sun showers freshened and cooled the air. The sunsets following the thundershowers colored the sky with a magnificent palette. By morning, the roads were again firm and dry.

Shortly after leaving Danville, Hampton Riley and Lt. MacBeth found and confiscated a second abandoned wagon. Two of the horses were hitched to the new wagon and Billy and Troutman loaded it with supplies, bedding and hay. The shabby Gypsy caravan rolled south with only an occasional Confederate soldier seen walking or riding in silence, stoically bearing the weight of personal tragedy and the shame of failure. If any of them recognized Mr. Trenholm it was unspoken or only acknowledged by a nod of the head.

Because of General Grant's generous terms, most of the former Confederate soldiers were still armed which brought an odd order to this final retreat. The former soldiers had already seen too much brutality and would not tolerate any more. Trenholm assumed a Federal warrant had been issued for his capture. The charge would be treason and possibly written "dead or alive." Secretary Trenholm, however, was confident that the Federals would want the financier of the Confederacy alive. Regardless, the reward would be substantial. Trenholm wisely spent the day out of sight in the back of the ambulance.

Occasionally, small groups of war-hardened men riding with more purpose passed by with saddlebags heavy with booty. They lacked the shame of the individual troopers trudging their way home. These C.S.A. veterans had made the quick career transition to highwaymen or bounty hunters. Slouch hats were pulled low to cover their eyes, revealing only set jaws, stubbled chins, and unkempt hair. They had thrown away their Confederate tunics in favor of simple cotton shirts with necks banded by a combination of sweat, skin oil and road dirt. Muddy boots dug into the sides of their over-galloped horses who had belonged to someone else in the recent past. Canvas dusters covered rifles and revolvers and the stench of booze, body odor and frothy horse sweat enveloped them. They studied the wheel ruts for any hint as to the contents of the ambulance and wagon, they sniffed for the presence of women and they appraised the danger presented by boys in red-striped naval pants. Thomas Henry and George Chapman stared right back at the highwaymen and pointedly exposed the shot guns on their laps. The riders were looking for easy pickings. The boys made it clear they would not be easily intimidated.

If the riders lingered too long, Lt. MacBeth and Hampton Riley would drift back toward the wagons opening their coats to reveal revolvers and sheathed rifles. Only a blind man would not recognize Hampton Riley's murderous capability. So far, each encounter had ended with the highwaymen choosing to ride on.

Each evening the caravan would find a spot off the road to camp. Mrs. Trenholm supervised the evening meal which was the highlight of each day. There was not much variety, but Anna Helen made each camp meal seem like a dinner party. They dined by lantern light on slices of sizzling salty ham with buttered biscuits, boiled potatoes, and seasoned field greens mixed with cider vinegar. On most evenings, Secretary Trenholm shared his collection of fine cigars and the travelers forgot their status as hunted fugitives and thieves. Secretary Trenholm seemed most contented of all which was surprising considering the substantial bounty he carried on his head.

The next morning was another brilliant April day with early morning ground fog giving up to mid-morning warmth. Billowy white clouds blew around the sky on a comforting breeze. The aroma of wildflowers rising from the roadside, the magnificent display of blooming dogwoods, the leafing and budding of oak and poplar trees made an argument for a future possibly better than anticipated. Their arrival in Charlotte disabused them of any of those notions.

In Charlotte, the news of Lee's surrender had been digested down to its elemental components of anger, vulnerability, and desperation. Grant was certainly bearing down from the North, but the greater fear was Sherman moving Northwest from Columbia. Stories of what Sherman had done to Atlanta and Columbia grew in fearsomeness with each retelling. The army had disbanded, and Charlotte lacked any civic leaders. There was no up-side to taking charge or having any association with the color gray. The strategy of every man for himself had descended simultaneously on the entire population of Charlotte.

George Trenholm was quickly recognized as the small wagon train rolled through the city. Groups of people gathered along the street to curse the Secretary and vent their rage. Jefferson Davis was the primary target of the crowd's wrath. However, he was not with this small caravan and George Trenholm would make a fine substitute. Another of the many rich, slave-holding bastards responsible for the deaths of friends, family, and the ruination of their lives.

They demanded that Trenholm, as Secretary of the Confederate Treasury, reimburse them for lost personal fortunes. Lt. MacBeth forcefully announced to the gathering crowd that the Confederate Treasury was being carried by train for safekeeping and would be deposited into the banks of remaining unconquered Southern states. Trenholm stood in the driver's box of the ambulance and used his considerable charm and oratory skills to convince the crowd that, sadly, he had no ability to serve as a roadside bursar exchanging Confederate bonds and paper for specie. They all understood that if Secretary Trenholm was not believed, and the gold hidden beneath his feet discovered, they would be torn apart. Finally, the crowd broke up and allowed them to pass.

The mood of the city darkened further when telegraph reports arrived announcing that President Lincoln had been assassinated the night before at Ford's Theater. By afternoon, word arrived that Lincoln had died. General Grant proclaimed that the treacherous Southerners responsible would pay with their lives. Neither sorrow nor rejoicing accompanied the news of Lincoln's murder. The only emotion was the numbing realization that any hoped-for rapprochement or leniency for the rebellious Southern states had also died in that box above the stage at Ford's Theater. Northerners who championed retaliation would now be recalibrating the profundity of their vengeance. Secretary Trenholm took the news hard.

"Fools. Such a waste. Assassinating President Lincoln will prove to be the South's greatest blunder."

Without saying anything to his traveling companions, Trenholm also considered that whoever killed President

Lincoln could potentially be a Confederate agent in Secret Service employ. He prayed for himself, his family, and the others in his company that there were no C.S.A. Treasury Department promissory notes carrying his signature in the assassin's coat pocket. Even if not, the intensity of his pursuit would now be redoubled. Secretary Trenholm retired to the back of the ambulance for several hours.

Fearing retribution as possible collaborators when either Sherman or Grant arrived, several hotels and even some former friends turned away Secretary Trenholm and his family. Eventually, Confederate Major General John Echols found accommodations for George and Anna Helen with William F. Phifer and his wife on North Tryon Street. That night, Trenholm declined an offer to meet with President Davis, and the remaining Cabinet, again citing ill-health. He instructed Lt. MacBeth and Thomas Henry to have the wagons ready at dawn.

"We need to get out of Charlotte before the Yankees arrive. The treasure train has already been off-loaded into the Charlotte mint. Sooner or later, someone is going to investigate the remaining boxes and wonder what has become of the gold bullion. We don't want to be here when people start looking for missing gold."

"Yes, sir, Mr. Secretary," Lt. MacBeth replied. "If it's going to get uglier than it already is, then I'd prefer not to see it."

"From your lips to God's ears."

"Do you think there is a place where the Yankees won't find us?"

"I wish there were, but there isn't. They'll catch up with us sooner or later. I'm confident of that."

"Then where should we go, sir?"

"When there is no place left to run, the only place to go is to go home."

"Back to Charleston, Mr. Secretary?"

"No, home to Abbeville."

Chapter 28

May 2, 1865

Purloo

The road from Charlotte to Abbeville was a dramatic change in scenery. The caravan was now traveling along the ragged edge of Sherman's foul will. The corn and cotton fields had been reduced to scorched stems and stalks. William Tecumseh Sherman had correctly surmised that it was far easier to wage war on unarmed farmers and defenseless crops than to engage hostile armies. Sherman's black hand had meandered its way across central South Carolina leaving behind a wide path of ruination.

Sherman's cavalry seized anything they could eat, anything their horses or mules could eat, anything of value they could carry and left everything else in flames. His men rode as high and wide as necessary to find new farms and towns to plunder. They took crops from the fields, fruit from the trees, hay from the barns, and corn from the cribs. They looted beans, onions, turnips, potatoes, cucumbers, and tomatoes from basements and root cellars. They took beef cows, milk cows, mules, goats, chickens, women, and girls. They slaughtered fat hogs in front yards, feasting in front of famished farm families. One room shacks and enormous plantation houses alike were ransacked for cash, jewelry, silverware, liquor, and family heirlooms before being put to the torch.

Trenholm and his party travelled south in stunned silence. Blackened foundations and tumbledown chimneys marked where families had once lived. Not a single chicken poked around an empty yard. Feral, half-mad coonhounds with exposed ribs skulked away sideways, eyeing the horses hungrily from the edge of the pinewoods. South Carolina had been turned into a wasteland of cindered dirt stained with innocent blood.

The caravan passed refugees with blank expressions. Elderly men and prematurely ruined women walked in muted silence without a horse or mule among them. Small push carts were loaded with cookware, quilts, and the occasional younger man. Children marched along dragging a reluctant shoat by a rope. They appeared dumbstruck, not yet understanding that they would never go to school, play with a friend, or have a childhood. Some groups were mixed, both white and black. Societal rules of master and slave no longer applied. The South's initial experience with a post-slavery existence were these directionless and hopeless bands of refugees.

Thomas Henry figured the white families had been burned out and were moving toward family who had hopefully been luckier. They had learned the hard lesson that Judeo-Christian charity was an illusion and only family relationships offered reprieve amid true anarchy. Thomas Henry also wondered about the groups of former slaves. Lincoln had granted them freedom, but they had no idea of what that meant. They were now free to find their own way, but without any maps, money, weapons, or understanding as to how things worked. They wandered the roads between Charlotte and Abbeville in search of a red-haired Union general they assumed would answer all their questions.

Thomas Henry shook his head and whistled. "I sure hope them blacks don't find what they're looking for."

"What they lookin' for?" George Chapman asked.

"They're seachin' for General Sherman, but he ain't slowin' down one whit for them. He will pluck them like a chicken and leave'm in his dust. I hear Sherman detests the blacks even more than Jeff Davis."

"Out of the frying pan and into the fire I guess."

"Maybe so."

Secretary Trenholm estimated that the caravan was about another day and a half from Abbeville. The party stopped for an afternoon shower that passed through from the west. Hampton Riley found a comfortable camp site about one hundred yards off the road. Anna Helen prepared a delicious purloo out of rice, onions, collard greens and ham. She also grilled some salt and peppered mushrooms that Hampton had spotted clustered at the base of a tree.

The purloo and mushrooms were delicious and most had a second helping. A full belly and an after-dinner cup of peach brandy caused George Chapman to drift while on watch. He never heard the horses on the roadway or the cracked twigs in the woods. It was a lethal mistake.

Thomas Henry awoke to the presence of five armed men well-spaced around the campsite. George Chapman had a knife to his throat. The black man they had encountered alongside the Richmond-Danville railroad line who called himself Carson Wolf stood the closest leveling a shotgun at George Trenholm. His new partners were scavengers who had deserted from Sherman's army. Carson Wolf had the same lean and hungry look as before, but the Yankees were unmistakably remorseless killers.

"Good to see ya'll again," Carson said with a shit-eating grin. "Glad you made it safely down the road." No one mistook his pleasant demeanor as reassuring.

Hampton Riley had already slid his hand down to the knife handle rising from his boot. He had hidden a shotgun behind the buckboard of the ambulance and began to ease toward it.

One of the Yankees with an unkempt black beard festooned with red ribbons, cocked his rifle and spoke from the edge of the campfire light. "I'd advise your big man to stay where he is. There don't need to be bloodshed here." Nothing suggested his statement would prove correct.

George Trenholm spoke next. "Stand down, Hampton. Mister, you could also take things down a notch by removing that knife from my nephew's neck."

"Okay, sir. Good to know who's in charge." The man with the black beard nodded toward a tall, gangly, and greasy man holding a knife at George Chapman's throat. He sat George down roughly, sheathed his knife and drew his pistol.

"How is that, sir? Little more of a tea-party now. May I ask your name?"

"It's George. What may I ask is yours?"

"Well, that ain't nothing you need worry about. We want to take a little look at what you got inside those wagons. Ya'll just stay settled while we poke around a bit. Ain't no need for anyone to get hurt."

The man with the black beard smiled, putting on a mask he hoped would be reassuring. George Trenholm smiled back. Despite George's privileged life, he was not naïve to the fact that these men would take what they wanted and then kill them for the cold-blooded fun of it. That was even more certain if they found the gold which they surely would.

Trenholm glanced briefly at Hampton Riley. The look on Hampton's face indicated he understood the same set of facts. George trusted that Lt. MacBeth was arming himself quietly in the back of the ambulance and that Anna Helen already had her derringer in hand. Billy and Troutman had bedded down under the supply wagon and were now sitting cross-legged in front of a squat, barrel-chested Yankee with thick muttonchops and a military-issued revolver.

The other Yankee was a tall, skeletal man with pale, almost translucent skin. His eyes were sunken, moist, and red-rimmed. He had a long sad face and a thin scraggly beard that called Don Quixote to mind. He wore a heavy wool blanket over his shoulders inappropriate to the relatively warm and humid night. He carried a shotgun tied with a rope at both ends and slung around his neck. He stood closest to the campfire. The awkward silence was broken by the sound of the gaunt Don Quixote coughing into a handkerchief stained red with lung blood.

George Trenholm jumped on the opportunity to prolong the conversation and seek advantage. "You know we've got some medicine in the ambulance that could help your man. Dover's opium powder is good for bad coughs. We'd be happy to share with you."

The black-bearded Yankee laughed. "I'm sure you would. While that is mighty neighborly, I'm afraid there might be something else in the back of that ambulance which ain't as healthful as a tincture of opium. Best we check out that ambulance ourselves."

"I wouldn't do that if I were you. My wife's tending to a couple of young boys with the smallpox. Good news is that they are doing better, but they've still got plenty of scabs running down their backs, shins and calves. If any of you boys ain't had the pox, then it's about fifty-fifty on whether it'll kill you. The lunger won't make it for sure."

The possibility of smallpox created the expected pause. Black beard studied George to determine whether he was telling him the truth.

"The past few years we've damn sure seen a lot worse than the pox. We'll take our chances if it's all the same to you. We're anxious to meet that wife of yours. Her purloo smells delicious," black beard said with a lascivious grin. Carson Wolf also smiled lecherously, and the others laughed.

"Sir, your prurient suggestions are not welcome. We are more than willing to be hospitable to fellow travelers, but any indecent intent will be vigorously resisted. Nor will you find my wife to be a willing companion," George replied while stepping forward toward black beard.

The bearded deserter raised his rifle and aimed it at Secretary Trenholm. "Step back, old man. To be honest with you, I don't think my boys and I are really concerned with that willing companion part."

As if on cue, the consumptive Yankee leaned into the fire and coughed again, spewing blood between his fingers into the flames. Sweat and tears gathered around his eyes as he bent forward coughing again with his hands on his knees. His shot gun now hung freely around his neck. George looked quickly from Hampton to Thomas Henry to wordlessly ask if this might be the moment.

George Trenholm's silent interrogation was interrupted.

George Chapman screamed as the Yankee behind him grabbed his hair and regurgitated bright red blood all over him. There was a gurgling in the Yankee's throat as he toppled over George Chapman with a large Bowie knife buried to its hilt in his upper back.

All heads turned as a tall man emerged from the shadows behind the fallen Yankee. Captain Jack calmly leaned over and removed the twelve-inch pig-sticker from the Yankee's back and wiped the blade on the man's tunic. The Yankee with the black beard shouted something inaudible as gunpowder silvered the air from a hail of rifle fire. Carson Wolf took a bullet to the forehead and crumpled where he stood with the same stupid grin plastered on his face. The barrel-chested Yankee standing beside Billy and Troutman took a mini ball to the neck and went to his knees, hands attempting to cover his wound. His efforts were futile as blood geysered between his fingers. He was finished by

Lt. MacBeth who exited the back of the wagon with flame flashing from revolvers in both hands.

The Yankee with the black beard caught a bullet in the shoulder as he attempted to raise his rifle toward Captain Jack. The bullet spun him around and up against a pine tree. He got off one poorly aimed shot using his only good arm that flew harmlessly into the trees. An effort to draw his pistol was interrupted by the knife thrown from Hampton Riley's boot that found the soft spot in his throat just above his breastbone. The Yankee stood there with the confused look of a man who could not understand what had gone so wrong, so fast. He looked down at the knife handle in his throat as his festooned black beard filled with blood. His befuddlement was ended by a rifle shot to center chest.

The consumptive Yankee, captured by a paroxysm of coughing, never even responded to the gunfire. Unarmed, Thomas Henry ran up behind him and shouldered him into the fire. In his thrashing, he accidentally pulled the trigger of the shotgun he'd fallen on top of. The gaunt lunger laid quietly in the fire after the blast took off the right side of his face and half of his skull.

Thomas Henry and George Chapman ran to their father who hugged them both. "Can't say I've ever been as happy to see you, Pa," George Chapman said.

"Happy to see you boys as well. Thought you might need a bit of help with these jacklegs."

By this point, Copper Joe, Caleb and Ezekiel emerged from the cover of the dark pines and joined them at the fire. Only Ezekiel had missed with his first shot. Anna Helen climbed down from the ambulance and gave her brother a relieved, long hug.

"Thank God, Jack. I've been looking for you for the last twenty-four hours," George Trenholm interjected.

"We've been following you for the last day and a half but decided to keep our distance. This scum started trailing you about mid-day today. Turns out they were just waiting for young George to fall asleep while on picket duty. We'll talk about that later."

In the darkness it was not possible to see the redness bloom on George Chapman's face. He offered no excuse. Thomas Henry came to his brother's rescue by changing the subject. "Poppa, how is the *Will O' the Wisp*?"

"Docked back home on the Abbapoola. I am looking forward to getting back to her. These damn horses are rubbing a sore spot on my butt-bone."

George Trenholm spoke next. "Let's bury this trash, get a few hours of sleep and try to make it to Abbeville tomorrow. Hampton, please take the first watch. George Chapman has had enough excitement for one night."

Everyone laughed, and George Chapman shook his head. It would be a long time before he'd be able to live this down.

"Anna, do we have any purloo left? It looks like Jack's men could use something to eat. Might also be nice to celebrate this reunion with a little peach brandy."

Anna Helen took Ezekiel's hand. "Come with me little man. Copper Joe, Caleb, happy to see you both again. Go down to the creek, wash up, and then come back up here for some supper."

"Sounds great Ma'am. I'd love some good purloo, but mostly I want to try that peach brandy. I've heard some prodigious stories."

"Joe, it'll have you dreaming about being back on the *Wisp*."

Chapter 29

May 23, 1865

Legareville

The killing of the five outlaws was not discussed again or regretted. The addition of Jack, Caleb, Ezekiel, and Copper Joe made the traveling party simultaneously more suspicious and intimidating. They took some hard looks from passing riders, but no one opted to stop and chat. Bandits and thieves have a finely developed sense of self-preservation.

In Abbeville they were reunited with Trenholm's daughters, Helen and Eliza, and midshipman James Morris Morgan who had accompanied them out of Richmond. Also awaiting them in Abbeville were Trenholm's son, William Lee, his wife, and his friend and business partner, Theodore Wagner.

Trenholm owned a fine large house on a two-acre wedge of land in the center of town. The two-story home was surrounded by a broad shady gallery, a breezy second floor piazza, and a burst of purple, white and pink azaleas at the base of the porch. Abbeville had somehow been spared Sherman's marauding cavalry. Faces on the street still flashed prideful anger rather than the ubiquitous despair they had seen in Charlotte. The men and women of Abbeville puffed up with indignation and defiance at any mention of approaching Union occupiers.

Unwilling to disclose their hidden gold, they resorted to a barter economy for sustenance. James Morris Morgan and Lt. MacBeth went on daily foraging excursions. Bolts of cotton cloth from the Graniteville Mill, partially owned by George Trenholm, along with horses and weapons taken from the Yankee highwaymen were traded to local farmers in exchange for food.

Jack convinced George that he and his men should continue onto Charleston with the stolen gold given the inevitable arrival of Union forces. Trenholm agreed. Trenholm also separated out a cache of twenty- dollar Liberty Head double eagle gold pieces and hid them in a large portmanteau.

The next night, Jack Holmes, his two sons, Copper Joe, Caleb, and Ezekiel left with the ambulance for the long trip to Charleston. Thomas Henry and George Chapman loaded the back of the ambulance with more bolts of cotton cloth from the Graniteville Mill. If stopped, they would claim to be traders delivering finished cloth to Charleston. Their backstory would not fool anyone but the dullest inquisitor. They did not look like merchants, they were armed like a death squad, they were pulling a military ambulance, and only had twelve bolts of cotton to trade. "Better we take the backroads and travel at night," Jack correctly surmised.

The first night they took an Indian path known to Copper Joe down to Aiken where they stopped and camped at the cool, freshwater Coker Springs. They melted in well with the large number of refugees, former slaves, cattle, and horses gathered around the brick and stucco springhouse. From Aiken, the group travelled south through Barnwell, Ehrhardt, Walterboro and then to Jacksonboro. The night travel, backroads and Indian trails were slow going and exhausting. They decided to rest for an extra day in Jacksonboro before crossing the Edisto River by ferry.

Jack feared that Union forces might have taken control of the ferry crossing point and decided to go down to the river to investigate. He was relieved to find only a single disinterested ferryman. The ferryman wore a tattered straw hat and the cotton pull-over of a farmer, but also the red-striped, gray pants of a Confederate regular army officer. He was unbowed despite a missing left arm and a wooden half-mask hooked over each ear that covered an absent lower jaw. He communicated with hand signals and unintelligible grunts. He waved off the offer of a note pad.

The ferryman communicated more elegantly with his chestnut mare who pulled the ferry rope. The mare responded to softer and gentler sounds and touches that bespoke their long friendship. Before his relegation to ferry duty, the horse had been a fine animal. The mare's coat, now thinning with signs of mange, no longer gleamed when hit by the sun. She had the same exposed ribs of every other animal south of Richmond. However, like her officer, she stood proudly refusing to acknowledge her diminished station. Her leather saddle was a frayed and scarred tapestry of every battle they had fought together.

After crossing, Jack gave the ferryman two twenty-dollar gold pieces. Jack spoke to him quietly away from the others and they embraced. It was probably the last time the ferryman would ever be treated as the man he was, instead of as the half-man he had become.

Once across the Edisto River, they turned northeast toward Charleston through inland farm country behind Edisto and Kiawah Islands. The muddy Lowcountry bottom-land and black-waters brought back bad memories of the Kiawah River. The only prying eyes were former slaves who watched from abandoned plantations and the dark edges of heavily wooded alligator swamps. They watched without understanding or particular interest as long as the white men moved on.

Mosquitoes were so thick that you killed two or three with each slap. George Chapman fell ill with febris. His energy ebbed, his face turned sallow, and dark circles raccooned his eyes. While the malarial mosquitoes were annoying, the slithering water moccasins and belching bull alligators were fearsome. Each evening, the sunken alligators kept watch on the ambulance, reflective eyes glowing just above the flat black waterlines. Their gaze was also without understanding, but with far more interest. A cooling breeze capable of rustling the dense Spanish moss draping the live oaks or riffling the still black water against the mango roots was a scarce as hen's teeth.

The ambulance finally reached some higher, drier ground in Rantowles where they again decided to rest before crossing the Stono River to John's Island. The Abbapoola was a tidal creek that emptied into the Stono River surrounded by dense forest and brackish marsh. However, as it approached the Stono, its water began to run fast and deep. Its name, Abbapoola, came from the Indian word for "running water." The *Will O' the Wisp* was hidden on a largely forgotten curve of Abbapoola Creek.

The small town of Legareville had stood on the point where Abbapoola Creek emptied into the Stono River. Legareville had been a summer retreat for the rich planters on John's and Edisto Islands who did not wish to travel to the North Carolina mountains for relief from the summer's sweltering heat. Legareville was known for its cooling cross breezes which blew off both the Stono River and the Abbapoola keeping the mosquitoes at bay. It was a small town of twenty to thirty homes arranged around a narrow curling lane lined by tall pine trees. There was a schoolhouse, two churches, and a small store. Homeowners represented Charleston's most prosperous families including the Walpoles, Whaleys, Legares, Ropers, Stevens, Tennants, Townsends and Fripps who stayed until the first frost. Its deep-water dock offered a fast and easy sail back and forth to Charleston.

Legareville had seen a smidgen of military action earlier in the war but was now razed and deserted. When Battery Wagner fell in September of 1863, Union forces swarmed over all the sea islands probing for weak spots that might be exploited in a coming attack on Charleston. Union gunboats patrolled the Stono River initiating skirmishes with rebel batteries on shore. Ultimately, the inhabitants of Legareville were forced to flee.

On Christmas morning 1863, Confederate artillery batteries and infantry tried to retake the town in a battle that made up for its lack of importance with its intensity. Most of the Confederates were local boys who had spent their childhoods fishing the creeks and hunting the woods around Legareville. At daybreak, Confederate batteries opened fire on two Union gunboats, the *USS Marblehead* and the *USS Pawnee*, who responded with their own large guns. For about an hour and a half the air crackled with sharp artillery exchange. The Confederate infantry was never able to advance on the town because of the inability to drive off the Union gunboats. Eventually, the rebels withdrew, ending the Battle of Legareville.

Subsequently, it became known that the homes and churches of Legareville were being cannibalized by Yankee troops. Their wood planks were being used to build Union camps on Folly and Morris Islands. The Yankees were also using the deep-water Legareville landing as an embarkation point for Union troops. In August 1864, Major John Jenkins and his Stono Scouts raided Legareville and burned it and the landing to the ground. Many of the Stono Scouts were burning their childhood homes, but that was better than watching their childhood memories be usurped by the damn Yankees.

By May 1865, Legareville had disappeared from the face of the earth and Union gunboats no longer patrolled either the Stono River or the Abbapoola. The Stono ferry was now manned by former slaves who had simply stepped into a void created by the disappearance of Southern authority. Rumors of free land for former slaves were rampant, but no one knew how to pursue that dream and feared the danger of inquiry. Many continued to work the same patch of dirt and only house they had ever known. Seizing the ferry was a bold move and the former slaves were suspicious and fearful of Jack and his heavily armed men. They had no idea what to charge or whether they might be killed for their effort on the other side of the river. The sin of human ownership had so perverted the relationship between black and white it seemed unlikely to ever be untwisted.

Arriving at the Abbapoola, Jack was relieved to find that the *Will O' the Wisp* undisturbed. She was tied to a sagging, weathered dock with decayed barnacle-covered posts and gray-white sun-bleached deck boards curling up at the ends against their rusted nails. It would take two days to clear away the debris they had used to conceal the *Wisp* and restore her seaworthiness. They had no time to waste. Eyes were on them and information about a ship like the *Wisp* was worth hard U.S. dollars to Union occupational authorities.

By the following evening, the Confederate gold had been loaded and the *Will O' the Wisp* prepared for sea. It was the smallest, but most valuable cargo the *Will O' the Wisp* had ever carried in its hold. It was actual treasure, and an entire nation was searching for it.

Caleb and Ezekiel talked to the men at the Stono ferry and were able to recruit a crew of former slaves receptive to the idea of escape and hard money payment. They selected men without families who had no reason to return. Believing more in good food than bad luck, Jack also recruited two mammies to serve as cooks and their children to work as galley hands.

With the arrival of a king tide, they floated the *Wisp* back out into the river. Captain Jack used his secret back door down the Kiawah River one last time. Once at sea, there was not a ship in the Atlantic that could catch the *Wisp* which would be flying without the added weight of tons of cotton. There was still a quarter moon, but it was obscured by clouds. Jack ordered Copper Joe to fire the boilers just as the distant clouds bloomed with spider-like lightening followed by faint rolling thunder.

Thomas Henry steered the *Wisp* on its familiar run down the Kiawah River while Captain Jack studied the nautical maps. He had never sailed to Saint-Domingo, but it didn't appear difficult. He reviewed maps of Saint-Domingo itself and the formal letter of introduction given him by George Trenholm. A second document provided precise directions to the Comte de Greffin plantation, the French ancestral home of George Trenholm's mother, Irene de Greffin.

As the *Will O' the Wisp* moved down river and through the slip between Kiawah and Seabrook Islands, Copper Joe and Ezekiel joined Captain Jack on deck to watch the Lowcountry pass behind them. They knew it might be years before they saw their home again, if ever.

Chapter 30

July 16, 1865

Susan Petigru King

George Trenholm held no illusion that his service to the Confederacy would just be forgotten. Friends suggested stealing away to the Florida coast and escaping to Cuba. George and Jack had a plan, however, and fleeing was not part of it. Chances would have to be taken.

The South Carolina military governorship would sooner or later get its wits about itself. Trenholm's business partner, Thomas Wagner, had already been threatened with a charge of treason by the Charleston provost marshal. Wagner avoided arrest by paying a $10,000 bribe. George assumed he would not be far behind and the price would be higher. George had no intention of wasting precious gold on greedy Federal administrators. Instead, he would rely on a lifetime of positive relationships with people both above and below the Mason-Dixon line.

Eventually, Trenholm was summoned to Charleston to answer Federal charges. George and James Morris Morgan, along with a portmanteau full of twenty-dollar gold pieces, traveled by train to Charleston. George asked James to check the portmanteau believing that he would be arrested, and possessions confiscated, immediately upon his arrival. As expected, George was met at the station by a company of Negro Union soldiers who marched him unceremoniously over the rough cobblestoned streets to the

Charleston city jail. When James Morgan tried to follow, he was struck in the stomach by a gun butt and fell into the street vomiting. George knelt beside his young protegee and stared at the private who had struck him. The private slinked away, unwilling to confront the imperious man glaring at him from the gutter.

"James, are you all right?"

"I'll be okay, Mr. Secretary. Just have to catch my wind."

"Don't get up," Trenholm whispered. "I'm going to be fine. The provost is going to offer me the opportunity to make reparations for my offenses."

"Are you planning to pay, sir?"

"Certainly not. The only thing more disgraceful than soliciting a bribe is paying one."

"Why am I not surprised, sir?"

"Once I inform them of my refusal to pay a single cent in exchange for my freedom, they'll arrest me. Find a room nearby. When things quiet down, take the portmanteau to Mrs. Susan Petigru King. She'll know how to make the best use of the money and the Provost won't deny any requests she makes to visit."

"What can I do for you, Mr. Secretary?"

"Just lay low. Can't have you getting arrested as well. Understand?"

"Yes sir, you be careful, sir."

George Trenholm was roughly pulled back to his feet and pushed on down the cobblestoned street. On his arrival at the city jail, Trenholm was ushered into a cell with filthy straw on the floor. Even the Negro guards found it incongruous for the elegant Trenholm to be standing in such a room. George Trenholm would make no complaint, nor compromise.

Susan Petigru King was one of many Charleston widows. She was the daughter of the recently departed James L. Petigru who had been the attorney for Trenholm's firm of

John Fraser and Company. James Petigru always said what he pleased and had been the last Union man in Charleston. He had staunchly opposed secession even during the hot-tempered pre-war days. While many in Charleston loathed Petigru, George had always held him in high regard for his earnestness, loyalty, and intellect. George also valued the many connections and friendships Petigru maintained with Northern leaders.

Petigru owned slaves but was opposed to the expansion of slavery into new territories. He fiercely litigated against the South Carolina Negro Seaman Law which allowed the incarceration of free black seamen from the North while their ships were in port. Petigru regularly invited U.S. Army officers stationed in Charleston to his home for dinner and brandy. Among his guests was a young officer from Ohio stationed at Fort Moultrie named William Tecumseh Sherman. Abraham Lincoln counted James L. Petigru among his few Southern friends.

James L. Petigru passed in 1863, and the same year his daughter, Susan Petigru King, was widowed by the war. Susan King turned to George Trenholm for help during the desperate final two years of the war. George's generosity supported her family and he managed her small estate. Before his assassination, Lincoln ordered the occupying force in Charleston to extend every courtesy to the remaining Petigru family.

The night after George Trenholm's arrest, Susan Petigru King hosted a dinner party inviting both the provost marshal and the commanding general. Also attending was James Morris Morgan whose vest, pants and coat pockets were stuffed with heavy coins. Spotting Morgan, Mrs. King excused herself and took James upstairs where they emptied his pockets. Mrs. King carefully laid out the gold double eagles between the mattresses of her widow's bed. She also charmed the commanding general into giving her a pass to visit the imprisoned Trenholm.

Flummoxed by what to do with the former Confederate Secretary of the Treasury who wouldn't pay for his freedom, the Union commander in Charleston wrote to his commanding officer for advice. The orders he received were to transfer Trenholm to Fort Pulaski, Georgia, via Hilton Head.

The Hilton Head garrison was under the command of the Union General Quincey Gillmore who had been close friends with Trenholm before the war. On his arrival in Hilton Head, General Gillmore dismissed Trenholm's guard and invited George and James Morgan to dinner at his cottage. Concerned over his friend's declining health and grateful for the kindness Trenholm had shown to Union prisoners during the war, General Gillmore granted Trenholm a parole and sent him home to Abbeville.

The military governor for South Carolina was infuriated and took his complaint directly to Secretary of War Edwin Stanton. General Gillmore was relieved of command and Trenholm re-apprehended with orders for immediate transfer to Fort Pulaski. At Fort Pulaski, Trenholm was reunited with most of the Confederate Cabinet save Secretary of State Benjamin and Secretary of War Breckenridge who had escaped to England.

During Trenholm's time at Fort Pulaski, Susan Petigru King orchestrated the outpouring of good will that he had counted on. Both she and her elderly mother wrote President Andrew Johnson begging mercy. They recounted how George Trenholm had provided them food, clothing, shelter, and protection in the wake of Judge Petigru's death- a generosity made even more remarkable by her father's known Unionist leanings. Prominent citizens and clergymen from Richmond to Charleston also wrote President Johnson pleading for his release. The letters touted his meteoric rise in business without the benefit of a formal education, his reputation for integrity, and history of kindness to those in need during the war, regardless of the color of their tunics.

Unstated, but understood by President Johnson, was the importance of men like Trenholm to bringing order out of the current chaos of Southern reconstruction.

President Johnson was a Southerner and had already offered amnesty and a return of non-human property to all former Confederates who pledged loyalty to the Constitution. The Tennessean argued that it was his duty to hasten Southern reconstruction for the benefit of the entire nation. Radical Republicans alleged that Johnson was simply taking care of his own and that the former Southern planter elite, the architects of secession, were reclaiming their land, homes, and status as a political force. Johnson was now under immense pressure from rabid abolitionists to resist any further Southern accommodations. Bending to the political backlash, President Johnson issued a second proclamation outlining amnesty exemptions. That proclamation clarified that any Southerner who owned more than $20,000 in taxable property and virtually all Confederate public officials would need to apply directly to him for a pardon.

The prisoners at Fort Pulaski were treated well. They had cots and blankets, but the prison was built over a tidal marsh which exposed them to heat, humidity, and the sour odors of low tide. The damp conditions aggravated Trenholm's neuralgia. Trenholm was interrogated at least weekly and the questions invariably focused on the missing Confederate gold. His story never wavered. Due to weak fiscal policies and the effectiveness of the Union blockade, the C.S.A. was essentially bankrupt at the time of Richmond's fall. Despite his earnestness and charm, the Union lawyers never believed a word of it.

George accepted his fate stoically and with dignity. His suffering was necessary so that other, less culpable, citizens of South Carolina might be dealt with more generously. The prison commander did not believe Trenholm either but respected his honor and unbending principle. He allowed Mrs. Trenholm to send articles of clothing and food that helped sustain both George and the other prisoners. Anna Helen wrote George regularly, keeping him updated, especially regarding plans for the upcoming wedding of his daughter, Helen, to her beau, James Morris Morgan. Anna Helen also confided that she had heard nothing regarding the whereabouts of Jack or his family. She feared for their well-being.

On October 11th, 1865, President Johnson authorized paroles for the former Confederate Secretary of the Treasury George A. Trenholm, former Vice-President Alexander H. Stephens, John H. Reagan, Charles Clark, and James Archibald Campbell. George was surprised. He had not requested a release but was grateful.

Chapter 31

November 22, 1865

Thanksgiving

George and Anna Helen returned to Charleston after his release from Fort Pulaski and took residence at 51 East Battery. Little money was available for repair and many homes south of Calhoun Street were uninhabitable. However, the small home at 51 East Battery had only been minimally damaged. It was offered to George Trenholm by the beneficent widow Susan Petigru King.

Most assumed there was little to be thankful for on this Thanksgiving Day. The Trenholm family home, Ashley Hall, had been commandeered. As a paroled former member of the Confederate cabinet, Trenholm was a man without rights or business opportunity. Once the wealthiest man in the South, George Trenholm was now officially bankrupt.

Thanksgiving arrived with a dreary gray sky and a cold drizzle. Slick brown mud swelled between the cobblestones of East Battery while weeds pushed their way between fractured sidewalks and cracked stucco walls. Still, thanks to Anna Helen's artistic sensibility, 51 East Battery radiated warmth and hospitality amidst a distressed lower peninsula. A large Magnolia tree dominated the front yard. Waxy brown leaves and woody cones studded with bright red seeds blew into small piles against a wrought-iron fence. Its oversized windows and window sashes were brightly illuminated. Anna Helen had decorated the porch with colorful Indian corn, pumpkins, winter squash and gourds.

George and Anna Helen were thrilled that their daughter, Helen, and James Morris Morgan, who had married on November 16th, were able to join them. Other close Trenholm family friends who added warmth to the occasion included Susan Petigru King, Christopher Memminger and their young Episcopal minister, A. Toomer Porter. There was a sense of optimism and joy in the house that was otherwise rare in Charleston in November of 1865.

Many of the men paroled from Fort Pulaski with Secretary Trenholm had significantly diminished. Former C.S.A. Vice President Stephens had wasted to almost ninety pounds and appeared as frail as a child with one foot on the other side. Postmaster General John Reagan looked feral with sunken eyes, hollow-cheeks, unkempt hair, and cracked, festered skin. Although thinner, Trenholm had been unbowed by his prison experience. The guests were moved by his personal resilience and unshakable confidence. Even among their closest friends, few appreciated how much strength George took from Anna Helen.

In the aftermath of the war, the Federal government was interested in more than just recovering the missing Confederate gold. The Federals pursued claims involving hundreds of millions of dollars in unpaid taxes on the goods run through the blockade by ships under the control of Fraser, Trenholm and Company. Arguing that his properties had been purchased with funds received from the sale of cotton and other contraband, the Federals impounded Ashley Hall, multiple outlying plantations totaling many thousands of acres, commercial warehouses, wharves, banks, printing presses, and hotels including the splendid Planter's Hotel on Queen Street.

Trenholm's bank accounts from South Carolina, to New York City, to London, Liverpool and Paris were opened, examined, and emptied of any wealth found by the

U.S. government. Trenholm spent many days testifying before one official board of inquiry or legal deposition after another. George incensed the Federal lawyers with his prideful arrogance. George sat for hours on end across the table from Union lawyers, hands on his knees staring at his inquisitors. He rarely spoke unless directly questioned. More infuriating than his muted impertinence, however, was the twinkle of mischievous amusement in his eyes.

George was entirely different across the Thanksgiving dinner table. He hosted a magnificent meal and regaled his guests with humorous stories from Fort Pulaski. Susan King was surprised by the continued presence of several slaves in the Trenholm home. Tall, well-dressed black men carried silver platters of puff pastry topped with minced shrimp, cucumber, and onion. The turkey had been shot by George himself and roasted by two black women. The same two women had prepared the Trenholm family mushroom and oyster dressing for more Thanksgivings than either of them could count. The same women also prepared a piping hot corn bread sweetened with molasses and topped with chopped pecans.

George sensed Susan's discomfort. "James, Samuel, Maddie and Rebecca are all now paid servants. They live here free of charge and remain only as long as it is their preference."

Mrs. King nodded approvingly. "That's wonderful, George. I lament that we were not more forward thinking five years ago. We could have saved ourselves such misery. I guess I'm surprised they wanted to stay."

"Anna Helen and I were pleased they did. I made it clear they were free to leave. They never questioned the money offered, but to be honest, I imagine they do not have a frame of reference. I will be sure to have a talk with James and Samuel about the fairness of our compensation. That will be a conversation I've never had before."

"Maddie and Rebecca too," Mrs. King corrected.

"Yes, James, Samuel, Maddie, and Rebecca," George corrected himself with an acknowledging smile and nod of his head.

"They also deserve a bonus for this cornbread," Christopher Memminger added licking his fingers hungrily.

After dinner, George, Christopher Memminger, George's new son-in-law, James Morris Morgan, and Reverend Porter retired to the study for brandy. George mentioned that he had just received word that the U.S. government had sent a Special Agent to London to supervise the prosecution of claims against both Confederate and Trenholm properties held by London and Liverpool banks. There was no invitation to contest the claims.

George smiled despite what must be crushing financial strain. "Don't they know I did the honorable thing and resigned my position in Fraser, Trenholm and Company when I became Secretary of the Treasury?"

Reverend Porter asked George what plans he had made to get himself back on his feet.

"Reverend, there's no need to waste your prayers on me. How to rebuild our city is what deserves our attention. I may be broke, but I have talents and I can accrue means. However, Charleston is spectacularly broken, and we must do something."

"But what can we do?" Christopher Memminger asked. "All you must do is look outside. The city is a shamble, the plantations are fallow, the boatyards empty, the lumberyard quiet and the streets filled with the helpless and hopeless."

"There is no denying our wretched state. However, I don't consider the South to be done. We still have rich soil, dense forests, inexhaustible reserves of iron and coal, and eight million emancipated people who need to work. Like James, Samuel, Maddie, and Rebecca, those eight million men, women and children share the common human desire for prosperity. If we can provide fair opportunities and establish mutual self-interest, then I have great faith in our future."

"George, God bless you, but we cannot save the entire South," Christopher Memminger responded.

"Absolutely, Christopher. We will start at home. Lowcountry soil will continue to produce a bounty of fruit, vegetables, rice, and our still treasured Sea Island cotton. The forests north and south of Charleston will provide not only timber, but also tar, pitch and turpentine. All these resources will need to find their way to Europe and South America. Charleston is still the finest harbor on the East coast. We must rebuild the railroads to Charleston and find new ships. Trade will once again flow through our city like a great river."

"Inspiring as always, George," Christopher Memminger quickly answered, "But maybe a bit naïve. Our natural resources may be the envy of the world, but we simply do not have the capital to get the coal from the ground, trees from the forest, cotton from the fields, build railroads or commission ships. Cotton made Charleston the richest city in the world, but Jefferson Davis squandered it all with his preference for conniption fits over reasoned judgment."

"Christopher, I know President Davis never listened to you, because he never listened to me. He bored us to tears with his intellectualizing about the Constitutional vagaries on property rights while allowing the evaporation of our accumulated national treasure. But history isn't going to blame Jefferson Davis alone." George sighed, wiped his upper lip with his forefinger and thumb and looked away at nothing before continuing.

"Collectively, we led the South into a war that was financially unsound, militarily negligent, and morally indefensible. We were too self-absorbed to pay our house slaves a dollar a day to serve us canapes and empty our chamber pots or to pay our field slaves a penny per pound to make us all wealthy beyond our wildest dreams. The responsibility now falls on us to make things right."

"Again, George, how do you plan to make things right without capital or investors?" Memminger responded. "The new South Carolina Constitutional Convention in Columbia did a hell of a lot more than just nullify the Ordinance of Secession. At the insistence of Washington, they repudiated the Confederate debt."

"The Memminger debt as I like to call it," George laughed.

"Very funny," Memminger continued. "Repudiating the debt absolves the Federal government of any responsibility for repaying the debts incurred by the Confederacy. Anyone who ever loaned the Confederacy money will not be repaid and has no recourse. There won't be any more European investment coming our way for quite a long time. As Momma used to say, 'Fool me once, shame on you. Fool me twice, shame on me.'"

George smiled and leaned back in his overstuffed chair. He paused to light a cigar and offered the same to his other guests. "Christopher, it might not be as bleak as you imagine. Toward the end of the war, I explored some loans against future cotton exports with a few European banks, particularly Paris and Brussels. It's not wise or necessary to mention any names. Despite the fall of the Confederacy, those bankers may still be willing to honor those contracts anticipating that the price of cotton is going to skyrocket in the aftermath of the deconstruction of the Southern plantation system."

Memminger persisted, "How do you propose to honor your part of the contract? The cotton fields are burned, the slaves dispersed, the wharves and ships confiscated. The Yankees aren't going to let you make a penny. Your new Parisian partners will sue you for everything you have."

"Well, they'll just have to get in line," Trenholm laughed. "Hard to squeeze blood from a stone."

"George, did you sustain a head injury at Fort Pulaski?"

"Worse, I had to eat mutton!"

Everyone laughed and Trenholm continued, "It will not be easy, but I have some ideas how to raise capital. I've done it before and I'm confident I can do it again. My question for you, gentlemen, is if we did have available capital could you prioritize a list of worthy projects? Projects that rebuild our infrastructure and agriculture and put the people of Charleston back to work. Projects that help both whites, freedmen and former slaves."

Reverend Porter interrupted. "Mr. Secretary, we need to ask President Johnson for a pardon. Without a pardon you cannot restore either your citizenship, your businesses or your property. To help Charleston, you need to help yourself first."

Trenholm responded sharply. "I'm glad to have been paroled so I might be back with my family, but I am not inclined to beg for Mr. Johnson's pardon. My hypocrisy extends only so far."

"Then how do you plan to achieve these noble goals?"

"Reverend, Christopher, there are other options available and I ask you to just trust me at present. However, if I were able to re-establish financial liquidity, could you develop an equitable system to make sure that investment money got where it was most needed?"

Trenholm knew that his challenge would appeal to Memminger's sense of civic planning and methodical manner. "We can, George. We can draft a document outlining the essential needs of both Charleston and the state addressing general welfare, health, education, infrastructure needs and the requirements for business self-recovery. Not having the money doesn't mean that we shouldn't have a plan."

"That's the spirit," George exclaimed, pointing his finger at Christopher. "Reverend, we also must not forget the importance of religious and moral leadership. That is where we stumbled most egregiously in the build-up to war. We cannot let that happen again. In fact, faith may be more important than it has ever been. Reverend Porter, I know that you've been doing all you can with your church, but similar efforts need to be made by the clergy in every corner of our city. Anna Helen has told me about your church's debt."

"Mr. Secretary, we are committed, but my church has given all it can. Like you said, there's only so much blood that can be squeezed from a stone. I have collected three hundred and twenty-eight dollars from my congregation along with three gold watches, several diamond rings, breast pins and even a wedding band. It's nowhere near enough to keep the church and our school going."

George blew a billow of cigar smoke toward the ceiling and waited several moments before he next spoke. "Reverend Porter, I was never more ashamed than when I asked the good people of Richmond to donate their personal treasures to the Confederacy. I do not intend to ever take another broach, ring, necklace or jewel from a woman or an heirloom from a family. If you return that wedding ring and all the other jewelry you have collected, I'll pay the balance of your church's debt."

"You are most gracious, sir."

"No, Reverend, just forward thinking. James Morgan here just married my daughter. My new son-in-law is not the sharpest tool in the shed. I know that his soul needs a good scrubbing. Without personal influence at your church there might not be anyone willing to take on this new Morgan branch of the Trenholm family tree."

Everyone laughed, except James Morgan.

Chapter 32

December 7, 1866

Saint-Domingue

The *Will O' the Wisp's* last steam from Charleston took her south to the port of Cap Haitien on the northern coast of Haiti. George Trenholm's maternal grandfather had been a large plantation owner on the northern plain of what was then called Saint-Domingue. Saint-Domingue, the "Pearl of the Antilles," was the most prosperous French colony in the West Indies. Thanks to 800,000 African slaves, the French plantation owners of Saint-Domingue exported 40% of the sugar and 60% of the coffee consumed in Europe as well as significant exports of indigo, cotton, and timber.

A slave rebellion had overthrown the colonial French creating the independent nation of Haiti. Fear of a similar revolt was never far from the minds of the numerically outnumbered Southern whites. Paranoia inevitably breeds brutality and the vicious slave uprising against the French in Haiti was used to justify the cruelty of Southern plantation owners.

Following their revolution, the Haitian plantation system was destroyed, and the sugar and coffee trade quickly collapsed. Without significant exportation, Haiti fell into massive debt worsened by the weight of huge reparations demanded by France and embargoes placed on it by other European nations. The country was rife with corruption and there was little that was not available for a price. With gold in hand, Jack Holmes had little trouble establishing legal residence.

Jack purchased the majority of what was the former de Greffin plantation and restarted the production of sugarcane. He also established the Holmes Shipping Company out of Cap Haitien. In registering his new shipping company, Jack solemnly changed the *Will O' the Wisp's* name to the *Mary Ann Gleeson* for her protection. In time, Jack added two other quality steamers, the *Eliza* and *Frannie*, to his flagship.

Jack Holmes became well-liked and highly respected in Haiti. He paid his sugarcane field laborers well using a productivity-based compensation plan. He designed and built more efficient mills for the crushing of the cane. Jack allowed the workers to use the trash cane to make a local clairin rum in large homemade stills. Jack provided his workers with gallon glass jugs so that the rum could be sold at market or exported. His only request was that the clairin rum be called Will O' the Wisp Rum. His field hands had no idea why but were more than happy to use the name and collect the profit.

The Holmes Shipping Company also enjoyed a positive reputation. Jack's ships were fast and reliable, but it was his reputation for honesty in business dealings that made Jack Holmes unique along the Haitian waterfront. Holmes' three ships began a regular schedule of sailing to America with holds full of sugarcane, tobacco, coffee, mahogany timber, cocoa, coconuts, and Will O' the Wisp Rum. Desperate for export income, the Holmes Shipping Company became a major contributor to Haiti's economic recovery. Between the shipping company, shipbuilding, and the sugar cane plantation, Jack became one of the largest employers in Haiti. Despite being a white face in a black country, Jack Holmes quickly established himself as one of Haiti's most influential businessmen and one of its richest.

His crew melted into Haitian society like chocolate. Copper Joe took a Haitian wife and discovered a green thumb. After years at sea, he found himself fascinated by growing things in the ground. Copper Joe came to oversee the sugarcane production and was as efficient at that as he had been in the boiler room. Jordan Ryan, Caleb, and young Ezekiel all started families. Most of the crewmen took interest in the clairin rum production. The crew had come to terms with their expatriation to Haiti. They would never make the kind of money they had during the war, but then again, no one was firing 32-lb shells at them.

Captain Jack's crew were proud of what they had done in service to the Confederacy. They passionately believed that without their efforts the war would have ended two years earlier. Other than Jack, none of the crew ciphered on whether an earlier culmination of the war might have been the better thing. They wore their reputation as a phantom ship as a badge of honor and saw their dredging of the Kiawah River as brilliant and unimaginable. Despite their pride in the *Will O' the Wisp's* accomplishments, the crew knew to never mention her former name. Once again, the phantom *Will O' the Wisp* would have to pass behind the veil and disappear. For a runner with as much notoriety as the *Will O' the Wisp*, the men understood that the alternative to their new life in Haiti could still be years in a Yankee prison.

Jack Holmes had established financial relationships with Brown Bros. and Co. of Liverpool and London and Drexel, Harjes and Co. of Paris while in Nassau during the war. Now, following the war, he was able to extend those banking relationships as well as open new accounts with other European banks. It was a simple matter for the ship company owner and sugarcane exporter, Jack Whitesides Holmes of Haiti, to visit a Caribbean branch of any of these banking houses and exchange his personal golden wealth for universally accepted bank notes. With a handshake and exchange of paper, the Confederate gold disappeared bar by bar, ingot by ingot, coin by coin into reputable European banks.

Captain Jack steamed the *Mary Ann Gleeson* into almost every port on the East and Gulf coasts of the United States except for Charleston. He did not want to take any chance that the sleek *Mary Ann Gleeson* might be recognized. Even a rumor that the *Will O' the Wisp* might be roaming the coastline would engender a still resentful Union naval response. No Union captain ever believed that the *Will O' the Wisp* had rolled over onto the bottom of Shem Creek. Both the *Wisp* and Captain Jack would always remain uncollected and highly coveted prizes.

Jack Holmes favorite port-o-call was New York City which allowed Jack, Thomas Henry, and George Chapman to reunite with the rest of the family. Mary Ann, and daughters Eliza and Frances, had fled to New York using non-combatant visas provided by Secretary of State Judah Benjamin and a $1500 gold warrant signed by George Trenholm to secure their passage. The family's hard currency was hidden in their clothes and baggage. Mary Ann bought a house in the Flatlands section of Brooklyn and started the Holmes Ambulance Service, taking advantage of Lizzie's nursing training and war experience.

Jack would soon turn Holmes Shipping over to Thomas Henry, who now captained the *Eliza*. George Chapman was more interested in the growing Holmes Ambulance Service than shipping and stayed in Brooklyn with his mother and sisters. Jack was already comfortable with leaving the sugar cane operation in the capable hands of Copper Joe. Jack longed for the day he could reunite with Mary Ann and his other children but feared that day had not yet come. For now, he would need to keep his distance. Retribution remained an obsessive interest of the Federal government.

Jack and Mary Ann Holmes opened a bank account with Drexel, Morgan and Co. of New York. Into that account

Jack deposited the bank drafts issued to him by his European banking connections. The Drexel, Morgan and Co. account grew quickly. The plan was working precisely as George Trenholm had explained it would. The stolen Confederate gold was mixed with the profits from the Holmes Shipping Company and Jack's sugarcane production and then exchanged for European bank drafts in Haiti. Those bank notes were then converted to clean U.S. dollars in New York backed by the full faith and credit of a major U.S. bank.

When Captain Jack visited the ports of Philadelphia, Baltimore, Norfolk, or Wilmington be would meet secretly with an old acquaintance, the still untamed Belle Boyd. Not only had she survived the war, but she married a much older, new U.S. Senator from Virginia. Belle provided him with female charm, wit, and Washington companionship that he would have never otherwise deserved. He provided her with an unassailable cover, an undemanding libido and a busy Congressional schedule allowing her ample time for travel and continued intrigue. Belle Boyd had never surrendered and never would.

As a silent partner in the new Haitian registered Holmes Shipping Company, Jack delivered George Trenholm's share of the profits on each visit to America. Included with those dividends were sizeable withdrawals of cash from Drexel, Morgan and Co. against the now banked Confederate gold reserves. The money was smuggled back to George Trenholm in the false bottom of Belle Boyd's carriage when she traveled to Charleston to see a sickly favorite aunt. Her fat and happy U.S. Senator husband never suspected that the mysterious Belle Boyd no longer had any extended family at all.

Only George Trenholm and Jack Holmes knew where the gold had gone or how it had been converted to U.S. dollars. Jack's accounts were never questioned, and Belle Boyd's smuggling was never intercepted.

Chapter 33

January 1, 1866

Bank of Charleston

George specifically selected January 1st for its symbolic importance. A new start was the message he wanted to bring to Henry Gourdin. Henry was a successful Charleston merchant who had opened the Bank of Charleston in 1834 and remained a member of its Board of Directors. More importantly, Henry had been George's long-time business associate and friend.

It was a bitter cold morning, but George still chose to walk from his East Battery home to the Bank of Charleston on the corner of Broad and State Streets. George was accompanied by both Jack Holmes and Belle Boyd. It was the first and only time that Jack had accompanied Belle on one of her excursions to Charleston. Jack was nervous to be back in Charleston but believed the uncomfortable woolen business suit he was wearing and Belle Boyd at his side would be an adequate disguise. Belle Boyd was with them for the adventure and that meetings tended to go well when she was involved. Henry Gourdin was no longer a young man, but the last time George had checked, he was not dead. As George walked, he tried to figure out the best way to approach the most scrupulously honest man he knew with an idea that certainly was not.

Yet, he was still the man that needed to be approached. George respected Henry's business acumen.

Henry was a man who knew how to prosper when others struggled. Under Gourdin's leadership, the Bank of Charleston had flourished. The newly formed Bank of Charleston built a close alliance with the Bank of Liverpool establishing themselves as a financial institution capable of supporting the city's growing trade with European markets. In short order, the Bank of Charleston became recognized in European commercial circles as the strongest financial institution in the Southeast. With its success, the Bank of Charleston dramatically grew its capital, declared excellent dividends, made loans at low interest, and became an even more respected bank of issue.

When the war started in 1861, the Bank of Charleston had branch offices in the coastal cities of Apalachicola, Florida; Mobile, Alabama; and New Orleans. Its notes were current from Maine to Texas and circulated seamlessly in Europe. Following secession, the Bank of Charleston lent $100,000 to the new South Carolina state government and, at the request of Christopher Memminger, Secretary of the Confederate Treasury, lent $1.5 million dollars to the fledgling Confederate government. Neither loan was ever repaid. The Bank of Charleston and the Georgia Railroad Bank were the only two Southern banks to survive the war. It teetered on the verge of bankruptcy but was able to honor with specie all the hoarded Bank of Charleston notes which flooded their offices once Confederate paper became worthless.

That miracle was a direct result of Henry Gourdin convincing the Board of Directors to invest most of their reserves into English pound sterling. Pound sterling rose substantially in value between 1861 and 1865. The Bank of Charleston had supported the C.S.A. but had not bet on it. While the bank had survived, George knew it to be hanging on by a velvet shoestring. George hoped that Henry's desire to renew the bank's fortunes might impart some moral flexibility for which Henry Gourdin was not especially known.

There had been terrible destruction along Broad Street during the war and from the sixty-one fire. George and Jack were impressed by the significant repairs already made to the Bank of Charleston building. Stucco had been reapplied to the masonry walls of the two-story building. Smashed arched window and door openings had been replaced. In what should have been recognized as an omen, the gold leaf eagle adorning the gable on the front of the bank had never been damaged despite months of bombardment. Jack smiled, recognizing that banks were always the first to accomplish significant renovation.

George, Jack, and Belle were shown into the Board of Director's Room on the second floor. It was a stunning room with a coved ceiling, pilasters with Corinthian capitals, and marbleized wood painted to simulate tan and black marble. Henry rose from an elegant dark mahogany conference table in the center of the room and greeted George enthusiastically. George had not seen Henry in quite some time and wondered if maybe Henry has assumed he had died.

Introductions were made. George presented Jack as one of his former business partners in New York City by the name of Pendergast and Belle as his wife. Belle spoke to Henry in fluent French, uncaring as to whether he understood her or not. Her smile and coquettish curtsey revealed ample décolletage which was clearly understood.

"Mister Secretary, to what do I owe the honor of this unexpected visit?"

"Henry, I only go by George these days. No sense in getting even more people angry at me than already are."

"Of course. Please accept my apology. What's on your mind, George, and how can I help you?"

"Henry, I want you to help me rebuild Charleston, rebuild the state and, in the process, rebuild the Bank of Charleston."

"Well, that sounds good. I was worried you might have something overly ambitious in mind."

"I'm serious, Henry. The war was an earthquake that shook the entire South from center to circumference. If we do not act boldly the South may never recover. The war has resulted in a loss of life and property beyond computation. You must be feeling the pinch of the millions of dollars in lost currency, bank capital, and bonds that vanished with Lee's surrender. The forfeiture of slave property rights alone approaches $3 billion. The railroads are destroyed, the docks dilapidated, and the merchant fleet burnt to the waterlines. We've got to get our city back on its feet and back to work."

"George, I promise you that I'm intimately familiar with all those numbers. However, there's very little we can do. We are literally hanging on by our fingernails. We are perilously close to insolvency."

"Henry, with all due respect, I believe that your definition of 'perilously close' is far different than most other's definition of 'perilously close.' I may be off a bit, but I understand you're currently lending at fourteen percent."

"Fifteen."

"Fifteen percent! That will never get us anywhere. Rebuilding the railroads, steam lines, and cotton economy will require huge amounts of borrowing. At those rates no one will ever turn a profit. We can't incentivize investment with interest rates at fifteen percent."

"George, we're not insensitive, but what can you expect us to do. We no longer have sufficient capital to be liberal with our lending policies."

"I expect you to place the welfare of our city above the welfare of your investors. Your friends and neighbors have been reduced to poverty and left forsaken. In the footprints of our foolishness we have scattered the seeds of famine and pestilence. The fruit of those vines will be misery and crime."

"George, I'm reminded of how eloquent and persuasive you can be; however, you forget yourself. I have lived here all my life and feel the same sorrow for what has become of our city. But this, sir, is not city hall. It's not the General Assembly. It's not even a church pulpit. This is a bank. We have obligations that exist to prevent us from falling victim to sentimentality. Had we chosen sentiment-tality; the Bank of Charleston would be shuttered as were all the other Southern banks. I resent being asked to choose between being a banker and being a human being, but in this building, and in this room, I'm a banker. We cannot loan more than we have, and we cannot lend our investors' money without a high probability it'll be repaid."

"Henry, I didn't mean to offend. I've been a banker as well. My God, I was the banker for the entire Confederacy. Never a day went by that I didn't worry I'd lost my soul."

Appreciated or not, Jack stepped into the conversation. "What if I could offer you a way to both help your community and build your assets?"

"I'd be interested to hear what you have to say, Mr. Pendergast. Skeptical, but interested."

George continued with his pitch. "Henry, we will provide the Bank of Charleston with regular cash donations with a ceiling in the low seven figures. You will record the deposits as being from an anonymous Northern donor to a fund for Charleston Relief and Southern Reconstruction. The bank can keep five percent for administration of the fund. When appropriate, the bank can also negotiate a small percentage, and I mean small, of any profits reasonably anticipated to accrue from the investment of those donated monies. However, I want to be clear that much of this money will be directed toward missions of a purely civic nature such as the restoration of schools, churches, orphanages, and housing for widows. I have asked Christopher Memminger and the Reverend A. Toomer Porter to create a prioritized list of needed community investments. You will provide money for those efforts for as long as the money persists. You are, of course, welcome to invest other bank monies in these projects as suits your Board."

"And?"

"There will be no record of our involvement in these donations and it will never be discussed outside of this room today. Whatever paper trail you want to create is fine with me so long as there is no way it can be traced back to myself, Mr. Pendergast, or our families. It had better be a good one though. Sooner or later, nosy people from Washington will show up and start poking around in your ledgers. I have lots of new Federal friends."

Henry Gourdin was silent. This was the moment. George was asking him to violate every rule that had governed his life since he stopped playing mumblety-peg. Henry was a man who lived rigidly by rules and he was now being asked to ignore them all. George wondered what kind of man Henry Gourdin would turn out to be. The answer took almost three minutes.

"I suppose I shouldn't ask any more questions," Henry Gourdin finally offered.

"That would be best," Jack quickly interjected. Belle smiled and curtsied again for Henry.

"Understood. The Bank of Charleston is honored to join this partnership. Let me get us all a glass of sherry to toast our agreement." George could not remember ever seeing Henry Gourdin beam.

The men toasted and then shook hands. To George's surprise, Henry embraced him again. "I hope we can make a difference, George."

"I think we can. That's why I came to you."

"I'm glad you did. When can we start?"

"Mrs. Pendergast will return tomorrow with an initial three hundred thousand dollars for deposit. The money's first use should be to build new warehouses in the burnt district for the storage of cotton. We'll also need a new cotton press. We can't bring cotton to Charleston if we don't have anywhere to put it. I also want to rebuild the Charleston Iron Works. We'll need iron, plus it employed almost two hundred skilled men we cannot afford to lose to other cities."

"Who will do the construction?"

"I'll leave those details to you and your staff. You know who's capable far better than I. Again, I insist, there cannot be any trail leading back to the Trenholm or Pendergast families. I want the line of builders and workers clamoring at your door, not mine."

"Of course, you can trust in the bank's discretion. Would it be better that in the future we meet at some other location?"

"Good idea, Henry, but my hope is that we may never meet again. Reverend Porter and Christopher Memminger will meet with you soon to help guide the selection of projects. All future deposits will be brought directly to you by Mrs. Pendergast and placed only into your hands."

"Well, I will certainly look forward to seeing Mrs. Pendergast again," Henry replied as he looked at Belle who smiled broadly in silent response.

George continued, "Other than the three hundred thousand that you will receive tomorrow, I don't want to know how the funds are handled. I trust in your industry, economy, perseverance, and, of course, discretion. Honorable ambition will stimulate you to use those talents God has bestowed on you to their fullest."

"Thank you for your trust in me, Secretary Trenholm. It means more than you will ever know. There has been such an overturning of society I wasn't certain if it was wise to remain in Charleston. The welfare of my family is paramount to my every consideration. I feared that Charleston was neither a safe nor desirable place for them to be. I feared for their future but could not bring myself to cut and run. This is the first day I've felt comfortable with that decision."

Henry Gourdin refilled the sherry glasses and toasted again, "To a brighter future, Mister Secretary."

"Please, Henry, just George.

Chapter 34

October 15, 1866

Stinking Stones

Christopher Memminger and Reverend Porter completed the document George Trenholm had requested. It was prepared in two parts. The first was an outline of the major reconstruction projects needed for South Carolina and it was delivered to General Daniel Sickles, the military Governor. Sickles was more than enthusiastic as the document was a blueprint for everything that he was under pressure from Washington to accomplish. While there were still influential voices in the North bent on reprisal, there was also a growing sense of practicality, especially in the business and financial sectors. As George Trenholm had predicted, those voices argued for investment in Southern recovery as being essential to the overall economic health of the re-United States of America.

The second document was specific to Charleston's needs and was far more detailed. Memminger and Porter delivered that document to Henry Gourdin at the Bank of Charleston. Memminger was nervous about visiting Gourdin's office and mumbled something about owing him one and a half million dollars. Gourdin did not mention the C.S.A. debt and was excited about their prescription for revitalizing Charleston. He was anxious to start right away. Somehow, the ever-cautious Henry Gourdin had suddenly become a bold man of action.

Reverend A. Toomer Porter embarked on a quest to obtain a pardon for his prideful and reluctant friend. He carried petitions from Susan Petigru King and the remaining family of the late, but immensely respected, James L. Petrigru. The Sisters of Our Lady of Mercy in Charleston wrote, "In our efforts to afford relief to the Union Soldiers confined in the Prisons and Hospitals, we never applied in vain for aid to the Honorable Gentleman, and we can testify to the liberality and readiness with which he has always supported our works of charity."

Before traveling to Washington, Reverend Porter visited New York City and obtained more letters from several influential Republicans and powerful businessmen who could speak to George Trenholm's honor, trust-worthiness, and history of successful international commerce.

Ultimately, Reverend Porter gained an audience with President Andrew Johnson. He had met President Johnson earlier in 1866 when Porter acquired the Marine Hospital at 20 Franklin Street. The Marine Hospital had been severely damaged by Union bombardment, but the Episcopal Church had repurposed it as a school for black children. President Johnson spoke on the day of the school's dedication. "The education of the black man must not be neglected. Education will elevate them mentally, physically and morally. Only an educated man can become an enfranchised citizen."

President Johnson remembered the event and the speech. He was clearly pleased that Porter remembered it as well. Reverend Porter informed President Johnson that the transformation of the pulverized Marine Hospital would not have been possible without George Trenholm's generous donations. Although Johnson had been harshly criticized for the high number of pardons he had endorsed, especially for former Confederate leaders, he made an exception for George Alfred Trenholm and signed his pardon on October 15th, 1866.

Uniquely, it was a pardon that Trenholm never officially requested, never paid an inducement to receive, and never required a public admission as to his responsibility for either the war or its horrors. George used his Presidential pardon to return home to Ashley Hall and reclaim many of his other properties. He reorganized his companies and re-established a cotton brokerage under the name George A. Trenholm and Son. He partnered with Holmes Shipping Company out of Haiti to expand the number of first-class steamers available to him.

Regardless of the pardon, George Trenholm still faced innumerable Federal lawsuits. Although hundreds of companies were involved in blockade running, only George Trenholm had an exclusive relationship with the Confederate government. The United States government had long ago seized the assets of Fraser, Trenholm and Company, forcing it into bankruptcy. Pardon or no pardon, the government would continue to target Trenholm's money as recompense for unpaid tariffs on imported goods during the war. George understood that he would never be allowed to regain his pre-war wealth or power.

Both Porter and Memminger became known for their patronage of charitable causes and large heartedness. No suffering of which they heard went unrelieved, regardless of color. Christopher Memminger had been raised in the Charleston Orphan House. After the war, Memminger converted his home on the corner of Smith and Wentworth Streets into an orphanage for Negro children and donated large sums of money for the rebuilding of schools for both poor black and white children. Christopher Memminger's passion was for public education and he became the chair of the City Board of School Commissioners so he could personally direct the use of his donations.

Reverend Porter was able to expand his plans for a church school, thanks to the patronage of the oddest pair of former parishioners. A Federal arsenal and foundry sat on a former four-acre potter's field where Bee Street met Ashley Avenue. Just before the outbreak of hostilities, something between a mob and a militia of Charlestonians turned away a detachment of Union soldiers from Fort Moultrie who'd been sent ashore to collect the arsenal's cartridges and musket balls before they fell into secessionist hands. It was that arsenal, not Fort Sumter, that was the first piece of Federal property seized in the war.

With George Trenholm's financial backing and the endorsement of yet another former parishioner, William Tecumseh Sherman, the U.S. Government transferred the old arsenal to the Holy Communion Church Institute under Reverend Porter's direction. The only requirement was that the property be used only for educational purposes. A black brick mason, Holton Bell, designed and constructed a two-story Gothic-style chapel with a surrounding brick wall on the site of the former arsenal. The new church and school became a home for war widows and orphans.

About six months after their visit with Henry Gourdin, Jack Holmes paid George Trenholm an unexpected visit. "George, I want to introduce you to my younger brother, Francis Holmes. Francis is the book smart member of the Holmes family. For some reason he never took to the water like the rest of us."

"It is my pleasure, Francis. Anna Helen speaks of you with great affection. I do believe, however, that we have met. Possibly at our wedding or one of Anna Helen's parties?"

"Yes, I believe we have, Mr. Trenholm. I am honored that you remembered."

"Francis owns a small plantation near Georgetown," Jack interjected. "However, he considers himself a gentleman scientist. Francis is passionate about searching for prehistoric bones. Prior to the war he published an interesting book about Lowcountry fossils. I wanted Francis to tell you about what he has discovered in his fossil search."

"Please proceed. I remember having a keen interest in fossils when I was a boy in school."

Francis began to explain his discovery. "There is an odd smelling phosphate rock which accumulates around fossils. We always called them stinking stones and generally considered them a nuisance. I developed a process to separate the soft, sedimentary phosphate rock from the mineralized remnants."

"Tell George what you saw next," Jack added excitedly.

"Well, I noticed how lush grass became in the field where I dumped the wastewater used to clean away the phosphate rock. That got me to thinking, so I contacted Dr. N.A. Pratt, a chemist I know in Georgia. We studied these stinking stones and developed them into an effective fertilizer."

"And?" Jack prodded again.

"The new phosphate fertilizer more than doubled my plantation's cotton production."

Few crops depleted nutrients from soil more aggressively than cotton. Most farmers did not have large enough tracts to rotate their cotton or were too shortsighted to let their fields go fallow and refresh themselves over time. Only the wealthiest planters could afford to import Peruvian bat guano to replenish the soil.

"I didn't believe Francis when he first told me about this," Jack added. "So, I imported some of his new phosphate fertilizer into Haiti and saw for myself what it could do for sugar cane production. I would not have taken the risk to come back to Charleston if I had not seen what his fertilizer could do with my own eyes. It's remarkable, George. Tell him what else, Francis."

"The Lowcountry has more phosphate rock than anywhere else in the world," Francis replied quietly.

George ran his hands through his silver hair and looked back and forth between Jack and Francis who were both nodding. "You mean that previously no-account land can be brought back to a high state of production with phosphate-based fertilizer?"

Both Jack and Francis continued to nod their heads and smiled.

George finally responded. "Phosphate could be Charleston's next white gold!"

Over the next month, Trenholm introduced Francis and Dr. Pratt to Philadelphia investors and obtained the start-up money for the Charleston Mining and Manufacturing Company. Francis Holmes became the company's first president and George Trenholm sat on the Board of Directors.

Phosphate mining became Charleston's post-war financial salvation. As Francis Holmes had opined, immense deposits of phosphate rock and fossil bone were discovered between the Ashley and Cooper Rivers in the Charleston neck. It was a wealth of phosphate that would last for ages. Phosphate rock, however, was buried under several feet of topsoil, plants and roots. It required an army of men to dig it out. Even though the working conditions were brutal, phosphate excavation employed thousands of former slaves, poor white immigrants, Italians, and leased convicts. For the first time ever, there was a need to negotiate with a labor workforce and make compensation commensurate with effort.

By 1867, the Charleston Mining and Manufacturing Company was digging up more than ten thousand acres of phosphate deposits on both sides of the Ashley River. Beautiful antebellum plantation homes that lined the Ashley were razed and replaced by fertilizer mills with phosphate drying sheds, billowing smokestacks, and huge boilers needed to power the machines that washed, dried, and processed the phosphate rock into fertilizer.

In 1867, six tons of phosphate was mined in Charleston. By 1870, a half million tons, fifty percent of all global production, were being shipped annually from Charleston bound for both domestic and foreign ports. To move that tonnage, Trenholm and Son became one of the largest exporters of phosphate in the world, reestablishing the trading might of Charleston.

As he had always promised, Trenholm invested heavily in rebuilding the railroads leading to Charleston. George and his son took over the bankrupt Greenville and Columbia railroads and became directors of the South Carolina Railroad system. Although the project fell through, they also incorporated the Blue Ridge Railroad with a plan to connect Charleston to the American Midwest. George took advantage of longstanding business and shipping relationships in England, France, Spain, and the Netherlands to reopen the port of Charleston to foreign merchantmen. Relationships lubricated by both Trenholm's charm and generous enticements. Among the many ships trading at the port of Charleston were those owned and operated by the highly respected Holmes Shipping Company.

Jack Holmes read of George Alfred Trenholm's death on December 9th, 1876, at the age of sixty-nine, in a front-page obituary in the *New York Herald*. In a show of respect, more than a hundred ships in the Charleston harbor-Southern, Northern, and International- lowered their flags to half-staff upon hearing the news of George Trenholm's demise.

The obituary waxed poetically about how George Trenholm had accumulated great wealth and then lost it in misguided secession. Miraculously, he accumulated great wealth once again. The author opined that wealth can be a blessing or a curse depending on how it is achieved and how it is used. Somehow privy to knowledge that no one had, the author recounted how George Trenholm had used his wealth wisely and philanthropically to help restore the South following the war's devastation.

Jack Holmes approved of the obituary. He was pleased for the recognition of George's personal recompense. Despite innumerable lawsuits which had dogged him for the final decade of his life, the Federal government had never been to put a lien on his friend's honor. He was also pleased that none of the inquiries or lawsuits had ever revealed how they had liberated the Confederate gold, where it had been hidden, or how it had been used. The names of Jack Whitesides Holmes and George Alfred Trenholm would remain forever free from that reproach. Jack was comfortable with that anonymity.

EPILOGUE

In the spring of 1871, Reverend A. Toomer Porter accompanied George Trenholm on a trip to New York City. Porter was fundraising for his church school while George was having meetings with bankers, financiers, and philanthropists who might be able to support his commercial and political ambitions. While no longer the King of Cotton, George's success in resurrecting his shipping company and in the exportation of phosphate once again enabled the Trenholm name to open any door on either side of the Atlantic.

On their second night in New York, George invited Reverend Porter to dinner at Delmonico's Restaurant at 2 South William Street. Lorenzo Delmonico's steakhouse was the finest dining experience in the United States. George informed Reverend Porter that they would be joined by his brother-in-law, Jack Holmes. Porter had not seen or heard of Jack since the surrender of Charleston. The family was gone from Christ Church and the Shem Creek ship building business long shuttered. George had always said he lost track of Jack after being imprisoned at Fort Pulaski. Reverend Porter had assumed the Holmes family had fled to the islands, however, being killed or scattered were also possibilities.

From Jack and George's animated conversation, it was clear that they had not been lost to each other. The years had been kinder to Jack than to George, but together they lit up the room with energy, wit, and personality. For a few hours the two men were a decade younger. Jack explained how he had landed in Saint-Domingo after the war. His Holmes Shipping Company had been a success and Copper Joe had proven to be a wizard at growing sugarcane and distilling rum. When pushed, Jack admitted that the *Will O' the Wisp* was still a beautiful lady but now forced to travel under a pseudonym.

Jack was now living with Mary Ann and the children in Brooklyn. The pride on Jack's face was obvious as he reported recently turning the shipping company over to Thomas Henry. He also proudly described how Mary Ann, Lizzie and George Chapman had built the finest ambulance service in Brooklyn.

"While the Holmes Ambulance Service has been successful, it hasn't been Delmonico's successful," Jack chided George. "I assume you're paying. This place is beyond the means of a retired cane farmer and, I assume, a man of the cloth." George smiled and lifted his glass of Irish whiskey.

"Jack, I know you're going to order the Delmonico steak. You have all the imagination of the oldest barnacle on the *Wisp's* keel. But you, Toomer, I hope you will show just a bit more sophistication. Delmonico's chef was born in France and was training in Paris at age twelve. Before Delmonico's, he was the private chef for Prince d' Henin, comte d' Alsace. If you don't order something classically French, you're missing a wonderful opportunity."

"How about the Lobster Duke Alexis?"

"That's the spirit, Reverend. You will not be disappointed. Plus, it'll assuage the shame of Jack ordering boiled potatoes to go with his steak."

"I bet the boiled potatoes are good here."

The potatoes did not disappoint, nor did the steak. The thick porterhouse arrived sputtering on a scalding flat iron, seasoned perfectly with dashes of sea salt and fragrant pepper, and indescribably fresh butter melting over it. The meal, and the conversation, were memorable. The entire restaurant turned when Chef Charles Ranhofer came from the kitchen to speak with Mr. Trenholm. George had obviously dined at Delmonico's many times.

"Jack, Reverend Porter, please allow me to introduce Charles Ranhofer, the finest chef in all of New York, if not the country."

"*Merci*, George. I trust that you and your friends enjoyed the dinner."

"Magnificent as always, Charles."

"I had the Lobster Duke Alexis and I think it might've been the best thing I've ever eaten."

"That pleases me to hear, Reverend Porter."

"My steak and potatoes were great too," Jack interjected.

"Charles, I apologize for my brother-in-law. He's a Philistine who lives on a boat and guides himself at night using the dancing lights from swamp gas emissions."

"*Formidable*, maybe we can interest your barbarous friend in a new dessert I've been working on."

"I can do a dessert. What is it?" Jack asked.

"It's called omelette a' la Norvegienne. It's quite spectacular."

"But what is it?" Jack repeated. "A Norwegian omelet doesn't sound like dessert to me."

Charles Ranhofer looked at George who shrugged his shoulders.

"It is vanilla ice cream in a small pie dish lined with sponge cake and topped with meringue. After the dessert is constructed, I place it in an extremely hot oven for a few minutes which caramelizes the meringue. It has the heat of the mid-summer Florida sun and the coldness of mid-winter Alaska."

"Charles, we'll have three."

"Excellent, *Monsieur* Trenholm."

Reverend Porter had always wondered about George's surprising and unexpected post-war philanthropy but had never dared ask. After listening to Jack and George reminisce about their adventures and learning of Jack Holmes' emergence as a shipping magnate and landowner in

Haiti, he began to put two and two together. As they enjoyed their omelette a' la Norvegienne, Reverend Porter finally asked.

"George, did you and Jack steal the Confederate treasure at the end of the war? There is no one more aware of your generosity than I, but were the things you did for Charleston accomplished with stolen gold?"

"Reverend, I prefer to think of it as your church school and all our other building projects as being paid for by the Confederate States of America. Jack's amazing success in Haiti with shipping and sugar cane production was not anticipated, but also contributed substantially. We were partners in those profitable businesses. However, the C.S.A. did provide our initial investments."

"You are at peace with your appropriation of the Confederate treasury?"

It seemed like the entire dining room had gone quiet. George glanced briefly at Jack who wiped his mouth with a linen napkin and then answered definitively. "Absolutely."

George added to Jack's blunt response. "Reverend, you would probably be surprised, but as a banker and financier, I've never really believed that gold, or currency of any kind, held any inherent value. It is only a medium of exchange for things either needed or wanted. Jack and I stole the Confederate gold to make sure it was used for things needed, not merely things wanted."

"I'm sorry, George, but that sentiment could be a justification for any thievery. Stealing is a moral issue, not a financial one."

"I agree, Reverend," Jack interjected with his typical imperious intensity. "The accumulated Confederate treasure represented a huge moral issue, but one far bigger than the question of theft. Men who had accrued personal wealth using slave labor began this war to protect their own prosperity. Everyone else died or suffered in the effort to make it so. The overarching moral issue was that we should have never allowed that suffering to occur. Secession was pushed by a bunch of grifters. Those with the most to gain gave the least, and those with nothing to gain lost all they had. What they did not give was taken from them including fathers, husbands, children and homes."

"Jack is to fine a friend to say it, but one of those grifters he is talking about is me. It is a responsibility I bear with far more shame than the theft of Confederate gold. When the fall of the Confederacy became certain, Jack and I decided that whatever was left needed to be protected and given back. People we failed to protect from the misery of war should not have to suffer further if we any ability to alter its aftermath. If we had not taken that gold, it would have certainly ended up in the hands of either highwaymen, Union banks, or the limitless greed of Yankee carpetbaggers. None of those groups would have cared a whit about the people from whom that wealth had really been stolen."

"The gold came within minutes of being taken by five Yankee highwaymen who would have gladly murdered us all," Jack Holmes interjected.

"But?"

"We killed them first."

The coldness of Jack's admission was chilling. "You're both okay with that?" Reverend Porter inquired.

"I've never regretted those killings for a second. Jack saved my entire family."

"Assuming that your families didn't have to die, have you considered whether it might have been better for your souls to have allowed those highwaymen to take the gold?"

"Maybe we did," George countered with a laugh. "It depends on your definition of highwaymen. However, if I correctly understand your question, I am sharply aware that my family, Jack and his family, and other of my friends, have benefitted from the gold we stole. Our thievery was self-serving, and it gives me pause and occasional self-loathing. So, to answer your question directly, stealing the gold may not have been good for my soul, but I am comforted knowing that most of the treasure we appropriated served a greater good. We rebuilt railroads, commissioned steamships, opened schools, christened hospitals, and replanted cotton fields. Those efforts, however, required far more gold than we liberated from the C.S.A. treasury. It required that I reestablish my businesses and the businesses of others I trusted. Financing Jack's shipping company in Haiti alone probably tripled the money available for Charleston's reconstruction."

Jack continued, "We thought about just giving the gold away to those in greatest need, but we realized that would have no lasting impact. We were not clever enough to figure out any other way than to trust our business experience. To be honest, most of those business judgements came from George and almost all proved successful."

"Your church school is a fine example," George added. "With a relatively small act of charity you were able to start a sewing class open to girls of both races. That class grew into the first Industrial School for Girls in South Carolina. Then you started taking contracts for the sewing of plain underwear, pantaloons, and coats at ten cents per garment. You became self-supporting and were eventually able to purchase new sewing machines, hire men to do the cloth cutting and pressing, and pay for the fuel and light. Best of all, the leftover was divided among the seamstresses creating family income. That small act of charity has grown into something vital that has helped many."

Reverend Porter thought for a few moments and then responded. "I think I've given this sermon before. Give a man a fish and he'll eat for a day. Teach a man to fish and he will eat for a lifetime."

"My congratulations, Reverend, but I can promise you that Jack and I were not following gospel parables when we plotted to steal the gold. We just got tired of watching others pay for our mistakes. A miscalculation that was far greater on my part than Jack's. Reverend, did you know that Jack never owned a slave or paid a man less than a fair wage?"

"Enough, George. I chose sides the same as everyone else and failed to appreciate the folly."

"George, neither you nor Jack are responsible for the war."

"I should have been smarter, or maybe braver, but regardless, huge mistakes were made. We gathered on a High Battery piazza drinking brandy, smoking Cuban cigars, and thinking only of our own rewards. We failed to consider the despicable nature of human bondage or the destruction and despair that would invariably follow our attempts to preserve it. We allowed ourselves to be captured by self-interest and to be blinded by the presumed superior moral relativism of our race. Reverend, I know of another sermon you frequently give. Man's greatest sin is our hubristic presumption and ignorance of the humanity of all God's children. Whatever virtues we might have had, succumbed to our significant vices."

"You're still not responsible for the war."

Jack replied this time. "At the end of the day, people are what they do. Both George and I allowed ourselves to be swept up in the rush to armed rebellion when we should have thought it through and advised caution. We had both seen far more of the world than almost anyone else we know, yet we lacked vision. Nothing that George and I have achieved since the war's end will ever change the shame we feel for our inexplicable foolishness and the despair that we did not try harder to prevent."

George followed, "Consequently, Jack and I believed that we were obligated to do what we did. If a ledger is being kept, we wanted to relieve as much of that suffering as we could and put at least one tic mark on the positive side."

"Reverend, you know that I do not share George's religious convictions. I don't fear for my soul as George does. It matters not to me whether it was God, pixies, stillborn babies, or swamp demons who sent the Will O' the Wisp to light my way home. It's my responsibility to read the signs and find my way through the tangled roots and shallow bottoms. The crew is also my responsibility. If the heavens and earth are governed by a creator and all-wise Providence, I must believe that he expects us to be self-reliant and care for others not as able. The man who habitually neglects his duty and relies on Providence to do for him what he should do for himself, will never succeed, and hurt others in the process."

"Jack, for an agnostic, that's one of the most insightful explanations of the transactional relationship between God and man that I've ever heard."

"Accidental, Reverend. I promise."

Reverend Porter stared at the faces of his two old friends and then turned back to Jack. "Despite your words, I know the pangs of conscience that you and George carry are sharp. While you may not seek God's ineffable love, I do believe you fear his abandonment. I have heard you tell the story before of the Will O' the Wisp guiding you home. The Will O' the Wisp was there for you when you had lost your direction. You considered it a signal from God reserved only for sailors. I remember you saying that all God requires is for you to have faith in him and his signs."

Jack smiled wistfully and looked away. "I remember, Reverend. It seems like a long time ago, but I do remember," Jack replied quietly. "I guess I wonder if I am the same man who followed the Will O' the Wisp home and whether I'm still worthy of God's direction. I am sure that I'm not the same man I was back then, and I suspect that God isn't the same man either."

"A man's heart and his actions are not always aligned. God has always been a reader of men's hearts and not a scribe of their actions. I only ask that you consider the possibility that your redemptive deeds may have been guided by his invisible hand."

"Reverend, I will consider it, but it seems unlikely that God would soil his hands guiding a sinner like me."

"Jack, both you and George personify the priceless value of honor. Honor is not a gift or inheritance. No element of the human heart radiates more brightly, and it carries a power and influence that speaks to other men. Money cannot purchase it, and no man can be robbed of it without his consent. Accomplishments are meaningless without it. Ill winds eventually blow upon everyone. Those without honor will yield to distemper and an unaccommodating disposition, until nearly all the sweetness they had in life is gone. A man possessing honor brings light unto himself, his family, his companions, and walks with the eye of God constantly on him. Leave it to God to judge who is irredeemable and who is not."

"Jack and I appreciate those thoughts, Reverend. We know the good we have done. But we do worry about the sins we've committed along the way. At least I do."

"Maybe me too," Jack grunted softly while chewing.

"If it is of any comfort to you, George Trenholm and Jack Holmes, I am aware of the generosity in your hearts and the goodness of your intentions. I have seen what you have done for others. The tic marks you have accumulated on the positive side of the ledger are innumerable. The gold you stole would never have shined more luminously than it has in the eyes of the men, women, and children, black and white, for whom you provided a future. Gentlemen, I absolve you of the sin of theft and murder on behalf of our Lord Almighty."

Jack Holmes smiled and took another big bite of omelette a' la Norvegienne.

George Trenholm cried.

~*~*~*~

Meet Our Author
Roger Newman

Roger Newman, M.D. is a Professor of Obstetrics and Gynecology and Maternal-Fetal Medicine and the Maas Endowed Chair for Reproductive Sciences at the Medical University of South Carolina. Other than a two-year fellowship at the University of California, San Francisco, Dr. Newman has practiced his entire career in Charleston at the Medical University of South Carolina. He has enjoyed significant academic success as author of more than 160 scientific publications, and as national president of the Society for Maternal-Fetal Medicine. Beginning in 2014, Dr. Newman began writing fiction and has subsequently published a series of medical suspense novels entitled *Occam's Razor, Two Drifters*, and most recently, *What Becomes* which was long listed for the 2018 Chanticleer Mystery and Mayhem Award. Dr. Newman is also an author for the award winning and extremely successful *When You're Expecting Twins, Triplets or Quads*, 4th Ed. published by HarperCollins. This is Dr. Newman's first effort at historical fiction exploring the forces that bred secession leading to Civil War in his hometown of Charleston and the roles played by the shipbuilder/blockade runner Captain Jack Whitesides Holmes and the shipping magnate/financier George Alfred Trenholm who ultimately became the Secretary of the Treasury of the Confederacy. Dr. Newman continues to live in Charleston, is married, has 3 grown children, and happens to be a distant relative of both George A. Trenholm and Jack Whitesides Holmes.

www.ingramcontent.com/pod-product-compliance
Lightning Source LLC
Chambersburg PA
CBHW062150080426
42734CB00010B/1629